Wise as a Serpent; Gentle as a Dove

Dealing With Deception

A guide to surviving a world in deception.

By Peter F. Hyatt

Table of Contents

Introducton 1
   A Debt of Gratitude. 1
      Chapter One: The Pain of Deception...................................Page 5
      Chapter Two: The Cost of Deception in Business.....................Page 13
      Chater Three: The Pain of Deception in Sexual Abuse   Page 27
      Chapter Four: The Right Man for the Job   Page 45
      Chapter Five: Statement Analysis and Missing Persons   Page 56
      Chapter Six: Statement Analysis and Suicide?   Page 61
      Chapter Seven: What Happened to Hailey Dunn?   Page 90
      Chapter Eight: "Tot Mom"   Page 108
      Chapter Nine: Confession By Pronoun   Page 126
      Chapter Ten: The Reliable Denial   Page 140
      Chapter Eleven: Fathers Molesting Daughters   Page 163
      Chapter Twelve: Small Business Theft   Page 175
      Chapter Thirteen: Mid Sized Business Theft   Page 184
      Chapter Fourteen: Fake Hate   Page 187
      Chapter Fifteen: Coping With Deception   Page 207
      Chapter Sixteen:The Emotional Cost of Lying   Page 211
      Chapter Seventeen: The Insult of Being Lied To   Page 215
      Chapter Eighteen: The Trap   Page 233
      Chapter Nineteen: The Deceptive Among Us   Page 245
      Chapter Twenty: Crisis in Confidence   Page 253
      Chapter Twenty One: Even the Guilty Call 911   Page 271
      Chapter Twenty Two: The Conclusion of the Matter   Page 289

     1

;

Dealing
With Deception

Peter F. Hyatt

Dealing With Deception

A guide to surviving a world in deception.

Being deceived hurts.

Some hurts are worse than others. In dealing with deception, it is not always known just how much damage a liar may do. In fact, as the years have gone by and I have devoted my life to detecting deception, I have concluded that the damage done in life by the deceiver is without measure.

Traveling alone

What if you received a call from the police, stating that your daughter committed suicide, yet you found yourself being lied to by her fiancé?

What if you learned that the man you entrusted your children to was a pedophile?

What if you learned that your investment broker was deceptive, and had embezzled money from your company while you trusted her to safe guard the business?

What if the deception you experienced paled in comparison to these, yet, cost you money that you did not have?

For one, the simple sales transaction, coupled with deception, means the loss of money, which happens enough in life to 'write off' the pain.

But the same deceptive sales transaction for one leading to a loss of, less say, twenty five hundred dollars, may be something far more painful to another customer.

A German Shepherd puppy, from Germany, or from German import parents, is something special indeed. Due to the rarity, as well as the costs involved in importation, vet care, feeding, and housing, the price of the puppy is considerable.

Let's now say that two customers buy from the same breeder, and both puppies end up with very short lives due to hip dysplasia, an ailment that plagues large breeds today.

Did the breeder knowingly sell puppies from dysplastic parents?

Were x-rays ever taken?

If so, were the x-rays that came with the imported dam, or mother of the litter, authentic x-rays?

One customer seeks the recovery of his twenty five hundred dollar loss, as the breeder has a guarantee in place. The customer is naturally upset, but not, perhaps, as much as the second customer who has suffered a similar loss.

The second customer could not afford the puppy in the first place, but had promised his daughter an "authentic German German Shepherd puppy" as her very own to train, as she had been studying constantly how to train a working dog. His daughter had helped save her money towards the purchase, but even so, it went on a credit card at today's 19.8% interest. Upon learning that her pup might not even survive the surgery, if the father even had the money, she is devastated. The hurt of one is deeper and more penetrating than the hurt of the former.

But did the breeder willingly breed dysplastic dogs? What if, as is in life, two dogs with excellent hips, proven by authentic x-rays, still produced dysplastic pups? It happens. This is not a pain as the result of deception, but of the natural consequence of life's disappointments.

In the above case, there is much more to the story, and at the very heart of the story is deception. We will cover this story in our chapter on "Deception in Advertising" in detail.

The father of the 13 year old girl left bereft of the puppy, now saddled with unmanageable debt, was, indeed, a victim of deception that, had it been detected, would have saved his daughter's heart from breaking, as well as his own foolish indebted purchase.

A young man applies for a job in a dynamic, growing company. He is well spoken, articulate, and although he is only applying for the position of a driver, his appearance is more suited for management. He has little on his resume, and only a high school diploma, but with a handsome smile, he convinces the Human Resource interviewer to 'take a chance' on him, as he deceptively told of having to care for his young siblings when his mother developed cancer, thus spoiling his college ambitions. A year later, the company is out almost $100,000 in cash due to his theft, with police offering the only comfort of, "well, at least no one was hurt."

Young, pretty, but with a noticeable imperfection, she fell under the magical words of praise from the tall, handsome military hero's words of praise. When she asked him about his background, it was "that bitch of an ex wife" who made up the assault charges in order to smear his growing military career. He would make a fortune for his new bride, working in foreign countries, providing "security services" with "the United States' best military minds", from Africa to the Middle East, but could never tell her exactly where he would be, due to "security" reasons.

On the night she found herself awakened by the hands around her throat, cutting off her oxygen, and the pain riveting through her groin, the result of deception was long past evident.

13 year old Hailey Dunn, just another runaway problem child from small town Texas just might have been "taken" by someone when she walked over to her best friend's home for a sleep over.

Her dutiful and loving mother, Billie Jean Dunn, took to the Nancy Grace Show to highlight her daughter's plight, and seek the help of a nation who's collective heart broke at the young mother's tale.

Vigils, protests, and donations flooded the world of Charlie Rogers, who said that three sadistic men broke into her home, tied her down, carved hate slogans into her flesh, poured gasoline in her home, lit it on fire, and left her for dead. 5 minutes and 462 words on television brought the nation to unite in common denunciation of this horrific hate crime. In every internet news article, news group and blog that I, and a team of readers could find, not once did anyone question her story.

These cases, and others, will be covered with a consistent theme: deception could have been detected and no polygraph machine was necessary. All that was, and is, necessary, is the trained ear.

Gratitude

Special thanks must be delivered to those who's input into this book is invaluable. My wife Heather's undying confidence in my application of principle has allowed me to gain clarity, as her unusually gifted memory, and desire for truth, even in the worst of times, lifted me more times than I can count. She is the love of my life.

To my children, Peter, Joseph, Jonathan, Sarah, Christina, and Sean, who have all taught me the value of truth, forgiveness, and the bonds of family.

To Avinoam Sapir, the genius and "grandfather" of all Statement Analysis, who's careful consolidation of facts in such stark clarity is, indeed, rare genius today.

Chapter One: The Pain of Deception

Herein lies the mystery that I am unable to solve: how to measure the pain of deception. There will be more than a few stories in this book that speak to the topic of pain in deception. Even as I avoided statistics such as "business estimate that x billions of dollars are lost in shrinkage" because I did not want to de-personalize financial loss into numbers that lose meaning, so it is that I am acutely aware that those of you who have suffered because of deception, have your own unique, personal story to tell. I cannot quantify it in a statistic, nor should I try.

It is likely that if you found this book, you did so through the Statement Analysis blog I have authored the last several years. Readership has steadily grown, and judging by the comments, readership is also loyal, therefore, as I post a new story, I do not always have to give lengthy explanations of how the deception is detected; I often simply <u>underline</u> a particular word, and the 'regulars' know. They know. They go by some unusual names just as many commentators do so "anonymously", or change their names, yet the writing style eventually reveals that "Bob" is really "Rob" who is really "Sue", and so on.

We give ourselves away, as I will touch upon in the chapter regarding Anonymous Letters analyzed.

Yet, what is it that unites us? The comments reveal conservative and liberal, religious and secular, educated and uneducated, old and young, male and female, all posting, sometimes passionately, about cases that contain elements of deception.

The unifying force may not be justice, nor even the quest to 'solve' a murder case, but it is my belief that readership is united by pain; the pain of deception.

Recall the story of the writer who had achieved success in life, having raised a family, and built a nice career for himself, suddenly finding himself blinded by a pain so acute, that the only escape was suicide.

He learned that his beloved wife, of whom he had always adored, was leaving him, having cheated on him with a woman. His world was shattered, his manhood gone, and he could find no hope nor purpose to live. He packed up a few belongings and went to his country camp, to set his affairs in order, and end his life.

He did not know his wife had a secret life. He believed that they were close and loving, and that she was, indeed, his best friend. The 'atomic bomb' of information destroyed everything within him, so much so, that every memory that he sought refuge within, such as Christmas of years past, was tainted, as he wondered, "When she said she loved me that Christmas morn', was that a lie?" He could find no comfort anywhere, as the trauma against the brain was more than he could bear.

With enough food for a few days, and the very means of ending his life, he set out to write letters to his grown children, so that they would not be left with the additional emotional pain of not knowing why he chose to end his life.

He began by addressing each, affirming his love for each of them, detailing their many talents and characteristics in life that made them so special. From there, over the course of a few days, he wrote about the shock that he experienced, and what the shock had done to him.

It was enough to save his life.

He released the 'pressure on the brain', through words, just enough to not commit suicide. Needless to say, where his wife had done this to him, deception had built up in their marriage, for a considerable amount of time.

Deception hurts.

The introductory story about the German Shepherd puppy was one in which deception was past on from one victim to another, with victim becoming perpetrator.

Wanting to "make a name for himself" in the risky business of dog breeding, a young man had convinced his wife and his mother-in-law that if they were able to purchase one of Germany's top stud dogs, he would recoup his investment in the first year, and make a small fortune in the following 5 years. All it would take is an incredibly large amount of money to convince the German Shepherd's owner, in Germany, to part with his prized award winning male.

How much money?

Without adjusting for inflation costs, it meant not only the family's life savings, and as many credit cards as banks would issue, he convinced his mother-in-law to mortgage her house for the purchase.

Pulling together money from anyone who would loan it, the man made the purchase and, perhaps, the most beautiful German Shepherd male I have ever seen, landed in the United States, with the promise of "stud fees" already backed up on the calendar for months.

The problem?

The original seller was deceptive about the males progeny. Talk of falsified x-rays and fertility tests along with an angry and suit-threatening mob of owners of females who had flown their prized females to the kennel for breeding yet with few puppies born, the pressure mounted upon the new owner.

His mother-in-law needed to make payments on the second mortgage.

Those who had paid stud fees often had no puppies, whatsoever, produced.

The deceived man was in dire straits, and the pressure was now on his marriage, as well.

The star stud dog was not producing, therefore, in desperation, the deceived became the deceiver, and began, at an early age, to use one of the star stud's own male pups, to breed the incoming females, while falsifying the documents as to which dog actually did the breeding.

When pressed, his language produced passive replies. Passivity in speech seeks to avoid recognition, or responsibility. In domestic homicide cases, it sounds like:

"the gun went off...", as if guns had a mind of their own.

In asking questions about the breeding, evasive, passive answers were given, until finally, one customer who happened upon the kennel early one morning to find the male in with his female was not the famous expensive stud dog.

"Who is breeding my female?", he demanded.

"Who is breeding your female? How can you even ask me? You've known me for years. Kennel help is so hard to find. Reliable workers are almost impossible to find!"

His response is deceptive, but, word by word, it isn't a lie. You undoubtedly noticed that he answered a question with a question, meaning that the original question is "sensitive" to him. When someone answers your question with a question, there is sensitivity attached to your question. This sensitivity can be anything from the subject not hearing you, all the way up to needing time to think because he wants to deceive you.

What was the intent of the response?

The intent of the answer was to lead the owner of the female German Shepherd to believe that a careless worker had, unreliably, put in the wrong male with his female.

He did not come right out and say this, however, which leads us to a principle in detecting deception:

People do not like to lie outright.

You may have read somewhere online that "the average human being tells 250 lies per day…" or something along those lines.

It is not true.

In fact, the average human being tells very few outright lies in life. More than 90% of deception comes from withholding information.

Why is this so?

Do deceptive people really feel so badly about lying that they avoid it? If so, what about sociopathic types, who lack a conscience?

Direct lying is something that causes internal stress and a human will avoid it, so as to avoid the direct confrontation of "you lied!"

This is best seen by former President Bill Clinton when he looked right into the television camera, pointed his finger, and said, *"I did not have sexual relations with that woman, Ms. Lewinsky."*

He did not lie.

In fact, had a polygrapher asked him, "Did you have sexual relations with that woman, Ms. Lewinsky?" and he said, "no", he likely would have passed the lie detection test.

Yet, the stained blue dress and later 'mea culpa' (which lacked some 'mea") tell us otherwise.

This leads us to understand an important principle in Statement Analysis:

Each one of us has our own personal, subjective, internal dictionary. In lie detection, our goal is to "decode" this personal, subjective, internal dictionary.

In training, I offer the following as proof:

In a training seminar, we seek to keep each class no larger than 20 attendees. The material and pace is intense, and when there are more than 20 in attendance, the pace can be slowed down.

I ask 20 attendees to write down what they picture in their minds when I say a word. I begin with the word "boy" and then ask for volunteers to tell what they have written.

The answers range from:

1. My newborn grandson, with a blue blanket, in the hospital;
2. My seven year old son holding a baseball bat;
3. My twenty-one year old soldier son in Iraq.

Here we have the single word "boy" giving us a range of answers coursing 21 years! A principle we follow in Statement Analysis is: Do Not Interpret.

We do not interpret; we listen.

In the case of "how hard it is to find reliable workers", the deceptive kennel owner is counting on the listener to interpret his words to mean something he did not say. He did not say "An unreliable worker put the wrong male in with your female!", because that would be a direct lie, which is rare. If caught, the stress of being found out to be a liar would be too much for the brain to bear, therefore, in less than a second, the kennel owner came up with his deceptive response.

President Clinton did pretty much the same thing, except he had plenty of time to think about his answer.

Each attendee in the training had their own personal view of the word "boy" and it is only through follow up questions that we learn what the word "boy" meant, in context. Remember: we do not interpret; we listen.

For President Clinton, his personal, subjective internal dictionary's meaning of "sexual relations" was "intercourse."

He did not have "intercourse" with Monica Lewinsky, therefore, technically, he was not lying. He was deceptive, but not lying. Later, he admitted that he was "technically truthful" though he "intended" to deceive.

After the finger-pointing appearance on television, President Clinton was seen with a black eye.

When pressed for an answer, he said, *"I like to rough-house with my daughter, Chelsea, on the White House lawn."*

He did not lie.

He also did not say *"I got the black eye from rough-housing with my daughter, Chelsea, on the White House lawn."*

He did, however, wish to be interpreted as such.

I believe that it was something else that caused his black eye. I believe that his wife, Hillary Rodham Clinton did not share his personal, internal, subjective dictionary's meaning of "sexual relations."

Being lied to hurts.

A woman once asked for my assistance to learn if her husband had been unfaithful to her. They were high school sweethearts and they dated all through college and appeared to have the ideal marriage. In fact, both their families had looked to them, through the years, as the ideal couple, who exemplified what commitment looked like.

She then found some suspicious text messages between her husband and his co-worker. He dismissed it as foolish flirtation, but nothing further. This, alone, pierced her heart, she said, because she simply did not believe he would ever even flirt with another woman: they were that close.

One night while laying in bed, she could not help but cry. The feeling of betrayal ran deep. They had been "best friends" since junior high school, had gone to their proms and had never even dated anyone other than each other. He sought to comfort her and said, *"These lips have never kissed another, and this body has never been inside another."*

The words were just the healing balm she needed. She snuggled close up to him, and for a little while, the feeling of being "unsafe" disappeared and she found sleep and rest for her disquieted heart.

The next day she woke up wondering about what he had said.

"These lips have never kissed another, and this body has never been inside another."

She didn't accuse of him kissing the woman, nor of having relations with her. Why did he offer these two things to her?

She asked for Statement Analysis. I repeatedly refused until she finally said, "*Listen. I am going to drill him with questions, anyway. I would rather learn the truth, so just give me some guidance on what questions to ask. I cannot go on not knowing. It is killing me. Day and night, night and day, it is all I think about.*"

I asked her, "*Did you ask him if he kissed her?*"

She did not.

"*Did you accuse him of kissing her?*"

She did not. It never came up because she thought it was just foolish texting.

He had offered her two things, in the negative, and in Statement Analysis, this is considered to be very important.

That night she began the quizzing and kept up at it until he finally admitted that at the office Christmas party, he had kissed her.

She said that she was devastated to learn this, but since he did not sleep with her, she decided to stay in the marriage.

I let it go at that.

Statement Analysis deals with not only what one says, but what one does not say.

"*They said I was a rapist and a recluse. I'm not a recluse.*" Mike Tyson

Being deceived hurts.

What of all those people involved in the refinancing scandal a few years back? Many lost their homes due to deception and those who joined the class action law suit received checks to help offset their losses: the check amount was just under $35.

Deception hurts.

When a person lies to you, he presupposes that you are not intelligent enough to know you are being lied to. This brings its own emotional pain and the habitual or well-practiced liar actually holds the world in contempt. There is an inherent belief that the liar is smarter than the audience and will fool anyone and everyone; hence the contempt.

Children lie.

This isn't something to be debated because if anyone wishes to debate it, as a parent, there is but little hope for the child. All children lie and it is in childhood that the habitual liar is formed. If the child is not corrected, the liar will grow in confidence, with each juvenile lie strengthening, as it were, the "lie muscles", giving the child the false belief of superiority.

Law enforcement, at its best, must learn to exploit this pride. I will cite a marvelous example of this later, but suffice for now, the habitual liar will inflict pain, sometimes immeasurable pain upon its victim.

The liar puts himself first. Period. The liar's needs, wants, desires, hopes and dreams must all supplant the best interest of others. It is this childhood narcissism that is left uncorrected, and the selfishness grows. When hyper-self-esteem teaching is poured upon the child in school, the liar has no problem seeing himself better, or more worthy than anyone else.

The degree of damage done cannot be measured.

Chapter Two: The Cost of Deception in Business

In a world where people are more and more prone to put their own interests above the interests of the company which employs them, detecting deception in the interview process by trained Human Resources professionals is needed now more than ever before.

I was raised with 9 siblings, 7 sisters and 2 brothers. We embraced the early American Protestant Work ethic (though not Protestants) and learned early to work for the things we wanted.

I loved to read. I still do.

In the third grade, a scholastic newsletter went out where kids could order books and 6 weeks later, the books would arrive in school, and distributed to the student buyers. It ranged from 3rd grade up to 6th grade readers and I longed after such treasured ownership. In such a large family, there was little chance that I would have the money to purchase one of those treasured paperback books. I knew to not even ask my mother for the money.

In the 1970's, I considered myself one of the kings of "Whiffle Ball" that my brother and I played with the neighborhood kids when and where baseball was not available. The small plastic ball did not break windows, and with enough practice, precise curves, sliders, fastballs and even knuckleballs could be produced to the dismay of even older boys who could not touch the pitches. With hour after hour of play, the plastic miracle of a ball would eventually crack, and once cracked, the impact on control was evident, and the lifespan of the ball quickly eroded to its "last game."

To purchase a new Whiffle Ball, we needed 25 cents, plus another .02 cents for tax. .27 cents. .27 cents is all that stood between the glory of the home run, hit over the neighbor's fence, where it had to be retrieved away from the snarling Chihuahua, "Peanuts" who, in spite of his diminutive appearance, scared the daylights out of us. My brother and I took turns on which would enter the gate while the other ran to the other side of the yard to distract the raging monster, Peanuts, from tearing open our ankles. We became skilled at both raising the money, and keeping from being bit, in the summer of 1972 on Long Island, in New York. (Long Guylanders did not live "in Long Island" but "on" Long Guyland).

When we went to church, if we said our prayers and responses out loud, my mother would give us each a dime. She would not give us the dime if she could not hear our prayers, nor would she raise the stakes from the collective .20 cents to the needed .27 cents for the Whiffle Ball. The additional money had to be raised by doing chores.

We quickly learned that our older brother, a teenager who worked flipping burgers, would often leave his change out on his desk. Not daring to embezzle the needed funds for said Whiffle Ball, we knew that he could not go out of the house until his room was cleaned. Armed with this truth, we went into his room when he wasn't home, and wrestled on his bed, making a right mess of things of which he would then need to "hire" someone to clean for him.

The cost of cleaning up the mess we had inflicted upon him? .27!

Tony Soprano had nothing on the Brothers Hyatt.

This left us not only with enough money to buy the prized Whiffle Ball, but to get baseball cards, with its gloriously stiff and dated stick of gum, with the promise of landing a Willie Mays or Tom Seaver card; something to not be traded on the bus.

On Long Guyland, there were Met fans and then there were Yankee fans, both on the same bus to the same school but the twain did not meet. When one peace loving diplomat would say "I like both teams!", both groups gave him the Amish shunning treatment for not having the courage to choose.

Whiffle ball? .27 Baseball cards? .10 pack (I don't know why, but we were never charged tax, even with the stale gum awaiting us).

But to raise money for a paperback scholastic approved book?

This was beyond my abilities to extort money from my older brother. Plus, no one really likes a 10 year old Irish mug, shaking down family for book money.

I looked at that single paged but doubled sided scholastic book list with all of its pictures and blurbs and prices calling out to me with such utter longing that the pain on my face was not lost by Mrs. McKeon, my beloved teacher.

"I'll just order this one for you. You can pay me back by cleaning up the blackboards each day", she kindly said to me one day. I felt as if my heart would burst with love, and I wanted to give her the 'very bestest' hug a 5th grader could dare to deliver, but I caught myself, knowing that once before I had raised my hand and called her "mom" by accident, and endured the ridicule of the other students.

"I will have to ask my parents", I reluctantly told her, knowing exactly what their reaction would be, but the thought of landing one of those paperbacks, especially Encyclopedia Brown, filled me with the resolve of argument: I would be working for the book, not getting charity. Not only was the prize of landing the paperback before me, I also wanted to avoid the empty echo of pain that I would feel the day the books arrived, in the brown box, with all the eager faces ready to receive their treasures, and me left, bereft of the wonderful feeling of purchasing power, and cuddling up with a good book, taking imaginary journeys to far away places, or solving unsolvable mysteries that only someone who thinks like Encyclopedia Brown could think. It was almost too painful to consider.

My mother sternly lectured me that not only did we not accept charity, but that the same books were available, for free, from the school library.

"We work for what we get, Peter" she said. *"You know better than to even ask."*

Gulp. Did I feel guilty. I knew my father worked hard to support ten children, and when the 'blue laws' were lifted, our lives changed dramatically as Sundays were family days when my father was home, but now stores were to open and he was a commission salesman who could not afford to stay home on Sundays. My life would never be the same again. The Sunday roast beef family time became but a memory for us, and my dad would never be the same, either. Shortly after this, he suffered a heart attack and fell prey to Parkinson's Disease. Sunday throwing a ball, or swimming with him would only then live in my memory, something, to this day, I try to summon when I need a comforting memory.

When I was 12 years old, I got a paper route, and by 14, I worked part time in a butcher shop, sweeping up and doing various chores. When I wanted Converse Chuck Taylor sneakers and Levi jeans to match, I did not dare ask my parents for the money, instead it was my responsibility to save money in order to buy the sneakers I had wanted. It would take patience and self control, but it could be done. It meant delivering papers on time, being polite, and praying like crazy for my bicycle front tire to withstand the heavy load of a metal basket and a load of New York newspapers, afternoon edition.

Looking back, this lesson of "no charity" may appear to be extreme to some readers, and perhaps it was, but in not only teaching Statement Analysis and Analytical Interviewing (the interview naturally flowing from analysis) for companies seeking to hire the best applicants, the responses of the self-esteem culture is worth noting for its own extremity. It's almost as if an entire generation needs to be reminded to take a bath before a job interview.

For example, I interviewed one young woman for an entry level position. I had not been told, however, that she had already been hired. Human Resources simply wanted me to re-interview her, for the purpose of learning, without formal training, what an employment interview should look like.

The applicant was in her early 20's, and had decided not to go to college. She was living with her boyfriend, who was also recently hired (unbeknownst to me) and very much needed the job to pay the rent.

I ask open ended questions, and listen carefully to the responses. I follow the principles of Statement Analysis, and whether the interview is for murder, arson, child abuse, or employment, the procedure is the same.

I asked her to talk about her prior work experience.

She stated that she used to work for this company, but "got done" when she "stood up for my rights." ("Got done" is a regional expression, methinks, for "quit.")

Where one begins an answer is always important and often reveals priority. That her prior work experience had something to do with her "rights" caught my attention. She explained that she worked in a home where the patient had a cat. The cat got fleas. I don't have a cat, but I do understand that, every so often, a pet gets fleas. Pet owners usually purchase products, foggers, flea shampoo, etc, and take care of the problem.

"What of the fleas?", I asked.

She said that the company took the patient's cat to the groomers and 'bombed' the house. This is to "fog" the house. They moved the patient to a different home for the fogging and the next day, instructed the young woman to clean the house to prepare it for the patient's return.

She refused.

She said, *"I read the instructions on the fogger. It said it had to be aired out with the windows open for 24 hours. They didn't leave all the windows open."*

The supervisor did not know how to handle the young woman who "stood up for her rights" and refused to clean, so the supervisor simply went to the home and did what most of us would have done. She opened the windows that were not opened, took down the sheets and put them into the laundry, redid all the dishes, and cleaned the home.

The young worker "walked off the job" to protest the "unfair and unhealthy work conditions" and was "proud of herself" for doing so.

I wondered how her pride paid the rent.

No one wants to see someone sickened from flea fog, but I could not help but wonder what empowered her to not only refuse to do the work but to boast of it to me, one brought in to interview her. I sought to learn if she had offered any reasonable compromises to the supervisor, such as opening the few windows, turning on some fans, or anything like that.

Nope. Not going to happen.

The reason she mentioned this first, as a priority, was that she wanted everyone to know that she knew her "rights" and would not "be pushed around by anyone."

I informed the manager that I likely saved them trouble later by recommending: Do Not Hire.

I was met with a puzzled gaze. *"Didn't they tell you?"* (I always ask "who is they?" when I hear something like this). *"She's already hired."*

Less than one month later, she was accused of abusing the patient and under investigation. I explained that her priority was herself, and if tested, her best interest versus the best interest of the patient, or the company, she would win out.

Those who put themselves above the material needs of the company trouble the company and can be weeded out in the interview process by Analytical Interviewing.

The resultant allegation of abuse is accompanied by the possibility of a law suit, on behalf of the patient.

Today's work mentality is not the old Protestant Work Ethic of yesteryear.

When one is deceptive during the interview process, the deceptive person is many times more likely to:

File a fraudulent claim against the company;

Call out sick deceptively;

Steal, time, money, clients, etc;

Cause morale issues within the company.

In short, the deceptive person is not a problem solver for your company, but a problem bringer.

At no time is this better exampled than when, in the employment interview, the subject is found to be deceptive particularly when there **is no reason to be deceptive**. This is a strong signal of a habitual liar. It is almost as if the subject cannot turn it off.

That handsome, *"take a chance on me; I've been caring for my sick mom and raising my siblings"* young man, who, in the employment interview, said very little, but was a gifted listener and manipulator, got his driver's job.

Later, he was *"beaten at gunpoint"* by a 'gang of thugs' and forced to open the warehouse where, surprise surprise, a $100,000 of new lap tops and electronics had just been delivered.

"Oh, they beat me. They covered me with a blanket and beat me. They beat me in my head. They forced me to give them the key to the warehouse. Then we went into the warehouse and they stole all the computers…" he reported to police. He then needed to go on medical leave, not for his physical injuries, but for the psychological damage: he was too afraid to leave the home.

When I reviewed the police file, I pointed out:

Oh, they beat me. They covered me with a blanket and beat me. They beat me in my head. They forced me to give them the key to the warehouse. Then we went into the warehouse and they stole all the computers…"

Remember the teaching of Statement Analysis in which we all have a very personal, internal and subjective dictionary?

There are three exemptions to this principle that must be noted:

1. Objective time on the clock. When one says, "It is 1PM", it is one hour after noon, to each and everyone. It is objective information.
2. Articles. The words "the" and "a", as articles, are not subjective. *"I met a man in town. The man stole my money."* Before meeting the man, he was "a" man, but once met, he became "the" man. When a subject confuses articles, it is a signal of deception. *"I met the man and a man stole my money…"* reveals prior knowledge of the man.

3. Pronouns.

Pronouns are powerful tools in detecting deception. Pronouns do not lie. Pronouns are instinctive. In fact, pronouns often pre date our speech!

Listen to a toddler just learning to speak. Even as he learns the pronoun "my" he often communicates the word "my" even before he can say it, by opening and closing his hands, signaling what he wants as "mine."

Pronouns are intuitively used, millions of times by us, and do not need thought. When I tell a story from childhood, I do not struggle in starting my story with, "What should I choose? "I" or "We" in my story? " It is because I know if I was alone, or with someone else.

The word "we" speaks of unity, or cooperation. When a person is a victim of a crime, the word "we" is not likely to enter his vocabulary after the attack.

After a beating, especially where he was blinded to the blows (unable to protect himself from seeing the hits), he should have said, "they took me to the warehouse" or something similar. Eventually, you're going to read that pronouns even produce inadvertent confessions. Stay tuned.

I once had a sexual assault case in which, after interviewing all parties, I concluded deception on the part of the victim. Pressed against what seemed to be strong evidence, I stood upon this principle of instinctive pronoun usage. My manager asked, "Are you willing to base your entire conclusion on a single pronoun?"

I said, " *I bet my career on it.* "

The victim tearfully told an account that brought me to the edge of tears. Yet, after the assault, she said, "<u>we</u> *drove home, and I called police...* "

I said that after such an assault, it is not likely that the victim will use the word "we" in describing herself and the perpetrator after the crime. I suggested that the victim be confronted with this linguistic indicator in the presence of her therapist. A young man's fate was to be decided, as local police were set to arrest him. I sought just a short delay for this one opportunity.

In the presence of her therapist, she confessed to lying about the assault, angry and ashamed that her boyfriend had cheated on her, she was eager for retribution, even if it meant him going to jail.

Pronouns are a lesson in lie detection all within themselves.

When Human Resource professionals are trained in Analytical Interviewing, they are given tools of which, once employed, will save companies countless dollars, and countless headaches.

Unemployment Insurance Costs

Unemployment insurance is used to protect workers in a time of great need. It was not intended for those who wish to "game the system" and be paid to stay at home.

Deceptive individuals love to game the unemployment system, learning just how long to stay on the job, and exactly what words to say to an unemployment deputy or hearings officer upon being questioned.

When Human Resource professionals are trained to spot deceptive applicants, they are saving their companies quarterly funds, paid into the unemployment system, first by weeding out those who are statistically more likely to file a fraudulent claim, and then, secondly, they save money when the fraudulent employee goes to file. Here is how:

Statement Analysis.

In the trainings, we deal with odds and percentages. By constructing an employee interview specifically designed to discern truthful applicants from deceptive ones, there will be a reduction, over time, of theft, false filings of various types, and of those who apply for unemployment after ending employment for inappropriate reasons.

In some fields, particularly in entry level positions, turnover rate can be as high as 50%. These are often stressful, lower paying jobs where an employer cannot afford to pay a higher wage, therefore, finding himself or herself with heavy quarterly unemployment fees.

In a 50% turnover rate, this means that for every 10 hires, 5 will be gone by the end of the year. This is rough.

In one company with this type of turnover rate, Analytical Interviewing was implemented and then used, not only in the screening process, but in internal disputes, and then, finally, in the unemployment hearing, itself.

In a two year period, the company had a 100% success rate.

Why was this so? Wasn't this unfair to workers?

The reason for the 100% success rate is simple: the truth. The company told the truth, and documented everything. Where there was a temporary layoff, due to change in business, the company did not object to the employee filing, therefore, there was no hearing. But when an employee deliberately quit after staying the minimal amount of time (hoping to be on unemployment for the full 18 months), or failed to show up at work, or did something worthy of termination, the company contested the unemployment and was victorious. Good workers knew the company would not lie, and deceptive workers soon learned that the "gig was up" and that gaming the system would not prevail.

What about falling down on the job?

I teach companies that when they interview someone for a job, and the subject of the interview is deceptive in the interview, note carefully what triggered the deception. Was it a deceptive response about former employment? This is common. As I said earlier, the scariest of deceptive liars is those who are deceptive when there is no cause for it.

These are the most likely to...

Fall on the job.

Countless millions are lost on fraudulent claims of accidents in the work place. I once knew a woman who fell at Home Depot, Walmart and Kmart, which each of these large chains writing her a nice check for her "fall."

She was remodeling her home by gaming the system, and I wondered if those who negotiated with her had any training in detecting deception.

When is it appropriate for a person to use the pronoun *"you"* when the person speaks of himself? The use of the word "you" when speaking of oneself, is often found in both distancing language, as well as universal language (which is a form of distancing).

A while back, I fell down a flight of stairs. I broke my collar bone, toe, and bruised up myself pretty badly. I also tore my shoulder muscle, which took months to heal, and never healed completely. I had just received a new prescription for glasses: progressive lens glasses. I was struggling with them, and came down very early in the morning, and had left a book on the step the night before. I fell down almost the entire stairs, hit the landing, and fell down 2 more to the floor. The pain was acute.

Note the following statement:

"*It hurts when you break your collar bone.*"

This is not something you would expect me to say after the above described fall.

When was this said?

Herein lies the key: context.

A broken bone is very painful.

How close to the break was this sentence spoken?

When the pain is mostly a memory, it is appropriate to use not only distancing language, but 'universal' language: "you" is anyone who experiences a broken collar bone, no matter how the injury occurred

For me, it was the flight of stairs.

Now, a case to examine from several years ago in which an employee fell down stairs. I am always on alert for those who seek to "game" the system, and seek some form of compensation. The subject said:

"*Fell down a flight of stairs. I have to be seen.*"
I noted the missing pronoun, as I take notes, always. She did not say "I fell..." but "Fell..." This is distancing language. It could be because she was in severe pain. Having experienced a fall down an almost entire flight of stairs, the pain is blinding. Yet, "*I have to be seen*" is a legal responsibility an employer has. Besides "gamers", I also am concerned about health, safety and well being. No one in pain needs someone questioning their account, yet, my training has me on alert.

My response: "*Yes, immediately.*"

The subject continued to talk, therefore, rather than cutting her off with another insistence upon seeking medical attention immediately, I asked,

Q. "*How many steps did you fall down?*"

A. "*How many steps did I fall down? Well, uh, three.*"

I noted both the repetition of my question, and the number within the answer. This sensitivity (answering a question with a question) may be due to pain. I must always remain open-minded and believe what I am told.

Q. *What hurts?*
A. "*Everything. Everything. Everywhere it hurts. You hurt when you fall down the stairs.*"

Q. *Yes it does. You need to be seen immediately.*
A. *"Okay. I have to wait for my husband to drive me."*
Q. *"Do you want me to arrange a ride? Would you like to go in an ambulance?"*
A. *"No, I can wait."*
Q. *"If you choose to wait, you can ice it, and take advil."*
A. *"Yeah, that's true. I should be seen, but <u>I don't</u> like when they prescribe pain medication. It makes my head swim."*
I noted the introduction of narcotics. I noted that not only did she introduce narcotics, but she did so in the negative.

The secretary called the medical office contracted to see the employees, with the relevant information and the description of the injury.
The treating physician called me. *"I know your work! What do you think about this case?"*
I reported that I had my doubts, particularly for two reasons:

1. The number of steps was given as three. Of course, this may be true, but according to research by Mark McClish, "3" is to be flagged for possible deception. (I think that "two" might sound too little, for a deceptive person, and "4" might sound excessive, therefore, 3 is chosen. More on this later).

2. The distancing language within moments of the fall the subject used

I also told him that I had not asked about pain medications, but that by offering to me that she did not like pain medications, I was concerned that this may be a ruse to score meds. I told him that she may have very well fallen down three steps, injured herself, and hates pain medication, but that the linguistic indications mean I should verify.

He thanked me for my opinion, and said that he would report back to me the findings, including any work restrictions.

After the examination, he said, "*She reported global pain, and needed assistance to enter the office. I have ordered x-rays as a matter of routine, due to the report of such acute pain. Upon examination, there are no injuries. She requested pain medication but I only gave her a script for a single tablet, since there was no visible injury, and I also noted that when she was leaving, she did not know I was watching. I noted in my chart that she left with perfect gait. I told her that if the x-ray showed fracture, I would give her another prescription for pain medication.*"
She was sent to the x-ray facility, next building down.

She did not show up.
When an injury, or a physical attack happens, it is very personal. The distancing language comes into play as the pain or memory of the pain subsides. Emotion has a powerful ability to change

language, and in this case from

"*I hurt*" to "*you hurt*" when you break your...

Conclusion: Part of context is when the subject makes a statement. How often has the subject made the statement? If time has passed the subject is repeating his words, you make hear a "self reference" indicating the subject is no longer working from experiential memory, but memory of what he said earlier.

"*Like I said, when you break your collarbone...*"
As time and healing has taken place, universal, distancing language (2nd person, "you") is appropriate.

When the wound is fresh, or if the incident is not universal, distancing language should be examined for possible deception. Passivity and dropped pronouns should also be noted.

Lesser injuries will use universal language. When gender is not known, "their" or "they" is sometimes used, even when plural is denied.

Pronouns are instinctive. When something is universal, "you" is sometimes used. When something is up close and personal, we must question why one is using distancing or universal language.

Recall the Baby Ayla case, in which the deceptive grandmother took two unique, and terribly intrusive personal events and said:

"*When you're waiting for someone to call about your missing granddaughter...when someone is casing your house...*"
She did not lie.

People do not like to lie outright, instead will withhold or suppress information. No one likes to be seen or caught as a liar. When one is caught, rage is often the response.

The pronoun "we" always means "we", that is, not just me, alone. You'll see in the upcoming chapters, just how razor sharp lie detection can be if you simply listen to pronouns.

Dennis Dechaine took the stand in his own defense, on trial for the murder of young Sarah Cherry.

He has had a strong internet following of those who have claimed he was wrongfully convicted. These things sometimes even draw in celebrities, such as those who were duped, many years ago, by psychopathic murderer and rapist, Rubin Carter.

This week, Dechaine was denied a new trial.

In his testimony, he said, "*We were losing daylight*" while asserting to have never met, nor seen his victim Sarah Cherry, 12 years old.

Everyone of us has an internal, subjective personal dictionary. Therefore, if I say the word "bike", one of you might be referring to:

a tricycle for your toddler...

a motorcycle that you commute with...

an old fashioned Schwinn from yesterday...

and so on.

Therefore, it is follow up questions that are needed to clarify what "bike" actually means to the subject, unless the context makes it clear.

Everyone of us has an internal, subjective personal dictionary.

Pronouns, however, are the exception.

Pronouns are instinctive and take no thought. Even when recalling an event from 20 years ago, a person will know whether to start their account with "I" or "we"; that is, whether the person was alone, or with someone else.

Dennis Dechaine claimed to have been alone in the wood, yet what leaked out? The pronoun "we" found its way into his answer.

As he was describing the trees around him, he slipped into experiential memory, rather than the script he had given to his attorney.

In a recent statement, a business was held up at gunpoint by a crazed drug gang.

In the victim's statement, he said, "*They beat me and placed a bag over my head, screaming at me, saying "Where's the safe? Where's the safe." I said it was in the other room. We went into the other room and they got the money.*"
He knew the gang ad he was in on it.

The pronoun "we" entered his language after the beating.

Dealing
With Deception

The word "placed" is too soft for a violent drug crazed gang.

When something sounds 'off' there is a good reason for it.

The cost to business is far more than statistics tell us. There is a personal side to it, as well.

The small business owner who took tremendous personal risk, with his own money, to start up his business only to have it "take a hit" because someone was deceptive, takes this very personally.

People tend to view a business as its own face-less impersonal entity but it isn't. Unlike what President Obama so wrongly proclaimed when he said, "you didn't build this", the small business owner did built this.

Not only did he build it, but in many cases, across our country, the small business, fueled by one's own personal money, bears the owner's family name.

When one steals from a family business, it is like stealing from a family member. It is personal. It is hurtful, and it is something that is hard to shake off.

How about those who "bear the family name" in a business but who's demeanor, while bearing that name, is contrary to what the family believes. This, too, can be hurtful.

What of those who work their entire lives to build up a business and provide hundreds of families with bread on their table?

I met one such family when I was employed to train their company's human resources and security in Statement Analysis and Analytical Interviewing.

30 years ago, a man and his wife delivered goods to convenience stores, out of their own car. They used their own savings to buy items wholesale, and then competed with large companies, with large trucks, to even buy wholesale, but then "out customer serviced" the customer service of others.

They packed their car up earlier in the morning than others and were prompt, polite and gave excellent service. The convenient stores were pleased, and purchased more from them. Eventually, the back of their car wasn't enough to hold everything, so they used a second car, and with a drive to succeed that was more important to them than their own sleep, they forged ahead, meeting deadlines, beating deadlines, and continuing to provide excellent customer service which meant, at times, claiming the customer was "always right" even when the customer was certainly not. They took short term losses to win the long term contracts.

By the time I met them, they had huge warehouses, a fleet of trucks and employed more than 500 people.

What did this mean?

Let's say that each employee had a spouse and 2 children.

By the labor of their hands, with the risk of their own money, they began a business which now helped more than 2,000 lives be housed, fed and receive medical care.

What do you think it felt like when they found an employee stealing from them?

What do you think they felt when a customer called them and said, "Your driver just shorted me $500 in change?"

I may not be able to adequately portray how the husband and wife team (now joined by their grown son) felt, but I can tell you what they did:

They did not question their customer, instead, sent them an immediate funding of $500, apologized, and said that they would take it up with their driver.

It was far more than the $500 that was at stake: it was their family name. It was 30 years of hard work. It was the reputation of the business, which helps feed and house at least 2,000 human beings, that was foremost in their minds. Shrinkage? That's just a term. For them, it was, and is, personal, and it threatens the security of many others, including children.

They were trained to catch such thieves and let other employees know: We can catch deceivers. This is unnerving for the deceptive, but reassuring to the dedicated and hard working employees who love their company.

The cost of deception to a business is far more than just dollars and cents.

Chapter Three: Pain of Deception in Sexual Abuse

Pop Quiz:

Who is better equipped for choosing a prom date for a sixteen year old girl?

   A. The sixteen year old girl herself?
   B. The sixteen year old girl's father?

Hmm, let's see if I can reason with myself, and with my background as reference point.

If Hollywood has taught me anything, it is that the stodgy 50 year old father, having lived for decades on this earth, knows next to nothing about human nature, while his teenaged daughter, with impeccable precision in discernment, knows far more than any social scientist ever dreamed of knowing and is best suited to know how her life should develop and who's car is safe to jump in.

Such is the lesson of Hollywood to our daughters, and the incidents of date-rape appear statistically to be increasing, including the use of various intoxicants.

The results can be akin to a life sentence of pain.

Had the deceptive "Romeo" been caught, early on, the difference in life cannot be understated.

When the "funny uncle" molested the small boy, was there anything in his language that could have tipped off the family before hand?

"Out of the abundance of the heart, the mouth speaks" is truth eternal. The heart is the seat of the intellect and the affections; what we know, and how we feel about what we know. It makes no difference what you do with truth, it remains truth. Drop it in another time period and it si truth. Drop it in a different culture, and it remains truth. Call it something it is not, and it is still truth. Truth is timeless and outside the boundaries of culture or belief.

 Our words reveal us. Even those trained in detecting deception cannot deceive once they begin to speak freely for themselves. The pedophile is going to reveal himself, if you are listening.

It's a big "if" as so often people are not listening. Even the words we chose in unrelated conversation come from somewhere. Nothing comes from a void. (Did I really just say that?).

When we see the aftermath of sexual abuse, we know that deception was beneath it, fueling its ability to exercise its evil impact.

Jerry Sandusky presented himself as one thing, while he was really another. When he spoke, his words indicated deception. He wanted us to believe that he was only involved in 'horseplay' with young boys, while he was actually molesting them.

Even his own wife had to bear up his lies in order to remain in "denial" to protect herself from the creeping doubts within her own heart.

What is the cost of such abhorrent behavior based in deception?

Where do I begin?

What happens to a child who is molested? What becomes of the adult?

This is something that can be qualified with statistics, but is virtually impossible to conclude anything but pain; a life time of pain.

When a little girl is molested, for example, as a teenager, she is many times more likely to abuse herself. She is many times more likely to fall into substance abuse, depression, anxiety, promiscuity, and, in short, anything that can cause her to inflict pain…

Upon herself.

The child who is molested is sentenced to a life time of pain. Parents cannot be lax when it comes to allowing access to their children. Just a moment of distraction…

An investigator once told me the story of a man who had been diagnosed with a developmental disability to the point where, although he had molested children, he was not criminally charged due to his low IQ, instead was placed in a single development home where he had "24 hours a day eyes-on staff"; that is, he was to be watched every day, every hour, and every moment in life. The cost to taxpayers was incredible.

The company entrusted with his care had to train live in staff to be ever vigilant. Staff made his meals, did his laundry, made his bed, and in short, were his 'servants', and were barely above minimum wage. Due to the stress of live-in work, staff turnover was high, and each time new staff were hired, warnings were given to never take their eyes off of him.

As was routine, he went for daily walks with staff, careful to avoid schools. He was, however, allowed to walk, with staff, through the park when school was in session. The thinking was that since school was in session, the park would be empty.

On the fateful day, staff brought him to the park, as was the norm, and he asked to use the bathroom. The park was empty and staff had been trained to always go into the bathroom with him, just to make sure.

This was a less-than-pleasant assignment for staff and the man was a difficult and nagging sort, who's narcissism had only gotten far worse ordering around his "servants" night and day, which added to the high turnover rate.

On this particular day, staff decided to let him use the park's facility alone, seeing that the park was empty. Staff was glad to not go into the bathroom, check the stall, and wait inside. This short break was welcome relief for staff, who thought he could have a cigarette and catch his breath from the constant demands of his employ.

When the man did not emerge from the bathroom in a few short minutes, staff burst in and found the stall door locked, with the man refusing to unlock it.

Beneath the door he saw the sneakers of a young boy.

Who can say, with any certainty, what the life long suffering of this young boy will be like? A compromised immune system, leaving him open to disease, a self-loathing that could express itself in violence, substance abuse, or crime. Would he marry, and if so, would his wife suffer with him? What of his children? Would he take out rage upon himself, others, or even other child victims? Depression, anxiety, suicidal ideation…

It is not known what he will suffer from this momentary neglect of duty, but suffer he will.

What about the crime of rape? We employ Statement Analysis in rape cases and have seen how false accusations can be discerned, but this can take the focus off the horror of the actual crime, itself.

While no one holds a monopoly on suffering, it is in this realm that the crime of rape should be understood, that like a child who is molested, for the rape victim:

the suffering never ends.

Like a fire seeking to spread, the emotional toll of rape is something that, in unassociated rape, the death penalty should be considered. I care little for the cottage industry that says otherwise:

the suffering never ends. It may be mitigated, or, at best, managed, but it never ends.

Rape is about violence and it targets the woman's single most sensitive portion of a woman's body, taking that which is for intimacy and childbirth, and targeting it with violence. Human sexuality and violence are geometrical opposites. One is not to be associated with the other, except in the mind of the reprobate. It is a crime against sexuality and its ramification goes long after the physical violence impact has "healed" with medicinal intervention and time. In fact, it is my assertion that the impact never ceases and it spreads like a quiet cancerous trek through the loving connections of family and friend, as if it can sense a loving bond, and exploit it. Rape strikes at the very soul of her sexuality, and it destroys the depth of who she is, a woman.

In the previous account, we saw that in just a moment's neglect, a child's life can be ruined as the vigilance rests just for a second, and the guard is left down. That's all it takes. Here, we look at what happens when a woman is raped.

Question: Did she fight back?

Answer: Her entire life might be impacted by her response to the attacker.

a. If she fought back, the damage may be lessened by the very activity of fighting back.
b. If she froze in fear, the damage to the brain is likely to be far more severe, and the consequences of such will show.

This is something easy to explain. You may read of studies, going back 60 years, of victims who fought and victims who froze, and how the suffering changed among victims. You may take to this task on your own, as I will limit myself here, with a simple, basic explanation.

It also can help explain why Domestic Violence is so dangerous to young children, even babies, who are not physically hurt, but witness the violence.

Think of a time when you were driving in your car and were either in a car accident, or in an almost accident. You may have been sliding in the snowy road, or worse, had that white knuckle feel of hydro-planing on a wet road.

You squeezed the steering wheel and for a few moments (seconds) you felt an incredible flush of hormones, and held your breath. As you were able to "reason" within yourself that you were safe, the hormone levels quickly dropped, and you exhaled. You were okay.

Now picture those hormone levels elevated, but with nothing to bring them down, going on for 1 minute, 2 minutes, or even more. The imprint left on the brain is what we recognize as "Post Traumatic Stress Disorder."

The brain has a lifelong imprint due to the hormones ('fight or flight') not receding quickly, in a matter of seconds. The longer the hormone levels were extreme, the more damage done.

The PTSD shows itself in nightmares, hyper vigilance, outburst of violence, raging thoughts of suicide incessantly re-victimizing the victim, even when all in life is going well. Sudden rushes of the hormone triggered by sight or even smell, can quickly, in the brain, transport the victim to a frightening place, and can be, even just momentarily, like madness and insanity, with a sudden recovery.

Some 'light' examples.

In World War II, my father was on an escort destroyer in the Sea of Japan, and as a signalman, had to remain above deck and was scared by the kamikaze raids by the Japanese. This was a last ditch attempt by the Japanese navy to discourage the coming American invasion of Japan by deliberately flying suicide runs into ships. My father was on "high alert" during these times, as the planes, flying in excess of 350 mph, hit without much warning.

He suffered nightmares for the rest of his life. As a boy in the 70's, I recall him screaming, "The Japs! The Japs!" while sleeping or even napping, and would wake up sweating. He, like so many other vets, refused to talk about it. The length of time on high hormonal alert, scarred the brain.

Another veteran, in Viet Nam, was scared out of his mind lying in the jungle at night. He was more scared of the jungle cats than of the enemy because he had heard some of his buddies screaming, being dragged away by the jungle cats in the utter darkness of a jungle. Just a teenager, 40+ years later, the suffering continues.

Did you ever see the video of the "shell shocked" veterans of the First World War? They were video taped in England and it shows young men, even teens, who were unable to stop themselves from shaking. Strong, athletic, smart, they were reduced, by the elevated hormone levels to the brain, to quaking invalids. They were not cowards, they were victims of their own brains' attempt to protect themselves, finally shutting down after being over-loaded. They were strong athletes, used to controlling their bodies in extreme circumstances, now shaking uncontrollably and wetting themselves.

Did you ever read studies of hours of combat and PTSD? There appears to be a breaking point for all soldiers, at a certain number of accumulated hours of combat, and then they have nothing left. This is not moral, nor an act of the will, but of the human brain.

These are 'light' examples of PTSD. The word 'light' is used only as a comparison, and not to minimize their suffering. My dad worked his entire life and his suffering, while real, was not that of a woman who is raped. Hers is so much the worse.

In the history of humanity, no where was the impact of rape illustrated like it was in 1945 in Berlin, Germany, as the "Red Army" (our allies) entered into Berlin and sought to "pay back" Germany by wantonly raping women and children. (For those of you who believe we should have, while there, and so well equipped, stopped the Soviet advance as Winston Churchill wanted, there are some strong moral arguments to be made). Estimates of suicide by rape victims is in the thousands, though it is difficult to imagine formulating an exact figure among the chaos, as well as the shame in reporting by the family. I have read of Soviet soldiers who raped children and elderly nuns, and some were raped until dead. The Soviet propaganda called for such "punishment" of all the German people, and fueled by vodka and abandonment of restrictive law, the Soviet soldiers debased an entire city of women.

I. **The woman's suffering**

This is the area of unimaginable. This is the area in which few of us can understand, as even the victims cannot always find the words to not only what they experienced, but what they experience, day by day. I believe that most of the suffering will never be known, as her stomach tightens, her lips go dry, and her throat closes even as she attempts to find words to describe her pain.

She may suffer nightmares and night terrors for the rest of her life.
She will likely have "triggers"; that is, certain sights or smells, or even words, which will signal the brain to raise memories that were etched deeply within the recesses of the brain by the elevated hormones.

She may become promiscuous, impacting her self respect, dignity, and even her health. She may destroy her own reputation, as she seeks to "punish" herself. This is why, at times, victims of childhood sexual abuse put themselves, deliberately in dangerous situations: they wish to be punished for what they perceive as their own fault. So much time is spent attempting to convince them that they are victims, not assailants. I don't know of another crime where this disparity exists in this manner.

Speak of showering? Some loved ones of victims remain on high alert, 24/7. In Statement Analysis, we note where someone speaks of "water" or "showering", especially when it is not necessary to say so, and see an association with a desire to be 'cleansed'; just as observational evidence shows.

She may see herself as hideously ugly, worthy of punishment, no matter what others tell her. Given the chance, she'd slash at her face, if she could get away with it, only to catch herself, and know how terribly irrational such a thought is.

She may seek to break mirrors in her home.

She may become asexual, that is, incapable of having intimacy, even for a gentle husband who loves her. She may see herself as "dirty", and tainted, forever, by her "filth" and "unworthiness." It is not as though she can be talked out of this, either, as it is something deeply embedded in the brain.

The rape victim is not, therefore, "fishing" for compliments. When she sees herself as ugly, it is not an attempt to get her husband or others to tell her how beautiful she is: this is how she sees herself. There may be a distinct inability for accurate self-perception due to the violent crime perpetrated against her.

She may fear crowds, and for some, the smell of alcohol can make her come close to passing out.

She may develop substance abuse problems in a way of not only self-medicating, but in a way of slowly killing herself, something she lives for, and something she thinks of, perhaps, every day of her life; good days and bad days.

She may despise her own femininity and even her own body parts and seek to cover them excessively.

She may develop an eating disorder, as starving herself causes pain; the pain she thinks she deserves, which actually comforts her in a strange and perverse way. Food smells, and even food textures can set her off.

She may gouge herself with food, seeking to make herself so unattractive, that no man, including her husband, will approach her or find her 'attractive.'

She may become irrational, over a .99 item, while spending with abandon, and not understand why.

She may be extremely intelligent, so much so, that she can see these signals of irrationality, yet feel helpless in the face of them. This can compound her suffering.

She may work tirelessly to help others avoid dangerous situations, or become over protective of children at risk, then suddenly want to run away and know nothing of the life she once held dear.

She may become incredibly dedicated to a cause, and use her suffering to fuel her energy, yet, at times, want nothing to do with it, only to question herself even more so.

She may become deeply upset watching one walk in through an exit door rather than "following the rules" that exist, as "rules", that is, order, gives her comfort as once she felt that everything was "out of order" and "out of control."

This is where we seek blankets and water within statements, just as the victim may wash incessantly (or avoid washing in some) or 'cover' herself, constantly, including bringing a small blanket to work. It is in both life and language.

She may vomit without warning, with some feeling such anxiety that they vomit every morning, just as routine as a cup of coffee.

Her immune system is forever compromised.

Susan Murphy Milano was raped by her own father. She was a woman of dynamic nature and constitution, had book deals, movie pilot shoots, radio programs, and 1001 ways to help victims of domestic violence when she was diagnosed with cancer.

Why does one yield to cancer so easily while another, it may remain dormant and ineffective to destroy?

I believe Susan's sufferings left her vulnerable to its ravages because if I ever knew a "fighter", it was Susan. I used to say that if cancer ever feared someone, it had to be Susan.

I wept when I read how she deliberately chased her sister away from her drunken father, knowing full well the consequence of her action of saving her sister from rape.

I don't know if I have ever known a braver woman, though when I think of Carrie McDonigles' confrontation with her daughter Amber's killer, I pause, and feel inadequate as a man, knowing of such a brave action, not knowing if I possess such character and presence of mind to control myself in the killer's presence.

The physical suffering in a compromised immune system is something too vast to tackle here. Suffice it to say that fatigue, depression, stomach ailments, urinary tract infections, vomiting, aches and pains, and on and on it goes. Imagine, if you will allow, what this does to a social life.

II. **Her husband's suffering**

Imagine living with a woman you love, respect, honor, and protect, only to know that each day she wakes up, she thinks of killing herself, day after day, week after week, month after month, year after year. No matter how you love her, no matter how often doctors intervene, and no matter of circumstance, holiday, celebration, or blessing, the thought of shame never leaves her.

The husband is left ultimately impotent against the rapist's power. Whether it be from childhood sexual molestation, or rape, the suffering can even become generational.

All the love, protection, extra trips everywhere to accompany her so she does not fear, all the changing of life to accommodate the incessant anxiety, the cutting of her steak so she does not hold a sharp knife, the buying of beautiful clothing and jewelry...yet nothing ever completely wipes away the stain of what she feels in a place that he cannot ever reach.

Need I say more? Let the intelligent, or the caring, reach deep into this principle, and think it through.

Her suffering is shared with him, as the two became one at marriage. It is far more than I could ever describe, including feelings of guilt for not having protected her, no matter the dating of the crime. Even if it occurred before he met her, his shame is not mitigated by fact. When he took her as his wife, for better or worse, he took upon himself her rape, her suffering, and her damaged soul. Men have expressed guilt over the knowledge that their wives had been sexually assaulted in childhood. Guilt. How can this be?

He will never get over not being able to protect his wife from a sexual assault. Never. It is with him daily, and it will be with him to the grave, even if it happened before he met her.

For some victims, there is little or no social life. Plans made are often cancelled, not by her, who feels such shame over her anxiety, but by him. He becomes a master of excuse making and feels that this is but a small way of helping protect her from her own embarrassment. He does so out of love, but hates hurting those disappointed that social plans are never followed through.

Sexual abuse dominates his life, every day, every night, Christmas, and holidays, too. It never goes away.

III. **Her parents' suffering**

I would rather experience the pain than my child.

This is the cry of so many parents, and even the indulgent King David, who created the monster of a son, upon his death uttered words so terribly painful to read, "*Absolam, my son, my son! Would I have died for thee, Absolam! Absolam! My son, my son...*"

One of the cruelest of punishments I have ever read of was a man having his sons brought before him where they were murdered in his sight, and then the perpetrator blinded him, leaving for him the last sight in life that of the killing of his sons.

Loving parents would take upon themselves the suffering of their children.

Every mother of every sexual abuse victim has her own **hell**. She was created, deliberately, with protective instincts, yet it is these same instincts that torment her soul, for her entire life, no matter how removed the circumstances of the abuse, even if she was in another state at the time.

Every father of every sexual abuse or rape victim has his own **demons**, too, wondering what he could have done differently in life that would have changed the circumstances of his beloved daughter's torment. "*Had I taken that job in Ohio, instead of moving to California, my little girl...*"

At every age, she remains his "little girl" and he may be plagued with homicidal thoughts for the rest of his life, even as her husband may be as well. We were made, by Design, to be protective of our children. Is there anything worse than being incapable, for whatever reason, including ignorance, time and geography, of protecting one's little girl?

IV. Her children's suffering

Generational suffering can take place as well.

On the outskirts of something few could ever understand, the rape victim may develop an acute need to "control" her environment, melting into despair over 'losing control' over the remote, the laundry, the hairbrush. The children do not understand how a simple change of plans can cause darkness to descend upon her, nor can they understand. They do not understand why she turned pale, in the mall, when she lost sight of them, or how her voice grew angry when her child asked to use the public bathroom, or how a certain odor in a restaurant can cause her to burst into tears.

They are, after all, just children, and shouldn't know of such things. Santa Claus would never allow such things, and on television shows, everything always works out before the half hour is over. The football team wins, the ugly duckling becomes the swan, and Rocky wins his title and dignity.

Only your children, sister, know the myriad of things that you think are hidden from them, and that they do not understand, but because they so deeply love you, they know something is wrong.

V. **Her friends' suffering**.

"I'm not up to it today" is often met with, later, *"Why do you always cancel on me? Every time I invite you, you always say you're coming, but you always cancel."*

It's just something she can't tell you about. It's not that she won't tell you, she can't. She has wanted to, many times, but she can't get her lips to frame the words. I have seen her try.

A dissolved social life, constant excuses, last minute cancellations, abruptly leaving early, and so many other 'rude' behaviors are often what accompany a rape victim, always unintentional, as she does care about the feelings of others, but is sometimes so filled with panic, or so very ready to burst into tears, wishing only to spare her friends or hosts the drama of uncontrollable crying, so she leaves.

Her husband knows, however, and does not object, no matter the cost of the tickets, the time lost, the length of the drive, and so on. He knows and wishes he could tell her friends and co workers

Many abuse victims go their entire adults lives until they let out what they consider their own dirty little secret.

Why must it be a "dirty" secret? Why should it even be a secret?

If she had been hit with a weapon, or held up at gunpoint, she'd enjoy the comfort of those who seek to help victims, but because it is rape, it has to be a goddamned secret? A secret that poisons her entire life and her health, her husband, his health, her children...

and on it goes. Her despair of life becomes his despair of life.

The poison of the secret is, indeed, toxic.

As she suffers mentally, if she had cancer, she could seek comfort, but because it is mental suffering, she thinks she must hide her pain and simply lose everything around her. If it was a physical illness, she could receive "get well" cards, and visitors to stop in, hold her hand, and kiss her forehead. Because she was raped, the silence has to rule; a silence so very cold that it is difficult to describe. 20 years could go by, and she cannot enjoy a simple trip to a shopping center without something out there to remind her...remind her of the pain. She grips her husband's arm until the nails almost cause blood to flow.

He knows, and let's the grip tighten, just the same.

Divorce, substance abuse, pain and sorrow, inflicted upon her, and everyone who loves her, by a man worthy of nothing more than death in this world. Nothing but death.

In unassociated rape, a judge should have the option of imposing the death penalty. Our society does not take rape and sexual assault seriously enough, and does not count the cost to the life of the victim, and everyone the victim loves, and everyone who loves the victim. We've made progress, but there is still too much stigma attached that is grossly unjust.

It is almost too much to describe, but it is that husbands, parents, children, family and friends, all suffer, yet feel that they cannot even mention the suffering because of our stigma in society.

It's wrong.

Sexual abuse can never be "paid for", ultimately, because the suffering is life long.

In analyzing the statements of Woody Allen and his daughter, signals of deception were found in his, while indications of veracity were found in hers. She used language that is often found in adult victims of childhood sexual abuse. He used passivity and an unreliable denial.

My conclusion of their statements: She was telling the truth. He was deceptive. When I posted y findings on the Statement Analysis blog, there were few who thought otherwise.

In trainings, we cover sexual abuse and rape, even in corporate trainings. Why? Why cover it in corporate trainings?

The first reason why is that Statement Analysis is the study of words. No matter what the activity, the words are the lens for us to view what happened and we use a variety of circumstances to highlight that deceptive people speak one way, and truthful people speak another way.

Secondly, the training has proven invaluable to companies that must decide, even within the realm of Human Resources, sexual abuse or sexual harassment cases. Statement Analysis gets to the truth of what happened, or did not happen, and can help those in authority be better prepared in decision making.

The suffering of a victim of a sexual assault is life long. I have spoken to too many fathers who just "knew" that the young man that came into their lives was "not right."

I have spoken to too many parents who also felt that something "was not right" with the adult who entered into their child's life and wrought destruction.

There are linguistic signals, and even with rudimentary understanding of Statement Analysis, deceptive individuals can be seen for who they are.

Once the liar is identified, the best practice is:

Avoid.

When I speak to Little League coaches, teachers, youth ministers, or anyone else who has access to my children, I ask them, "Tell me about yourself" and I listen carefully.

Our words reveal who we are.

If I have stumbled upon a pedophile, for example, and he knows that I am asking him about himself for a good reason, what do you think will *be on his mind* while he talks?

He will be working overtime at concealing his nature. It is here that the training pays off: it is called "leakage"; that is, where the brain knows what it knows, and even while attempting to conceal information, words chosen can reveal what it is the subject is trying to conceal.

More on "leakage" to follow when we view a statement made by a man who had been accused of molesting his own daughter.

The linguistic signals of sexual abuse mirror those in which social workers often describe as possible signs of sexual abuse, including "hand washing" and other references, often needless, to water and cleansing.

I once had a case in which would have been easily been dismissed as 'incidental touch', which I wish it had been, yet had it not been for Statement Analysis training, I cannot affirm that I would have found the truth.

A young male with mental retardation had claimed that a bus driver sexually molested him while attempting to remove his seatbelt.

Adults with developmental disabilities are, statistically speaking, many times more likely to be sexually abused than the general population. This statistic is confirmed in every state in our country.

It would not be uncommon for someone with developmental issues to misconstrue a helpful bus driver, and even perseverate about a past exploitation and input it to the driver, today.

Thus, I was prepared for such.

What I found, however, was something I was not prepared for.

When I teach investigations, I teach the "Reliable Denial" fully prepared that most in law enforcement will struggle with something this simple. "I didn't do it", spoken in the free editing process, is highly reliable.

Before I went to schedule the interview with the driver, someone close to the situation took me aside.

"Hey, Pete, I've got to tell you about the driver", he said.

"No, please don't. Let me just get a statement, analyze it, and then you can fill me in before the interview", I said.

He knew that I did not want anything to influence the analysis of the statement, including the driver's employment record, background, or even personality. The statement must speak for itself.

When I conduct the interview, it is then I am equipped with the analysis of the statement, collateral testimony, personnel file, evidence, or anything else that will help me in the interview. Yet it is the statement, foremost, that is, the very words of the accused, that will guide me.

"I know, I know, but listen, please hear me out. This guy is a virtual Santa Claus!"

This caught my attention. He continued, "He is a retired medical doctor, has a long white beard, and is a volunteer driver. He is known for 60 years in his neighborhood. He is 86 years old and he would not hurt a fly."

Although the rule of influence was broken, I was relieved to hear this. "Just another case of misunderstanding", he said.

It was music to my ears.

I was glad to hear that the adult with developmental disabilities was not molested. I have had too many such cases, and have talked to too many frustrated prosecutors who know they cannot bring someone like that on the witness stand to be ripped into shreds by a defense attorney.

I called the driver to request a statement and set up a time for the interview. "It'll be short", I assured myself.

The bus company told me that they did not say anything to the driver about the male rider's complaint, which is best. This way, the innocent will not be defensive, nor even know the reason for the call or interview.
The music in my ears suddenly went dark when he answered the phone.

"I know why you are calling! Those *&&(looney tunes! They'd just love to accuse me of something. I am a normal male!"

There were two indicators of sensitivity in his opening sentences:

1. His need to denigrate the victim.
2. His employment of the word, "normal."

The guilty often feel a need to blame or disparage their victims, particularly in sexual abuse cases, often saying the victim "asked for it."

In this case, he took to ridiculing his victim's intellectual disability. This would be something he would "need" to do in order to cast doubt upon the victim's words.

Next, he called himself, "normal."

In Statement Analysis, we flag the word "normal" in all settings. It is used in two contexts:

a. Routine
b. Sexuality

In the first, a deceptive person will often write, "It was a normal day, like any other", or "I was doing my daily routine, like normal…"

Even an elementary school reader knows that when a story starts with, "it was a normal day, like any other", something very abnormal is about to take place. It is a technique for story-telling; that is, the telling of a story.

When someone has done something wrong, they often use this in hopes of concealing their crime. We flag "normal" or "ordinary" or "routine" in every statement for examination.

Secondly, we see the word "normal" as a "red flag" when it is used in sexual abuse cases. In this case, the 86 year old "pillar of the community" called himself a "normal" male.

Question: Who calls themselves "normal"?

Answer: Those who have been called or thought of by others, as not "normal."

In the first seconds of the call, I believed he "did it."

He refused to write a statement, and he refused to be interviewed. He did, however, want to know what I knew, therefore, he "kept me" on the phone.

I listened and took notes.

I barely had to speak, for he went on, for almost a half an hour, about himself, using the language of deception.

He did not say, at any time, "I didn't do it."

We have a rule that we follow in investigations: If a subject is unwilling or unable to say he did not do it, we are not going to say it for him.

He had not simply assisted the young male with his seatbelt, he molested his victim.

The victim, known to be happy-go-lucky, refused to leave his room for weeks. He showered twice a day, rather than having to be prompted every morning. He went into a terrible depression.

The perpetrator?

He got a lawyer and a "deal" of sorts was worked out: the "Santa Claus" would not be around adults with developmental disabilities ever again.

Why wasn't he prosecuted? What about justice?

The prosecutor was beside herself. She wanted to prosecute but knew, exactly, what 'Santa's' attorney would do to him on the witness stand, in defense of his client. There would be no way to get a conviction, but in the least, we could take steps to see that the driver was in final retirement.

I wish I had a happier ending of this story, but I don't. It was not the fault of the prosecutor for the inability to obtain justice; it was the reality of the situation.

Do you believe it could have been avoided?

I do.

I know that, depending upon what State you live in, that you are limited in the questions you can ask during employment interviews, but we can be trained and listen for linguistic signals of sexual perversion. We can screen out those who's very lives are deceptive in nature, and who prey upon others.

The training takes time and it takes effort. The employment interview itself cannot be a short interview. One can simply not look at another and conclude that just because someone looks like a gentle soul means that he is a gentle soul.

I find that appearances can be deceiving, just as sociopaths can be charming.

The key is to get them talking. Remember, the brain knows what it knows, and even when it is trying to conceal information, words are chosen purposely. You will see in upcoming chapters, that these words that "leak out", sometimes even in humor, can reveal the intentions of the heart.

God help us help those who cannot help themselves.

\

Chapter 4: The Right Man for the Job

Sometimes the right man for the job is a woman. At least that is what my daughter, Christina tells me. She's a budding lie detector in her own right and is a strong advocate for justice.

Statement Analysis, by careful listening, can match the right person for the right position in a company, something that appears as a lost art today.

How we speak reveals who we are.

A few years ago, a company capitalized on this fact claiming to help improve one's vocabulary, in order to make a better impression upon others. They were selling a product to build one's vocabulary in order to help get promotions, or gainful employment.

Unfortunately, good vocabulary comes from reading and reading takes time and effort, and is not the 'past time', culturally, that it once was. Reading to children, before they are able to read (or even speak), seems to help create a love of books, which whether it be in electronic or paper form, remains key to education and language growth.

A poor vocabulary leaves a poor impression. We can complain that we should not be judged, all the day long if we wish, but people will continue to judge us, first on appearance, and then upon our language.

In the very least, we should consider that since we cannot stop others from judging us, we can influence that judgment.

Did you ever notice how people that are dressed a certain way have an easy time in stores when they are making returns?

It's true.

I've tried it, in both jeans and a t-shirt, and in a suit. It's always easier, even without question, while wearing a suit.

Language reveals us, and coarse or inappropriate language, for example, in a business setting, will leave an impact upon peers, customers, or our superiors, whether we like it or not.

As language reveals us, a personality trait may appear. This is, in effect, a kind of profiling, that is, of collecting data (if only in our brains) about the type of person speaking to us, as we listen to his words.

I. Personality Type: Impulsive Control

Have you ever met someone who is very impulsive? This is the kind of person that often "leaps before he looks" and will jump in, both feet first, often with enthusiasm, but little pre-thought. Where might this person fit in your company?

Impulsive individuals can be successful, for example, when the right fit is made, according to their personality type. Some might do well in environments where aggressive sales is necessary, whereas other sales positions might be better suited for pensive, thoughtful, careful employees.

Personality types do emerge from language.

In studying pronouns, we sometimes see that those in positions of authority, often drop the pronoun "I" in their memos, or emails, opting for either a missing pronoun, or the pronoun, "we", which can be, in some settings, distancing language.

But what of the impulsive type of personality that may even be aggressive, or disagreeable?

What of a subject who lacks impulse control? Can he be identified in the employment interview?

In Statement Analysis, we have noted that the word "but" is often used to compare, via a form of negation, two or more things. *"I'd like to do that for you but..."* and we say: *"Always note the words that follow "but" as very important."*

This can negate that which preceded it, or it can minimize, via comparison.

What if your position requires someone who is thoughtful and pensive, and must use critical thinking but specifically, "look" before one "leaps" and make careful decisions?

Language can identify poor impulse control in people.

The "Adversative" words are: "but, however, nevertheless..." and so on.

Subjects with poor impulse control are noted to use these words in abundance.

It is not likely that you counted the number of times you heard these words from someone, but I am betting that you have met someone like this, and you felt a certain uneasiness about the person, and wondered why.

You would likely not be surprised if later on you learned that the person you thought to be "difficult", even though you only spoke a short time, is actually one with poor impulse control, and the "adversative" words were 'getting to you' a bit.

These are often found in intuitive individuals who do very well with training in Statement Analysis and in Analytical Interviewing. Studies have shown, even among hospitalized individuals with poor impulse control, an excessive use of such words.

II. **Personality Type:** Obsessive Compulsive

What about someone with Obsessive Compulsive tendencies?

Again, a person with obsessive compulsive traits can be very useful, particularly when placed within the proper work environment, just as they can drive others crazy when placed in inappropriate or ill-fitted situations.

The person with obsessive compulsive tendencies can become quite anxious when attempted to resolve himself to stopping the habit. Many are "logical" to a fault, and must find a "reason" to repeat apparent senseless acts, such as hand washing, or checking and rechecking to see if the back door is locked. These types will often argue, even to himself, to justify or find a reason why the repetitive behavior is maintained.

What do we hear in their speech?

"So, since, therefore, because...." and so on.

They continually offer reasons for what they do in senseless repetition. These are words we highlight as sensitive, if the subject is asked, "What?" rather than "Why?", while feeling the need to justify action.

In what may appear to be 'mind-blowing' tedious labor, can be actually fulfilling to the subject, which is why the manager or supervisor must not project his or her own personality into the subject, particularly while attempting to be empathetic.

The poor impulse subject has a need to "oppose" others, and act upon the first impulse (poor "over the board" chess players, yet better at "Blitz" chess).

Human Resources, skilled in interviewing, can, therefore, find proper placement for the prospective employee (if the subject has been truthful in the interview process, therefore, not weeded out) that will benefit both company and employee.

How can **Human Resources** accomplish this?

a. open ended questions

b. specific exercise

a. open ended questions.

In Analytical Interviewing, we ask questions beginning with the legally sound, open-ended questions and move on to the analysis questions (from the written statement) and so on. This is exciting in training and quite useful. Even questions such as:

"What is your favorite movie?" will get someone speaking, with the goal to have the subject enter the "Free Editing Process", where he chooses his own words and we listen.

b. *The Ten Minute Exercise*

This can be a lot of fun.

Using your stopwatch, timer, or your iPhone, ask someone to speak, non-stop, about anything they wish to talk about.

Both healthy and individuals with mental illness can do this for about 10 minutes without difficulty. (Recently, someone did this to me, without stopping, for 48 minutes).

As the subject speaks, the Interviewer (HR, investigator, therapist) writes down the critical words and will be able to get a start on a profile of the subject by the words the subject uses.

The Interviewer is taught to write down adversative words (even in a number count!) as well as the "why" words, and note any words that are repeated.

It is not as difficult as it might sound, as the Interviewer becomes more experienced, since this is an exercise that can be practiced at work. (Recall the counting of words that follow "no" in a "yes or no question" format, and how this can reveal deception.)

The interviewer will soon learn that based upon the words, alone, gender will arise.

Do you have young children?

Do you have grown children?

This is something you can even do with your children, noting how the younger the child, the more use of "I" versus "we" and, you may even discover, that when you view old video tapes of your children who are now grown:

they will be able to differentiate which voice belongs to them and...

speech patterns will show similarity to the adult child.

In employment interviews, we ask questions that are designed to get people to reveal who they are. Here are some examples that we use in our training.

First, we find it critical to get a "writing sample" prior to the interview. By asking a few simple questions before we schedule an interview, we can already weed out deceptive individuals.

1. Tell us about yourself. Please use the entire page, and the back, if needed.

This strikes people as strange but it allows the subject to begin to talk about himself or herself precisely where the person chooses. You would be amazed at what people reveal about themselves before even getting to the employment interview.

Even in this single question, we have had samples where people were almost warning us that they had every intention of finding someone to sue! They had an agenda, and were "proud" of that agenda and if the company did not agree with that agenda, look out!

I had one "lecture" me about guns. I don't own a gun, but I don't have a political issue about guns (Dex watches the house for us), but this one applicant's statement was a "rant" against guns. Although her written statement should have been enough to preclude her from an employment interview, I urged the company to let me interview her: I just had to know!

Sure enough, she was terminated from her last job because her company sold a hunting magazine that featured a gun on its cover.

Yep.

Imagine her representing your family business? She lacked the self awareness to know that not everyone agreed with her view point on guns, especially in a job where there were no guns. On the "emotional intelligence" scale, she scored very low.

Another applicant I just had to interview left the page blank. I wanted to know why.

In the interview, she talked about how she had gone about sabotaging everything in her life and she had so wanted this particular job (an investigator) that she knew that by leaving it blank she would not get her "dream job." It was terribly sad, but leaving the interview, we talked about her issue, and about getting professional intervention. Perhaps something good came from it.

Another question is:

"Have you ever stolen anything in your life?"

With this question, we use the "prompt" system, in the interview, to get them to answer truthfully.

Many people will answer "no" to this question because they think of stealing as walking into a store, putting something in their pocket, and walking out. Therefore, we use the "prompt" system to see if they will be honest, for, after all, we have all taken something that did not belong to us.

Here is an example of an interview of a thief:

"I noticed that on your pre-application screening, you wrote "no" under the question, "Have you ever stolen anything in your life."

Applicant: "That's true. I've never stolen anything in my life. I wasn't raised that way. You don't steal, that is just it. You don't steal. "

I noted that she said, "you" don't steal and not "I don't steal."

I then shared a short story, sadly, a truthful one, in which I was sixteen years old and working at McDonald's and when a pretty girl would come through the drive through, I would put something extra in her order, hoping to land a date.

I then listened for the response.

Nothing.

Result: Prompt One: Nothing.

I then shared that I recalled (another true story) that I was in the bank one day, and left with the bank's pen in my pocket. I did not intend to steal it, but when I got to my car, realizing that it did not belong to me, I drove away rather than go inside. The pen was stolen.

Response: "I never stole anything in my life."

Prompt Two Result: Swing and a miss.

I then said, "Well, I guess it is why we have the 'paperclip' laws because we all, even by accident, take something that does not belong to us. The issue, however, is when we learn from our failures. Especially as children. We take things that we should not have, but learn from our mistakes."

Response: "Not me."

Strike Three. Three prompts and yer' out!

The company owner, however, was not convinced. She thought I was being "a bit over the top" on this "theft thing" and wanted Mrs, Three Prompts to be hired, just the same.

Later, one of the employees came to me and said, "Hey, did you recommend that woman for hire? I know her! I said, "No, in fact, I recommended against hiring her."

"Oh," she said, "she is terrible! I knew her from years ago. She was arrested for shoplifting. Did you know that?"

I didn't, but I suspected as much.

The company was not a big company, and even small theft would impact its bottom line as well as its morale.

When someone lies in the interview process, it is as if a red light is going off saying, "Do NOT hire! Do NOT hire!", yet we sometimes do not pay attention to the statistics that tell us that liars put their own interests above everyone else's, including the company's interest.

It is also by the wording within an interview, that we can properly match people with a proper position.

I once had a young woman outscore all other applicants in an emotional intelligence screening, yet, she was terminated from her previous employment. She said that she did not know why she was terminated, which is something that does not sound credible.

Yet, her language showed no deception.

How could she be terminated, from a large hospital, and not know why? I pressed her but her pronouns told me: she was truthful.

Today, businesses are reluctant to give out references, good or bad, as they are fearful of being sued.

I always find my way around this, however, when the person on the other end says, "I can only confirm that so and so worked here from such and such date…" by a simple method:

Listening.

I find a way to strike up a conversation and if the person on the other end is reluctant, I know the magical formula of which to employ to get one talking, and I will share it with you now.

When Menachim Begin was in Soviet custody during World War II, he was tortured into giving up information. He later said that although he gave out some information under torture, he gave out far more information from a very different tactic used by the Soviets.

He said that they cut him off, utterly, from all human contact.

He did not see anyone, or talk to anyone, for weeks on end. His food was placed on a tray and slid into his cell, where he was isolated from all human contact.

The moment they took him out, he began to blab and could barely contain himself.

Humans have been created to communicate.

When someone is reluctant to give answers, in our seminar, we teach how certain questions will eventually get responses, but there is one thing that humans have a very hard time resisting in speech:

Talking about what they do.

When your son or daughter comes home from school, what is the first thing they talk about (after asking for a snack)? It is about what they did.

It is virtually irresistible.

"What do you do there?

"What did you do today?"

"What did you do in the last hour?"

We all love to talk about what we do, whether it is what we do for a living, or what we do during the day. We struggle to resist it.

Loneliness comes from the inability to share what is is that one has done.

If you saw a terrific movie, but were alone, it would be almost as if it did not happen, unless you had someone to tell. This is why people often rush to Facebook or other social media.

What is the number one thing reported on social media? It is what one has just done!

"Just got back from…"

"I just got an A on my science paper…"

"I just learned that my aunt died…"

and on it goes: people with a need to tell other people "what happened" to them.

When I interviewed the young woman who had been terminated from a hospital, I was surprised because her statement and her interview revealed a highly intelligent, and hard working young woman who would be an asset to any company. At least, that is what my conclusion was.

I called the hospital and worked my way through the maze of departments until I got to the very department from which the young woman had been terminated from, and reached her supervisor. Her supervisor apologized for not being able to tell me more information about the young woman other than her dates of employment. Her politeness was my ticket to information.

"I understand. No one wants to get sued", I commiserated with her. "What do you do there?", I asked.

"Me, oh, I am the supervisor."

That's not what I was asking. I was looking for what she did, hour by hour, in her office.

"Yes, I knew that. You were her supervisor. I mean, what is it that you, yourself do there, in that department?"

On and on she went and it was the most methodically boring thing I had ever heard. I struggled to maintain interest almost as much as she struggled to maintain interest. "It is mind numbing boring work", she said.

Ah, there it is. She is talking.

As she talked, we became "friends" over the phone and she finally said, "This is the most boring work you can imagine. She was a good worker, but you have to understand medical records. The women here are all older, and from 8am to 5pm they barely say a word to each other. She was actually good at her job, but the other women hated that she kept talking all day, talking about her boyfriend, Downton Abby, her cat. She was outgoing, friendly, competent, and a great worker, but I had to let her go, as she was still on probation, and the other workers demanded quiet."

I knew it.

I knew that the young woman had been truthful about not knowing why she was terminated and I knew that the questions, from her statement, showed her to be competent and intelligent.

I recommended the company hire her and the last I had heard: she was a great fit. She needed to be in a position where her strong people skills would be best utilized. Being alone, or at least, quiet, in an office setting, was not for this dynamic young woman. Her personality was better suited in sales, or in negotiations, where her strong intellect and good self awareness would best serve her gifts.

Analytical Interviewing can help place the right person for the right position, and help avoid misfits, where square pegs are broken due to the attempts at forcing them into round holes.

Chapter 5: Missing Persons

When a young beautiful woman named Heather Elvis went missing, I received emails asking me to cover the case on the Statement Analysis blog.

The emails were not from the police or even family members, but from concerned citizens who could not bear the words of pain expressed by Heather's father, Terry Elvis.

Terry Elvis, a devout Christian, husband and devoted father, expressed his pain poetically. It is who he is.

I, too, felt inclined to turn away, afraid of the pain making its way into my own heart. I could not, however, turn from the case.

As a parent, there is nothing scarier for us than the "unknown." Stephen King could not write horror to frighten readers with the level that we, as parents, can frighten ourselves with our own imaginations running wild. With daily headlines of kidnappings, child murders, home invasion, and a strange trend upward in overall violence, parents need no assistance in giving themselves fright over their children.

The new parent who watches the precious little one getting on the bus, all by herself, for the very first time, might be inclined to follow the bus in her car, but will likely 'talk herself down' and convince herself, "nothing will happen." That is, of course, until she reads the news of a little five year old who fell asleep on the bus and went unnoticed by the driver.

The first time the child goes off to camp can trigger deep-seated painful worries that gnaw away at the parent's sleep.

I cannot enter into a place where I understand what it must be like to be the parent of a missing child.

When Heather Elvis was a baby and cried, Terry got up, wiped the sleep from his eyes, and attended to her needs.

When Heather was a little girl and fell, Terry Elvis picked her up, kissed her boo-boo and made it all better.

When Heather broke her favorite crayon, Terry was there, like a heroic knight of olde, to 'rescue' his little girl and present her with a new shiny crayon.

When Heather cried from not being picked for the grade school sport, Terry was there to wrap his arms around her and let her know how wonderful she really was, and how foolish the other kids were for not picking her...

Whenever Heather needed her daddy, Terry was always there.

It is not just Terry's story, but every father's story.

At just 19 years of age, Heather could not be found and Terry, who had always been able to "fix" things, was now left utterly helpless and without strength, as to what to do for his little girl, who, although young, wanted to strike out on her own and be her own woman.

To Terry, however, she was still his baby, and now, his baby, perhaps crying, could not be attended to.

How can such impotence be put into words so that I, as a father, might enter into Terry Elvis' suffering?

There is no way. All I could do was try.

I could pray, and did pray, but I could also use my skill as an analyst to help.

As is the case of missing children, young and old, I analyzed any statements available, including Terry's own. His statement, particularly about helping Heather buy a car, showed veracity. He was not involved in his daughter's disappearance. Like Clint Dunn, the father of 13 year old Hailey Dunn, he, too, would come under suspicion by the public, at least at first, while he sought to, by any means, publish Heather's plight, and find her.

Terry learned quickly how cruel people could be.

Next, I saw the statements made by Sidney Moorer, a married man who had allegedly had an "affair" with Heather. I put quotes on the word "affair" as Heather, still a teenager, was exploited by the middle aged Sidney Moorer, who had likely used Heather's desire for success and independence against her.

In Statement Analysis we presuppose that someone is truthful, and someone is innocent. By "innocent", I mean not only judicially so, but a "de facto" innocence: he didn't have anything to do with Heather's disappearance. My expectation is that he will tell me so, plainly.

This is called the "Reliable Denial" and will be covered in its own chapter. Suffice for now, if I were in a room with 20 investigators, left the room and came back and announced, "My wallet was stolen while I was out of the room", what would you expect to hear an innocent investigator say?

"On advice of counsel, I decline to address the issue of the allegedly missing wallet…"?

Hardly.

How about, "I ask for time, for the full truth to come out, and my innocence be proven in a court of law…"?

Nope.

You would expect an accused, but innocent investigator at the training to say, "Peter, I didn't take your wallet."

When we cover the Reliable Denial, you will not only see how incredibly simplistic this is, but how accurate it is.

My expectation from Sidney Moorer was that he would say "I didn't cause Heather's disappearance."

He did not.

We have a rule in Statement Analysis: If someone is unwilling or unable to tell us that he didn't do it, we are not permitted to say it for him.

But it was Sidney Moorer's wife, Tammy, who threw me a curveball.

While Heather was missing, Tammy posted a vile message, admitting that Sidney cheated on her, and smearing the name and reputation of Heather Elvis.

Analysis of the statement showed a very disturbed woman but here is what I missed. As I analyzed it, Tammy was truthful about Sidney's cheating, but used minimizing language. This is expected in the pain of infidelity. There was a blaming of the teenager rather than putting responsibility upon her husband.

Tammy slammed Heather, instead, saving her most venomous language for Heather.

This is not something that we would expect a guilty party to do, after all, with Heather still missing, why would a guilty party draw more attention to herself by showing hatred, hence, motive, towards the victim?

In fact, in Statement Analysis, we look for subtle hints of hatred or blame upon the victim, by the guilty, not overt hatred.

For example, in shaken baby cases, we find that the guilty perpetrator will in the most minute of ways, blame the victim, such as "she would not stop crying", or "she refused to let me change her."

We do not find open hatred and blame.

Tammy and Sidney Moorer have been charged in the kidnapping and murder of Heather Elvis. Tammy's open hatred of the victim 'broke the rules' of pattern, and stands as a reminder that principle is not established upon exception, but the norm. Guilty parties try to conceal their hatred, but the brain leaks it out. For Tammy Moorer, the hatred consumed her, and she was unable to control her tongue from lashing out. She is a defense attorney's worst nightmare, and a prosecutor's dream.

Terry and his family continue to suffer, and will suffer for the rest of their lives. But Terry also stands as a living monument to faith, in his belief that Christ will, one day, summon him home, and he will see his little girl, once again.

Until then, I hope his pain is mitigated by his ability to believe, which is a gift given to him, and that he continue his drive for justice for Heather.

She deserves it.

What can Statement Analysis offer the family of a missing person?

Wherever truth is needed, analysis can assist.

There is always a concern that someone might be withholding information on a missing persons case, for whatever reason. The deliberate suppressing of information will be picked up in the analysis, and can help uncover truth.

Is there a witness who has information but may be fearful of sharing it?

Sometimes in missing persons cases, there is 'crime attendant', that is, an association with other crimes, including drugs, in which one may selfishly want to remain silent, for fear of lesser charges.

Families of Missing Persons, forever haunted by the dark cloud of the unknown, can find some comfort in knowing that Statement Analysis can assist, even if just a review of the police file.

The police file, particularly on a cold case, isn't something that all detectives are willing to share, but some are.

It is worth a try.

A statement analyst will sign a confidentiality agreement, and review the file carefully, particularly when it comes to those who last saw the missing loved one, and gave statements.

Are these statements reliable?

This is something the analyst should be able to determine. If so, what leads were followed up, and what leads were not.

Many dedicated professionals in law enforcement do not mind their work being reviewed and reviewed again, for they concern themselves with the task at hand: locating the missing person.

Not everyone, however, is like that. Some departments are concerned about creating a crisis of confidence with constant questions, but no one wants an unsolved case.

In the very least, having an analyst review the case file is a start.

Chapter Six: Statement Analysis: Suicide?

Sheena Morris was a young, beautiful, vivacious woman with her entire life ahead of her. But that is not her story.

I met her mother, Kelly Osborne, a courageous woman brought to the very edge of living, still breathing, but with little life left within her, over the death of her daughter for whom justice remained unfound. Kelly attends the Center for Missing Persons Conference each year, to support other parents who have either suffered the death of a child, or has a loved one missing. She is a broken vessel that yields much refreshment to others, offering encouragement, tears, prayers and a shoulder to cry upon. She does so in the name of her daughter, Sheena, and continues the uphill battle for justice.

Sheena Morris was found dead, hanging in the bathroom of a hotel room. Police quickly concluded that it was a suicide, and that Sheena had a history of issues. Instead of this young, beautiful woman marrying and bringing her family grandchildren, her family is left bereft of not only the life that is not, but of answers, justice, and closure.

Statement Analysis gets to the truth. By principle, we listen carefully to what one says, and even to what one does not say.

At the Center for Missing Persons, Kelly asked me if I would look at her daughter's case, not knowing that I had already analyzed the transcripts from the Dr. Phil Show years earlier. Kelly is a powerful voice for justice for Sheena, and in spite of threats against her life, she continues to campaign for her daughter.

In Statement Analysis, we presuppose truth, therefore, when something appears "out of place" or "awkward", that is, something we did not expect, we are 'confronted' by it.

Yet we always begin presupposing truth and prepare ourselves for a truthful response.

If you were falsely accused of causing Sheena's death, it is appropriate for you to think how you would answer the allegation.

I would say, *"I didn't cause Sheena's death."* and in subsequent questions, I would add, *"I was not there when she died. I did not contribute to her death. I love Sheena..."* and so on.

It is this simple.

I recommend **not** reading the analysis before watching the "20/20" episode. It is persuasive about highlighting that this was not a suicide. My preference is to let the subject, Joe Geonese, speak for himself first. He appeared on the Dr. Phil Show, and on 20/20. He voluntarily submitted to a polygraph.

http://www.justice4sheena.com

The question at hand is simple: *Is Geonese truthful?*

The following is Statement Analysis of Joe Geonese appearance on the news program, "20/20", which included a short clip from the "Dr. Phil Show" in which the subject, Joe Genoese was given opportunity to speak for himself regarding the allegation that he had involvement in the death of Sheena Morris.

The method used is "SCAN", or "Scientific Content", and it is from the Laboratory for Scientific Interrogation" by Avinoam Sapir. As I said earlier, he is the 'grandfather' of all Statement Analysis, no matter what we label it. Investigators throughout the United States, along with analysts, themselves, are in Mr. Sapir's debt.

The quotations are in italics, with underlining and color added for emphasis, with the Statement Analysis in **bold** type.

On the 20/20 Transcripts, the subject is on pages 20-29. No changes have been made to the subject's words.

Lying is stressful.

People do not generally directly lie due to the internal stress it causes. Mostly, people will either mislead, in order to deceive, or will deliberately leave information out of their statement for the purpose of deception.
It is in the will to deceive that we find linguistic indications.

The Expected Versus The Unexpected

Statement Analysis presumes innocence. This is done so that we might set up the difference between "the expected" response from someone who "did not do it", against any response we receive that does not deny involvement. This is the "unexpected" from the subject.

By presupposing innocence (not merely judicial innocence but de facto innocence) Statement Analysis is confronted by words not expected to hear. This is how truth from deception can be evidenced.

An innocent person will not surprise us. He will say "I didn't do it", early, and often if necessary, and will not show sensitivity indicators within his speech. For example, he, the innocent person, will not allow weakness in his statement:

"I don't think I killed Sheena" would be to add weakness by the word "think" in the sentence. To say *"I don't think I killed Sheena"* allows for the subject, or someone else, to "think" differently. *"I didn't really kill Sheena"* qualifies "kill" with the word "really", something an innocent person would not say.
"I'm not guilty" is to deny judicial guilt; not the killing of Sheena. It is not reliable.

Short sentences are seen as best, with no need to buttress them with many words, in an attempt to persuade. It is the need to persuade that the analyst must take account of.

Sheena Morris is dead, found hung in a bathroom, in an apparent suicide. The subject is being accused by Sheena's family of murdering her.

We presume the subject did not do it, therefore, in being interviewed by national television, or by the police, he will, on his own accord say, *"I didn't kill Sheena"* freely.

Dr Phil: *These two people think you had something to do with their daughter's death.*

Please note that Dr. Phil Shows generally have an allegation presented so that the subject can speak to the allegation choosing his own words.

When a person speaks for himself, it is call the "Free Editing Process", that is, that the subject is freely choosing his words, what to add in and what to take out. This allows the subject the opportunity to say that he did not "do it" in a "Reliable Denial."

A "Reliable Denial" in order to be reliable, must come from the subject's own words. It consists of three (3) components. If there are less than three components, or more than three, it is no longer to be deemed reliable. The three components are:

1. The Pronoun "I"
2. The Past Tense verb "Didn't" or "did not"
3. The Specific Allegation Addressed

In this case, a Reliable Denial would be: "I did not cause Sheena's death." The innocent will simply make this statement, often not even waiting to be asked. It is to be deemed reliable.
Other denials that are not reliable include:

1. "*Didn't do it*", dropping the pronoun "I"
2. "I <u>would never</u> cause her death", with the words "*would never*"
3. "*I did not <u>harm</u> Sheena*", which now minimizes her death to "*harm*"
4. "I <u>never</u> caused Sheena's death" as the word "never" is substituted for "didn't" or "did not" and is not reliable.

The denial must be his own words. For instance, if asked,
"*Did you hang Sheena by a dog leash in the bathroom*" to which the subject says "*I did not hang Sheena by a dog leash in the bathroom*" would be to enter into the Interviewer's wording, and not freely choosing his own words. This is why leading questions are to be avoided in an interview. Best to say "How do you speak to the accusation?" and allow the subject to simply, without qualifiers, say, "I didn't do it."

In Statement Analysis we have a principle:

If the subject is unwilling or unable to say he didn't do it, we are not permitted to say it for him.
By Dr. Phil's laying out the scenario, we now have "The expected", that is, what we expect an innocent person to say. This is the perfect opportunity for the subject to say "*I didn't do it. I didn't cause Sheena's death.*"

Presuming innocence, we look for him to say so:

Geneose: "<u>All these things</u> are lies. They're <u>just</u>, they're <u>not</u> true."

Please note that "all these things are lies. They're just, they're not true" is not to say "I didn't do it."

He does not issue a Reliable Denial.

We do not know what "all these things" (plural) are that he refers to. He is accused of murdering Sheena Morris and it is expected that an innocent person will tell us that he did not do it. The subject fails to do so.

He says that "all these things are lies" but he does not tell us what things are lies, nor who is telling the lies.

Next, note the word "just." The word "just" is used when comparing two or more thoughts, with one being lesser. For example, if I sought to sell you a car for $15,000 but knew it was very expensive for you, I might show you a car that is $20,000, knowing that it is far too expensive. After you turn down the $20,000 car, I say,
"*Wait. Let me show you this other car. It is just $15,000.*" The word "just" is used to compare.
What is the subject comparing that which is "not true" towards? He does not tell us what is "not true" nor does he tell us what "all these things" are. This is to employ vague language, which avoids the simple, and easy Reliable Denial of "I didn't do it…"
The next context is that the subject voluntarily agreed to take a polygraph but failed it.

MUIR: *How do you explain those test results?*
And what it was that led to this…

GENOESE: *Can we cut?*

DAVID MUIR: *Tonight, as some of Florida's top investigators take another look at the mysterious death of Sheena Morris found dead in that hotel shower, the man she was getting ready to marry, who failed that polygraph, has decided to sit down with "20/20."*

JOSEPH GENOESE (FIANCEE OF SHEENA MORRIS)
Hello. How are you?

DAVID MUIR: *Nearly five years after he lost his fiancée, Joe says he is a victim too…*

So why sit down with me?

Topic: Failed Polygraph

The question is designed to allow the subject to defend himself. Regarding a failed polygraph, we expect an innocent subject to state:

"*I told the truth*" with three components:

1. **The pronoun "I"**

2. The past tense, "told", since the polygraph test took place in the past
3. The word "truth" should be in place. We note any inclusion of the word "lie" or "lying" as not reliable.

He is asked now to explain the result. The expected is "I told the truth", and it is that Statement Analysis is confronted by the "unexpected", that is, one that will not say "I didn't do it" and "I told the truth."

The subject can be nervous when he takes the polygraph, but a truthful subject is expected to say "I told the truth" and allow the blame to fall upon the machine, itself. The truth stands alone and it stands strong. It does not need extra words to buttress it, nor does it have need of persuasion. Better to hear, "I told the truth" than anything else. At this point, our expectation has been:

"I didn't kill Sheena" to be said easily, and regarding the polygraph, "I told the truth." He has been unable or unwilling to say either.

> GENOESE: *Because I have to tell you my side of the story. I'm being victimized 'cause I cared about <u>someone.</u> I was there for her when her family, a lot of times, <u>wasn't</u>.*

Statement Analysis deals not only with what one says, but also what one does not say. First, note that he does not say "I told the truth" in challenge to the results of failure. Instead of disputing the results, he says he has to tell his side of the "story."

One might question if he considers his account a "story."

Note that his fiancé is deceased yet he says "I'm being victimized." He also gives the reason for being "victimized" as caring about "someone." Please note that he does not say he cared for Sheena, but only "someone." Direct lying is internally stressful and often avoided by deceptive subjects. Here he does not use Sheena's name, which may suggest distancing himself from her.

Please now note that instead of saying that he did not kill Sheena, and that he told the truth, he disparages those who accuse him: *"I was there for her when her family, a lot of times, wasn't."*

Please note that he does not say he was there for "Sheena" but only "her", where he had previously used the word "someone." To call "her" from "someone" is to distance himself from Sheena. He does not assert that he cared about Sheena, nor does he use her name while attempting to disparage Sheena's family.

This is not expected from an innocent subject, but is the "unexpected" in analysis. When the victim or the victim's family is blamed, even in a subtle manner, it should be carefully noted as guilt.

Guilt causes stress, and a guilty subject might attempt to mitigate the guilt by:

1. Blaming others
2. Disparaging or blaming the victim
3. Share or "spread around" the guilt by using the pronoun "we" when the pronoun "I" is expected. This is something that parents of children readily recognize, especially where teens are concerned, as they like to "hide in the crowd" of "everyone doing it", reducing their own guilt or responsibility.

Thus far, we must note:
1. The subject has not denied killing Sheena
2. The subject has not asserted that he has told the truth
3. The subject has disparaged his accuser rather than answer the accusation.

DAVID MUIR: .put under the microscope, he says, by a mother determined to prove her daughter did not commit suicide.

BRENDAN MCLAUGHLIN (ABC ACTION NEWS): The story we've been following for years now.

DAVID MUIR: Joe says the portrait painted of his relationship with Sheena is not a true one.

REPORTER (MALE)   A domestic dispute between Morris and her fiancée.

DAVID MUIR: We've interviewed a lot of Sheena's friends.

JOSEPH GENOESE (FIANCEE OF SHEENA MORRIS)

Mm-hmm.

MUIR: *Many of her friends say that this was a <u>tumultuous</u> relationship.*

Please note that this is the perfect place for the subject to deny domestic violence, or even simply deny that it was a tumultuous relationship.

Interviewers should seek to avoid introducing language whenever possible.

JOSEPH GENOESE: *I <u>just</u> don't understand <u>where</u> they're getting at, <u>you know</u>?*

The subject does not deny that the relationship was tumultuous, but only that he does not "understand" where "they're getting at", or "where" the information, or the point is coming from, or "getting at."

This is to avoid saying "it was not tumultuous" or something similar, with, perhaps, a different word than "tumultuous" if he was not comfortable with it.

This is also the place where he can describe the relationship in positive terms. He has just heard the accusation: the relationship was negative, therefore, this is the perfect place to say that this claim is not true, and that the relationship was positive.

Please note that "you know" is an habit of speech. Like any habit, we note where it appears and where it does not appear. "You know" is an indication that the subject is acutely aware of the Interviewer's presence at this point, with this question.

This is the place for him to tell us that not only was the relationship not tumultuous, but that it was a good relationship.

He does not.

His answer appears not to be lost by the Interviewer, David Muir, who then specifically asks:

> DAVID MUIR (ABC NEWS) *There wasn't any fighting?*

The Interviewer asks this question in the negative, making it important for the Interviewer, himself. This may signal that the Interviewer may not believe that there was no domestic violence or "fighting" in the relationship between the subject (Genoese) and Sheena.

JOSEPH GENOESE

Well, in a relationship, there's always, there's always arguments and stuff.

The word "well" is a pause, which means that the question, itself, has caused the subject need to pause and think of his answer.

The question about "fighting" is now sensitive to the subject. One might wonder why a question about "fighting" would be sensitive to him, and cause him to need to pause to think longer before answering. It is another habit of speech and like all habits, we note what questions cause it to enter his language, and what questions do not cause it.

He says "in a relationship" and not in "my" or "our" relationship. This is to avoid answering the question. This is the second indication that the question is sensitive to him. It is to distance himself by moving away from "my" or "our" relationship.

Note "arguments and stuff" does not define what, besides "arguments" the subject is speaking of. This is where the Interviewer can ask, "What stuff?" and learn what the subject is thinking of, regarding "fighting" besides arguing.

It may be that in "fighting" there is "arguments" but for the subject, there is something else in addition to arguing.

This should be taken along with the two indicators that the question on fighting, itself, is sensitive, therefore, it is a likely a signal that there was domestic violence in the relationship.

Remember, people do not like to lie outright, and to avoid the internal stress, they will deceive by leaving out information instead. The interviewer senses that there was more than just "arguing" in his answer, and that he avoided speaking for the relationship itself,

instead turning to vague terms that might apply to others instead of himself.
He avoiding answering if there was "fighting" making "fighting" very sensitive to him.
Principle: When a question is avoided, the question, itself, is sensitive.

Muir: *It was never physical?*

This is a "yes or no" question, which is easier (less stressful) to lie in response. We note every word that is added beyond the word "no":

JOSEPH GENOESE:

No. You know, in a normal relationship, there, there was fights, there was, you know, back and forth. But there was no, never any violence. No.

Deception indicated.

The word "no", by itself, is a good answer. Instead, he continues, as do many deceptive individuals who are concerned that the simple "no" is not strong enough by itself. They feel the need to emphasize the denial, which actually weakens it.

Please note that in Statement Analysis, any word that is repeated is sensitive. We see that in this one answer, he uses the word "no" three times, making it very sensitive.

Please note the inclusion of the word "normal" in statement analysis is indicative that it was not normal. Even in early grade school readers when a young student reads, "it was a normal day like any other", they know that someone not normal, or extraordinary, is about to take place.
This is a strong signal that this was not a "normal" relationship within the context being domestically violent.

Note that he was said "back and forth" which appears to be a subtle blaming of the victim, that not only did the violence go in one direction, but in two. This voids his answer of "no" that he began with. Each word that goes beyond "no" is critical in analysis.

Note that "You know" appears twice in this answer. This is to be acutely aware of the Interviewer's presence while asking this question.

The word "never" in statement analysis is not a reliable denial unless the word "ever" is in the question. When the word "never" is added to "no", it is to be noted.
It is very likely that not only was this relationship domestically violent, but acutely so.

DAVID MUIR (ABC NEWS)

Nor was there ever <u>any violence</u> with his ex-wife, according to Joe, when we asked him about those battery charges that were dropped.

By simply stating the accusation, this allows the subject to say "there was no violence" and direct his answer to the relationship between himself

GENOESE: *It was a <u>push back and forth</u>. She pushed me, I pushed her back. <u>And</u> then she looked at me and <u>says,</u> "Now you're going to jail."*

Note that "push back and forth" is not "violent" according to the subject.
Note the order:
1. **She pushed me**
2. **I pushed her back**

This puts the priority upon her, that he only pushed her "back", which is to minimize.
Please next note that he said, "And"
Sentences that begin with the word "And" indicate that there is missing information between the sentence and the one that preceded it. After he pushed her back, and before she "looked" at him, there is missing information that he is deliberately withholding. This would be a good place to ask about it.
Note that when he quotes her, he does not say "she said" but moves into the present tense "says", reducing reliability. Note also that he does not say "she says" but "she looked at me and says", with "looked" in the past tense.
One might want to know what it is that is missing between the sentences that caused him to say "she looked at me":
When he pushed her, did she fall in such a way that in order to address him, she had to rise to her feet and turn around in order to <u>look at him</u> while speaking? This indicates that prior to her speaking, she was not facing him.
This may have been a serious assault or "push" that took place. This should be seen in light of the above conclusion of an acutely violent relationship.

DAVID MUIR (ABC NEWS)

And he points out his ex-wife dropped it all. And he says his fights with Sheena, including the one that New Year's night, were often caused by her jealousy of the family he already had. And he also says that Sheena was often depressed. Remember that Christmas morning video, where Kelly sees her daughter smiling and laughing.

SHEENA MORRIS (DAUGHTER OF KELLY OSBORN)

At least I'm (inaudible).

DAVID MUIR (ABC NEWS)

He sees something else, remembering the fiancée who couldn't get out of bed that morning, who didn't wanna spend Christmas, he says, with her family.

JOSEPH GENOESE (FIANCEE OF SHEENA MORRIS)

She wasn't out of bed for two days, <u>hadn't</u> eaten anything in two days. And...

Please note that he again avoids using Sheena's name, which suggests distancing language. Please note the missing pronoun, "hadn't eaten…', which reduces commitment to the statement.

When a name of someone as close as a fiancé is avoided, it is a signal of emotional distance. Why would an innocent, bereaving fiancé avoid using his love's name? We look to see, by the language itself, if there was trouble in the relationship.

DAVID MUIR (ABC NEWS)

Was she depressed?

This is another "yes or no" question in which we expect the subject to answer with one or the other, or an explanation why "yes or no" is not an appropriate response. "Was she depressed?" is very straightforward, especially in a suicide case.

JOSEPH GENOESE:

I <u>guess</u> she was <u>upset</u> with the fact, or depressed <u>with the fact</u>, that I was spending time with my kids over the holidays.

Please note that he does <u>not</u> answer the question about depression. This indicates that the question, "Was she depressed?" is sensitive to the subject.

Please note that he only says "guess" which is to express uncertainty and instead of using "depressed" he uses "upset."

Note that she is not "upset" but "upset with the fact"

Note that she was not "depressed" but only "depressed with the fact."

Principle: Change of language should represent a change in reality. If there is no apparent change of reality within the statement, it may indicate deception on part of the subject.

For example: *"The officer pulled his <u>gun</u> and fired his <u>weapon</u> at the suspect. He re holstered his <u>gun</u> and called for back up."*

The context shows veracity: it was a *"gun"* until it was being fired, at which time it changed into a *"weapon"*, but after it was no longer being fired, it returned to being a *"gun."*

"<u>The car</u> sputtered. I left the <u>vehicle</u> on the side of the road. After it was repaired, I picked up <u>my car</u> at the garage."

It was a "car" until it no longer operated, at which time it became a "vehicle", but once it was back running, it returned to being not only a "car" but "my" car. This is a sign of truthfulness in a statement.

In the subject's response, there is no apparent change of reality from "upset at the fact" and "depressed at the fact."

Conclusion: deception detected.

DAVID MUIR (ABC NEWS)

And Joe says that surprise New Year's trip was out of concern for Sheena because she had been down.

This is a statement. Best to ask questions, but the inference is, 'Did you take the trip to help her with depression?' but keep in mind that the subject (Genoese) did not assert that Sheena was either suffering from depression, or that she was depressed.

GENOESE:

And I <u>said to myself</u>, maybe we'll just go down there for New Year's Eve, since we had a crappy Christmas.

Here, it begins with "And", which may be an editing issue, as a sentence beginning with "And" is a 'connection'; that is, a signal of missing information between sentences.

Note that he did not state that she had depression, or was depressed, and that this trip was to help with depression.

Instead, depression is avoided, and it is not that "Sheena" had a "crappy weekend" but that "we" had a crappy weekend.

This is to avoid the depression issue and bring the focus to them, as a couple. They had a crappy weekend, rather than Sheena being depressed.

Remember, people do not like to lie outright, but will 'skate around' the truth, to leave an impression of deception, rather than lie.

Sheen lived with him.

He is unable to bring himself to say that she was depressed. We are not to say it, nor conclude it, for him, nor to match the police finding of "suicide."

It is not because of depression, but because of a crappy weekend. Follow the subject. Do not try to make his words fit any police theory, or murder theory ; just listen to him.

DAVID MUIR (ABC NEWS)

(VO) *And Joe says that Sheena was happy that New Years Eve night. He remembers, too, as she sat there texting her friends from the dinner table.*

We don't know if the Interviewer is quoting the subject or not. When body posture enters, it may signal an increase in tension. Is he quoting the subject?

Here is an example:

1. "*My boss told me to be at work at 8AM.*"

This is stronger:

2. "*My boss stood and told me to be at work at 8AM*" with the body posture a signal of increase in tension for the subject.

JOSEPH GENOESE

We went out to dinner at the place we were gonna get married at. She was texting and talking with her family most of the night.

Please note that even though they were out to dinner at the place they were going to get married at, there is distance between the subject and Sheena:
1. He continues to avoid using Sheena's name
2. He does not tell us that Sheena was talking with him, but instead, communicating with her family, which would leave him out of the communications, as he is not mentioned.

This was not likely a good night between them, even if Sheena enjoyed communicating with her family.
Note that she was not only "texting" with her family, but "talking" with them.
Note that this went on for "most of the night" which may make one ask if this angered the subject and gave occasion for "fights and stuff"

Next, notice the location of the dinner is important to the subject. It is unnecessary information, therefore, it is important. By using the location of the dinner, he is emphasizing that it was a special place for them to get married at.

During this special time for where "we" were going to get married at, she was both "texting" and "talking" with her family, not only during the dinner, but "most" of the night.

This is a signal of discord between them. This is the domestic fighting that is of primary concern; more than depression, which has not been acknowledged. Remember: listen to his words to guide you. If he is unable or unwilling to say it, we must not say it for him.

DAVID MUIR (ABC NEWS)
And he remembers their kiss at midnight.

The interviewer introduces the word "kiss." Better is, "What happened at midnight?" which allows the subject to choose his own words. New Year's kiss is something significant. Will he affirm the Interviewer's statement about the kiss?

GENOESE:

And then New Year's, you know, 12:00 came. And we - went out on the balcony and fireworks went off, and you know, we celebrated New Year's.

1. "And": when a sentence begins with "And" it is an indication of missing information between sentences.
2. "You know" as a habit of speech showing acute awareness of the interviewer at this point. Here, it enters his speech twice.
3. He does not say that they "kissed" at midnight. They "celebrated" but not kissed? It is likely that midnight was sensitive to the subject, as it is not something he wishes to disclose here.

DAVID MUIR:
A New Year's kiss?

The failure to mention "kiss" is not missed by the interviewer.

GENOESE :

Yeah. Exactly, yeah. Everything was great.

"Yeah" is to agree rather than assent. Then it is repeated, making it sensitive, but it is also described as being "exactly", giving us three indicators. The need to say "Everything was great", when he was only asked if they kissed should lead one to ask if they fought at midnight. The need to say "everything was great" may come from the fact that "nothing was great" at that point.

DAVID MUIR (ABC NEWS)

Great, he says, until he went back inside that hotel room to call his children, to wish them a happy New Year too.

He leads the subject.

JOSEPH GENOESE:

It lasted all about 15, 20 seconds that I was on the phone. <u>And as I turned back around</u>, she was right there. She <u>just looked</u> at me and said, "You just (censored by network) up the whole night."

Note his need to add in the time of the call.
Note body posture. "And" indicates missing information.
"And as I turned <u>back</u> around" This is an indication that physical maneuvering was part of his memory. He not only turned around, but "back" around, indicating that he may have turned from her deliberately. This was not a pleasant exchange.

DAVID MUIR:
Why did she have such a big problem with you calling your kids?

Please note that Sheena was not able to speak for herself and rebut this assertion. This is the subject's assertion, in the words of the interviewer. What will this topic reveal from the subject himself?

GENOESE:

She <u>just</u> didn't want me involved <u>with</u> my children. It was like another family to her. <u>And</u> she started getting <u>really</u> upset, screaming and yelling. <u>And</u> then she started punching the wall.

"And" indicates he is skipping over periods of time, withholding information that has to do with "really upset" and "screaming" and "yelling" and eventually, "punching" the wall.

The word "with" when it is between people, suggests distance.

My wife and I went shopping" is one way of saying it.
"I went shopping with my wife" puts, "I", as far away from "wife" as possible. This is distancing language.

Something like the above may simply be distance due to the fact that in the first sentence we were shopping together, but in the second sentence, I did not really want to go shopping with her.

Note that he says "she just didn't want me involved with my children" reduces the relationship to not parenting, but only being "involved" with his children. The distancing indicator is between the word "me" and "my children."

Perhaps it is he, himself, that caused the distance, and not Sheena.

DAVID MUIR: *Joe says initially, it was Sheena's idea to leave the hotel but that she suddenly changed her mind, refusing to go.*

GENOESE:

<u>She actually</u> at one point tried to grab the money that I had on the bureau so and - she said that I wasn't leaving. <u>And</u> I told her, <u>"I</u> am leaving. <u>We're</u> leaving." Because at that point, I, <u>you know</u>, from her punching the wall and screaming and yelling the way she did<u>, I, I</u> was afraid that, <u>you know</u>, cops were gonna come.

Every person has an internal subjective personal dictionary. When one says "boy" for example, one reader here might think of a new born baby boy, while another thinks of the fighting "boy" in the military at 21 years of age over in Afghanistan.

It is subjective and follow up questions, or context might be needed to give clarity.

Everyone one of us has a personal, internal, subjective dictionary. A good interviewer will "decode" it.

There are two exceptions:
1. Articles ("the, a, an")

Dealing
With Deception

2. **Pronouns**

   Pronouns are instinctive. They do not require thought and are reliable for analysis. Here he described "she" (he continues to avoid using Sheena's name) and said "I am leaving" but this changed to "we're leaving." Pronouns that are confused are often indicators that the subject is not speaking from memory but is being deceptive.

   Note repeated "you know" in context.

   "Stuttering I" in Statement Analysis.

   When a non-stuttering stutters on the pronoun "I", it is an indication of an increase of anxiety at this point of the statement. The pronoun "I" is used millions of times by us, therefore, the stuttering upon it is an indication that the topic the subject is speaking about is causing him anxiety.

   The word "actually" is used when comparing two or more items. "Do you like chocolate?" "No, I actually like vanilla." What is he comparing this response to? Sometimes it may be that the subject is comparing a deceptive statement to what actually happened.

   "Because."

   The subject was asked to explain what happened. When someone who is asked to explain what happened feels the need to explain "why" something was done, it is very sensitive. It means that the subject anticipates being asked why he did something and feels the need to explain it first, as he does not want to be asked. This is very sensitive information.

   DAVID MUIR: But guests were already placing that call to 911.

   CALLER (MALE)
   There's two people over there just screaming and yelling, a woman and a man, at each other.

   DAVID MUIR (ABC NEWS)
   And Joe told us what police say he's always told them.

   DAVID MUIR

   And where did you go?

   GENOESE:

Home, straight home. Straight to my townhouse, where there were people there, they were having a party, and at least five or six people saw me.

Deception indicated.

Please note that when he answered, "Home" it was a very strong answer, but he did not stop with "home."
Deceptive people say too much, and use too many words. They feel the need to explain and add words in order to sound convincing. It makes them sound deceptive instead of convincing, as it underlines the weakness in the assertion.
Instead of simply saying "Home", he adds, "straight home" suggesting that he could have gone somewhere else. But then he changes "home" into a "Townhouse" which we see what caused his "home" to change: a party.
Note that he adds that five or six people saw him:
This is alibi establishing.
This may cause one to ask why he feels the need to establish an alibi?
These additional words indicate that he has a need to be "seen" and that before going "home" to the "Townhouse" in order to be "seen", there is missing information about where he was.
Note that he does not say "we were having a party" but "they" were. Where? His "home" or his "Townhouse"?
He reveals that he needed to be "seen" suggesting that he knew what he had to do in order to establish his alibi.

DAVID MUIR:
On the drive home, Joe says Sheena was on the phone with him suddenly sinking into that depression.

"sinking into depression" is the words chosen by Muir, taken from the subject, pre interview. The follow up question should be:

"If she was sinking into depression, why would you leave your fiancé alone in a hotel room?

DAVID MUIR (ABC NEWS)

What was she saying to you?

If she was "sinking into depression", this is a good question. Was she begging him to return and help her?

Dealing
With Deception

GENOESE : *There was one thing that she did say. In a somber note, she said, "If I can't have you all to myself, don't wanna be here."*

Note that additional wording often gives away the deceptive subject. He was asked what was she saying to him and instead of simply answering it, he affirms only one particular thing with the wording, "there was one thing she did say", giving us the word "did" as unnecessary.
Note the editorializing: "in a somber note" is added.
The word "did" along with the editorializing suggests: rehearsed speech.

Please note that he is presorting to speak for her, but even here, we have a dropped pronoun:

"...don't want to be here."

Even in repeating this, he drops a pronoun. Was he quoting her accurately while dropping a pronoun?

If so, it may be the first time I have ever encountered such a thing.

I do not believe it.

It appears that the Interviewer did not either.

Even without training, a dropped pronoun sounds awkward. It may be that David Muir heard that, and did not even know why it didn't sound "right", but knew enough to ask about such a strange thing.

People drop pronouns when they are being deceptive -it shows a lack of confidence in the statement.

DAVID MUIR : Had she ever said that before?

This is a "yes or no" question. It indicates a strain:

JOSEPH GENOESE:

No.

Please note that he is able to answer a "yes or no" question with a simple "no" showing what a truthful response looks like.

This is likely a truthful answer.

He has no need to add any emphasis.

I believe his answer. I don't think she ever said that to him before, and, in fact, I don't believe he ever said it...period.

DAVID MUIR

And as for that 911 call Sheena made just after 2:00 A.M...

SHEENA MORRIS (DAUGHTER OF KELLY OSBORN)

He just made me bleed and left claw marks all over me and stuff.

The subject will now speak to the allegation, via 911, that he made her bleed and left claw marks all over her. "And stuff" indicates that he did other things to her, that may not have left visible proof, but were done just the same.

GENOESE: *The scrape on her, on her finger, we know that came from her punching the wall. And the scrape on her neck, when she went to grab the money off of the bureau and I grabbed her by her - her shirt, and - and it got her necklace and it, and left a little scratch on her neck. That's, that's it.*

Deception indicated.

Pronouns are instinctive. Here he says "we know" instead of "I know", since he was there personally. Sheena had reported where the injuries came from. He was there, alone with her. Who is the "we" he now speaks of? This is a very strong indication of deception. Note the admission of "I grabbed her by her her skirt" with the stutter.
Note that "that's it" is unnecessary, which gives us an indication, since he was not asked if that was all that took place, that there was much else that took place and that he has the need to stop the flow of information and end it with "that's it", yet stuttering on the word "that."
This is a strong indication that he is not truthful about this.

DAVID MUIR: And he says like the mother who loves Sheena, he was devastated, too, on that New Year's Day when they all learned Sheena was dead.

The interviewer uses the name, "Sheena" but her fiancé distances himself as he is unable to bring himself to use her name.

GENOESE:

And I <u>walk up,</u> and I - and <u>I look</u>, and I was like, what's going on? And <u>he looked</u> at me and said, "I'm sorry for your loss." And I, I fell to my knees. And I just looked at him. I couldn't believe what he said to me. Can we cut? Can we cut?

Please note that the subject speaks in the past tense about what has happened, yet now, he slips into the present tense with, "I walk up" instead of "I walked up", and "I look" instead of "I looked." Yet, when it comes to the activity of another, he appropriately says, "And he looked at me" in the past tense "and said", which is also in the past tense.
Speaking of himself, he slips into present tense, but speaking of another, he remains in the reliable past tense.
This indicates that his reaction is artificial, while the reaction of the other person is real.

DAVID MUIR:

And when he was ready to continue...

GENOESE:
She was a beautiful <u>girl</u>. I - this is a tragedy in everybody's lives, <u>you know?</u>

Note that she is a "girl", not a "woman."
Please also note that she is not "Sheena", the name he has consistently avoided in the interview, which is distancing language, but the phrase "you know" reenters his language, regarding it being a "tragedy."
The interviewer caught this fact:

DAVID MUIR: For you too?

This is a "yes or no" question.

GENOESE:

Absolutely. I was engaged to <u>her.</u>

Note the need for emphasis with "absolutely" while he continued to avoid using her name, distancing himself from her. See "Joey Buttafouco"

DAVID MUIR: Do you think everybody's forgotten that you felt this way too?

GENOESE:
No. I just think that they, they're on the Kelly train. And if you go against what Kelly says, then you're not an advocate of <u>Sheena</u>.

Here, he finally uses Sheena's name. This is a very significant point of the statement. What has caused him to finally say Sheena's name?

Please note that it is the entrance of "Kelly", Sheena's mother, which causes the subject, Joseph Genoese, to finally use her name. With Kelly present, she is "Sheena", a person with a name and identity. She is now close, because "Kelly" and the "Kelly train" is present.

It is the entrance of "Kelly" into his mind that gives "Sheena" a voice, life, and the respect that is rightfully hers. "Kelly" is a very, very important person in the life of Joseph Genoese. One may wish to learn why Kelly is far more important to the subject than his deceased fiancé.

The name "Sheena" is not in his vocabulary as:

his fiancé,
a beautiful girl
a suicide
a person involved in domestic dispute
the one he went to dinner with
the one who talked to and texted her family
the one who was left alone in the hotel room

She was never "Sheena" until a new atmosphere, or context arises:

She is now "Sheena" in an adversarial role.

This is highly significant.

His concern is the "obsessed" mother, Kelly Osborn. It is his worry, and the language reveals why: he is deceptive about the death of Sheena Morris, Kelly's daughter.

Kelly is demanding justice. Kelly has seen him fail his polygraph. Kelly has known he is lying and that he assaulted Sheena and caused her death in a domestic homicide and staged the hanging.

The presence of Kelly is enough to trigger closeness to Sheena.

He is distance from Sheena in all things, except in justice. Now, faced with accusations and guilt, Sheena is "close" and right in his mind.

This is a striking comparison.

DAVID MUIR:

A grieving mother out for answers no matter the cost, refusing to accept the possibility that her daughter could have taken her own life, or a fiancée covering his tracks?
We've talked to Sheena's mother, her family, her friends, and they all categorically say she never would have taken her own life.

This is issued as a challenge to Joseph Genoese, and the final place for him to say "But she did. I did not cause Sheena's death."

He has had many opportunities to

GENOESE:

My personal opinion is nobody ever thinks they're gonna take their own life. Does anybody presume that somebody's gonna take their own life?

Note that it is not only his "opinion" but his "personal opinion", which suggests that not only do others have differing opinions, but he, himself, may think otherwise.
Always note a rhetorical question within a statement as it may be that the subject is speaking to himself.

MUIR: *"Did she ever say to you that she was depressed or, or having suicidal thoughts?"*

This is a fair question. Was there a pattern of suicide? His answer is important:

GENOESE:

She told me she tried to commit suicide when she was 15 years old, took a bottle of pills.

Communicative language:
We note how one portrays communication. "Sheena said she tried to commit suicide when she was 15 years old…" is not what he said.

1. He avoided her name again
2. He used "told" and not "said." The word "told" is more authoritative. For example: "My boss said for me to be at work at 8" is not as strong as "my boss told me to be at work at 8"

One may wish to question why a young woman, confessing a weak moment as a teenager, would need to use authoritative language to report something embarrassing and even shameful, while confiding to her fiancé?
The language does not appear to fit well.

Muir: In fact, that's the same story police say Sheena's mother told them the day her body was found.

Had there ever been suicidal thoughts before?

KELLY OSBORN

She had gotten in some trouble with her dad and, and she kind of, like, said to her father that she took some pills. They checked everything out. She really didn't take anything. It was a false alarm.

MUIR   *Joe says he understands Kelly's need for answers but says she's looking in the wrong place. But how does he explain the mountain of evidence? The sand on Sheena's feet but no sand in the shower, her perfect appearance, her hair, her clothes, and that diamond bracelet on the wrong wrist.*

This is another place for him to say "I didn't kill Sheena."

GENOESE:
I let that, the professionals deal with that, the investigators and <u>everything else.</u>

Note that he does not bring himself to say "I didn't kill Sheena" though he has been given another opportunity to say so. If he is unwilling or unable to say it, we are not permitted to say it for him. Also note that he is not only leaving this to the investigators, but "everything else." What is "everything else"?

MUIR (ABC NEWS)
 He welcomes this new investigation because he insists he still has nothing to hide.

 And once and for all, <u>did you kill Sheena?</u>

This is a "yes or no" question, to which he should say "no" without the need for more wording. Every word after "no" can weaken the denial. We have already seen that he knows how to answer a "yes or no" question with the answer, "no", without the need to add words or change words for emphasis. The best answer is "no", with nothing added:

GENOESE: "*Absolutely not. What would be my motive, for God's sake? I'm 50 years old. I have three children."*

"Absolutely not" is to avoid saying "no"

"Absolutely not" is to show the need for emphasis, weakening the denial.

Please note that he then asks a question. This is sensitive. He challenges as to his motive, and this is not something that the "Kelly train" would struggle to answer, nor is it something an analyst, who knows nothing more of this case than this transcript: Domestic violence.

Note that having 3 children does not indicate innocence.

Muir: But what about the polygraph?

This same question would be asked on the polygraph, perhaps worded "Did you cause the death of Sheena?" so that he cannot say he didn't kill her, but the rope did. The polygrapher was retired FBI and well experienced.

DAVID MUIR (ABC NEWS) But why take the test?

This is another "soft ball pitch" where the Interviewer lets the subject say "Because I didn't kill her. Because I am telling the truth."

GENOESE: *Cause I had nothing to hide.*

Better is to say "I took the polygraph because I did not kill Sheena. I told the truth." If this was his response, the Statement Analysis would have been finished.

DAVID MUIR: *How do you explain those test results?*

This is where an innocent person will say "I told the truth" and need nothing else to add. Will he now, given this easy opportunity, assert that he told the truth using the three elements:
1. **The pronoun "I"**
2. **The past tense verb "told"**
3. **The word "truth"?**
Will he now make this simple statement that honest innocent people do?

GENOESE:

Well, I don't. I was uneasy with a lot of the questions he asked, first of all. Second of all, I was told by a professional the questions that he asked should never have been asked. They were setup questions.

1. He uses "well" as a pause, showing the need to think
2. "I was told" is passive. Passivity is used to conceal identity or responsibility.
3. The simple questions about causing the death of Sheena "should never have been asked" is something that "a professional" would not want his name attached to.

Please note that sample questions in a homicide are like these:

1. Is your name Joseph Genoese?
2. Did you cause the death of Sheena Morris?
3. Is today Thursday?

and so on.

There would be no surprise questions and the pre screen interview would make this clear.

DAVID MUIR: But now for Joe, there are new questions to answer, this time from those investigators taking a fresh look at the case with the real possibility that someone could be charged with murder.
When was the last time you talked to the investigators on the team?

JOSEPH GENOESE: Three weeks ago.

Note the short response is very likely to be truthful.

DAVID MUIR: Were you nervous?

GENOESE: Of course, I'm nervous. I mean, who wouldn't be nervous?

"Of course" is when one wishes us to take an answer without questioning it. Please note the rhetorical question as he may be speaking to himself.

When we come back, Joe's message tonight for Sheena's mother, what he wants her to hear. And we ask Kelly how she will react if no one is charged with murder in her daughter's death.

MUIR: Sheena Morris' mother gave up everything to become the lead investigator in her daughter's case when she says no else would, determined to find answers. The boyfriend who lost his fiancée says all these years, he's been asking questions, too, of the young girlfriend found in that shower.

GENOESE: *"I ask the question all the time. I - I asked her, "Why did you do this?" I don't understand it. I mean, I, I, who, who understands it? I don't.*

In this short response, he uses the pronoun "I" 8 times. This is a signal of anxiety.

Please note again that this is the perfect place for him to say "I didn't do it" but he is unable or unwilling to issue a denial.

Note also the stuttering "I" as an increase in anxiety.

Note that he is referring to Kelly. It was Kelly who's presence in a statement caused him to finally identify Sheena by name. Kelly brings Sheena close to him. Otherwise, he keeps her distant, in the statement. He has a need to distance himself from his own fiancé. This is not expected from an innocent person, but is expected from the guilty.

DAVID MUIR: What are you hoping to hear?

KELLY OSBORN (MOTHER OF SHEENA MORRIS)

I'm hoping my phone rings and it's the Florida Department of Law Enforcement and say, "Miss Osborn, we have a suspect in custody."

DAVID MUIR: Will this ever be over?

KELLY OSBORN (MOTHER OF SHEENA MORRIS)

When there's a trial and the jury finds the suspect guilty. That chapter will be over.

LEE WILLIAMS ("SARASOTA HERALD - TRIBUNE")

She needs some answers. The community, Southwest Florida would like to know what happened to Sheena.

DAVID MUIR: Do you think they'll ever know?

LEE WILLIAMS ("SARASOTA HERALD - TRIBUNE")

Yeah, I do. I would be very surprised if they come back with a, it was a suicide, because the evidence is overwhelming that it's not.

DAVID MUIR
Joe, as you sit here across from me, have you gone there? Have you thought about possible charges?

GENOESE: *I'm not guilty of anything, so...*

This is a truthful statement. He has not been convicted of anything.
It is also a statement that avoids saying "I didn't kill Sheena"

MUIR: You don't fear there are charges coming?

GENOESE:

No, <u>absolutely not</u>. As a matter of fact, if anything, <u>I think</u> I should bring civil charges against Kelly and her family.

Note that "no" is weakened by "absolutely not".
Note that "I think" is weak, as it allows for him, or someone else, to "think" otherwise.
Why would he only "think" he should bring civil charges against Kelly?
One might wonder if he is not sure he wishes to bring civil charges against Kelly because he would have to answer questions under oath.

MUIR: Do you plan to?

GENOESE: *We'll see how it - <u>I'm</u> gonna wait till the investigations is over with. <u>You know</u>, there's no reason why this family did what they did to me.*

Note the change of pronoun from "we'll" to "I'm. Note the blaming of the family what "they did to me" and not what "Kelly" or the "Kelly train" did to him. It may be that he is, here, adding Sheena into the equation, subtly blaming Sheena for the domestic violence that 'forced ' him to kill her, in his mind.

MUIR: If they clear you once and for all, do you think that will be enough for Sheena's mother?

Another great place for him to say he didn't do it.

GENOESE: *No. I don't think she'll ever stop.*

Agreed.

Analysis Conclusion:

Deception Indicated.

My opinion is this: The subject is deceptive and withholding information about what happened to Sheena Morris. It is my view that this interview reveals a domestic homicide in which Joseph Genoese is unwilling or unable to tell us that he did not cause Sheena's death.

We are not going to say it for him.

I believe he is deceptive about the nature of his relationship, and of what happened that night. He uses distancing language throughout, until finally "Sheena" is in the place of pursuing justice via her mother, Kelly Osborn, which provokes the name, "Sheena" to enter his language.

The Statement Analysis of this interview agrees with the result of the reported polygraph: Joseph Genoese is not telling the truth about his involvement in the death of Sheena Morris.

Kelly Osburn continues her quest for justice.

We stand with her.

Chapter Seven: What Happened To Hailey Dunn?

The Casey Anthony case got quite a bit of press, but not nearly as much press as her trial did. Casey Anthony was acquitted in a decision that shocked the country, as Casey reported her 3 year old "Caylee" missing, went out partying, and began a parade of silly lies and stories about a fake non-existing nanny, and had her own mother, Cindy Anthony, also lie on the witness stand, while swearing an oath to God.

The Casey Anthony verdict caused no small amount of emotion in the American TV public, but it was the disappearance of 13 year old Hailey Dunn that caused the most amount of "internet public" emotion that I have witnessed to date.

Yet the internet explosion began, interestingly enough, on television.

The Nancy Grace Show is a show for justice in which the former prosecutor hams it up for the camera, finds cute names to use (like "Tot Mom" for Casey Anthony), has shill guest attorneys who feign disagreement while trying to keep a straight face, and is, overall, a provider of cheesy entertainment while still highlighting the plight of missing persons, something near to my heart.

One evening, Nancy Grace covered the case of missing 13 year old Hailey Dunn, from Texas, which was then to ignite a controversial storm over the internet that still angers readers long after the case went unprosecuted.

At first, police thought that 13 year old Hailey had run off, but soon saw that no 13 year old girl is going to run away from home without her stuff. Teenagers love their stuff, and teenaged girls love their stuff even more so. Stuff means pocketbook, make up, phone, and, well, stuff. Leaving her "stuff" behind wasn't something that Hailey was likely to have done.

Yet it was the very first appearance on The Nancy Grace Show that we learned immediately, if we were listening, that this was no mere runaway, and, in fact, in the first few words spoken by the mother, Billie Jean Dunn, that this was no "missing person case" either.

How I found myself in the middle of this case, itself, is a strange story.

I had been writing the "Statement Analysis Blog" for some time, when this case broke, which was done in an instructive manner, but coupled with my own desire to write, share my ideas, learn from others, and dig deep, in any area, for truth.

At this time, I was not a full time Statement Analyst, but was working as an investigator into claims of abuse, neglect, and exploitation. I worked part time in Statement Analysis, including assisting various law enforcement agencies with analysis.

This case would not only draw me in emotionally, but would, sadly, provide me with an entire volume of training material for law enforcement, human resources, attorneys, business people, therapists, civil investigators, and a host of professionals who relied upon Statement Analysis to get "to the truth" in whatever capacity it was needed.

Billie Jean Dunn would not think highly of me.

With more than 10 million page views at the time, when a news story hit, and a statement was made, I was often at the ready to cover it. Nothing, however, including Casey Anthony, would bring as much blog traffic as the Hailey Dunn story.

That night, Heather and I were watching The Nancy Grace Show when she said, "*Uh, oh. Did you hear that?*"

I hadn't been paying attention.

"*You should rewind it, Peter. Another mother, another missing child, and another statement.*"

I didn't want to hear it. I knew from the look on Heather's face that what she heard had been disturbing.

Here is how it went.

Nancy Grace is a paid celebrity. She is not paid to get information, she is paid to get viewers. A legally sound interview is not good script for Hollywood. A great interview will have the Interviewer speaking only 10% of the words, with the Subject (or Interviewee) doing up to 90% of the talking, after all, it is the subject, Billie Jean Dunn in this case, who has the information, not Nancy Grace, the former prosecutor turned talk-show-news-thingy host.

But in the ratings game, in order to have a show, Nancy has to bring back viewers. She does this with a clever mix of face expressions, hyperbole, head bobbing, and some over-the-top commenters. She does, in spite of this, still get information.

The best question she could have asked the mother would have been "What happened?", which, in this case, was eventually asked. But first, there was the video over-dub, and the "bombshell" announcement, and the high pitched male voice, and then the introduction:

13 year old Hailey Dunn is missing. She went over walking to a friend's house to sleep over and was not seen again. Nancy Grace asked two questions, and although they are not in the best order, they revealed to us shocking information.

The first question was "How far did Hailey have to go?" to get to the sleep over, and then she asked, "Tell us what happened."

The true bombshell that exploded came from the lips of the mother, Billie Jean Dunn. I now use these, particularly in law enforcement or civil investigative training as a lesson in listening to what people tell us.

Here is how I set up the test. I remove the words "Hailey" and "Dunn" in the hopes that the students do not know the case. All they need to know is:

1. A 13 year old girl is missing
2. The mother is on television pleading for her daughter's safe return.

I don't want them to know anything but these two facts. When a statement is made, the only thing an analyst needs to know is why the person is making a statement. The Interviewer, as you know, is Nancy Grace, and the mother, redacted for training purposes, is Ms. Dunn.

Interviewer: 1. Miss *******, how far did she have to go to get to the little sleepover?

Mother: *Four to five blocks. It wasn't rare for ******* to walk a short distance during daylight. She wasn't allowed out after dark especially to walk, but she only had four to five blocks to go.*

2. Interviewer: Tell me what happened the day she went missing, Miss ******.

Mother: *She went missing on Monday while I was at work. My boyfriend - - he came home from work about 3:00 -- or he got to my house about 3:00. And he's seen Hailey. Hailey was there. She told him, I'm running across the street to my dad's house for a few minutes but I'm going Mary Beth's, and I'm staying the night there. Let my mom know. So that evening when he picked me up from work, we got home, we were getting ready for bed. I didn't get worried when I hadn't heard from Hailey. I thought she was at Mary Beth's. I was kind of upset that she didn't call and confirm it with me, but not worried at that point. Tuesday, I was at work again, I left my cell phone at home for my kids to use when I'm working. So Tuesday, I called my son. I said tell Hailey, text the little girl, her friend, tell Hailey she needs to go ahead and get home. This was around lunch. My son called me back within a few minutes and she said, mom, she said Hailey never made it over there. She never spent the night. So at that point I called Hailey's dad and found out she didn't over there and she didn't stay the night with him. I left from work and went to the police station in Colorado City and reported her missing.*

This is what Heather heard, and this is what upset her. This is what caused her to get me to rewind Directv and listen to the mother.

I heard her answers and said, "Oh, no, Heather. Another one!"

In Billie Jean Dunn's two short answers, we knew:

1. Hailey Dunn is dead.
2. Billie Jean Dunn needs an alibi.

I didn't want to get involved. I wanted to make excuses. It is just too awful to think that a mother could be on national television and make a plea for her daughter's return when she knows her daughter is dead.

"She will fail her polygraph, if she takes one" Heather said.

"Oh, she'll take a polygraph. She's got the nerve to go on national television, she is a habitual liar" I responded.

This is critical for law enforcement to understand: a habitual liar is one who has gained a false sense of confidence from lying from childhood and will, given enough rope, so to speak, hang herself. The liar cannot bear being called "liar" and will go down with the ship instead. Law Enforcement must be trained to not only recognize this kind of liar, but develop the strategy that gets the liar to "cut off her nose to spite her face" talk, talk talk.

How did we know that Hailey was dead and her mother needed an alibi? How did we know that she would fail her polygraph? How did we know drugs and pornography were involved?

We listened.

Q. How far did she have to go?

A. "Four or five blocks. She wasn't allowed to go out at night."

The habitual liar feels a need to persuade and press the story. The truthful often speak in short sentences and lets the burden of belief fall upon the audience, and not upon the speaker.

In other words, liars go too far.

"Four or five blocks" was enough. She answered the question. The question was "how far?" and "four or five blocks" stayed within the **boundary** of the question. This is a critical element in Analytical Interviewing.

The deceptive often go beyond the boundary as they feel a need to persuade.

"She wasn't allowed to go out at night.." told us two things, itself:

1. She is referencing Hailey in the past tense, while Hailey is missing. This is what we do when we speak of the dead: we reference them in the past tense. Not only that, but Billie Jean is the mother and a mother's natural denial will not allow her to accept her daughter's death so easily. Here, she has only been missing a few days and she is already telling us that Hailey "wasn't allowed" and not that "Hailey isn't allowed", as if Hailey is still alive.
2. Notice next, however, that Billie Jean Dunn had a need, while her daughter is missing, to portray herself as a good and conscientious mother, as if she would never be the kind of mother that allowed her young teenaged daughter to go out at night! This is a signal that neglect is part of the mother's life.

So the first critical point we learn:

I. **Hailey is dead.**

Next, Nancy Grace asked the far better question, "Tell us what happened" which is best because:

1. It gives Billie Jean Dunn no language to borrow from Nancy Grace, meaning that Billie Jean Dunn will choose her own words.
2. That Billie Jean Dunn can begin her account where she, Billie Jean Dunn, believes it should begin. This will give us her priority.

When asked the legally sound, open ended question of "Tell us **what** happened", the mother goes outside the **boundary** of the question to answer "when" something happened:

"She went missing when I was at work."

II. The second thing we learn after learning that Hailey was dead was that the mother, **Billie Jean Dunn needs an alibi.**

It was these two facts that hit both Heather and I in the heart. Neither of us wanted to believe it. The mother kept right on appearing, night after night, on the show, revealing more information. With each night's episode came my analysis posted in the morning. One Texas Ranger said to me, "You know more about the case than some investigators do. We read your analysis each morning to learn about the case!"

It is trained listening.

The mother's boyfriend used the word "looked" instead of "read", which Heather immediately said, "Uh oh, pornography is involved" because pornography is "looked at" and not read. We then heard the mother talk about her "toothache."

Now ask yourself this: If your little girl was missing, would you give a rat's arse about your personal comfort?

"Toothache" is very similar to "bad back" and often used by prescription pain killer abusers.

It was not magic, nor did it have anything to do with psychics that gave us the information that ended up, for the most part, being verified in the case. That no one has yet to be charged leaves the mother and her boyfriend, Shawn Adkins, as "unverified" but like others, we remain guardedly hopeful for justice for Hailey.

The case attracted the usual interest groups, including web sleuth types (some of which are highly intelligent), victims advocates, and even the small group of "groupies" who wish to be part of any form of spot light.

Billie Jean Dunn convinced Shawn Adkins to take a polygraph, drugging him so he could pass. When caught, she was forced to show up for it sober, or appear a liar.

She and Shawn Adkins both flunked their polygraphs.

Billie Jean Dunn had a child protective history, a drug history, and a history of stripping. This caught the attention of a small group of women who shared this set of less than noble characteristics, who went out of their way to defend her, even to the point of pulling her aside to remind her not to dress so like a slut at a rally, and put on a "help find Hailey" t shirt.

Marc Klass even flew to Texas and coached Billie Dunn how to 'speak to Hailey' in the camera, as if alive. Local police bristled at his interference with the case, and he was later forced to go back on the Nancy Grace Show and not only withdraw his support for Billie, but to call down "shame" on her for lying to police.

Billie did not search for Hailey, but instead threw a New Year's Eve party, just days after Hailey went "missing" and when pushed, finally said she would not search those "ugly fields" where the searchers were looking. This reminded me of Casey Anthony, the "Tot Mom" who, on prison camera, said to her mother, "in my heart, I know Caylee's close", only to have Caylee's remains found a quarter mile from her house. In the case of Hailey Dunn, she was found in the "ugly fields" perimeter, within the geographical route between her home and Shawn Adkins' route the next day.

Both mothers' words revealed the location.

Both mothers' words revealed, via the past tense verb, that the children were dead.

Both children were found dead.

The case had child pornography, bestiality, drug abuse and violence.

In her conversations with radio hosts, Billie Jean Dunn talked about her childhood sexual abuse and as an aging stripper, desperate to hold on to her looks, it may be that she saw her own child as a rival for Billie's younger boyfriend, Adkins. The lethality of drugs, violence and perversion brought not only Hailey's short life to an end, but brought Adkins and Dunn together, linked in a conspiracy of silence and lies, for the rest of their lies. Prosecutors are counting on the inability of them both to keep their deadly secret.

Mistakes were made, particularly early on, when the child pornography was found on computers that Shawn Adkins had access to, and probably should have handed over the case to federal prosecutors. Adkins, lover of scary masks, was terrified of prison and, judging by his words and ability to be manipulated by Billie Jean, would have folded and given up the details of the case, including where the body was dumped, early on in hopes of saving himself from being in prison as a pedophile.

Pedophiles in prison generally don't run for 'cell mate of the year' awards.

Clint Dunn was in an awful position. For whatever reason, he feared angering Billie Jean, which may have been born of a fear of not being permitted to see Hailey. He loved his daughter and after Billie reported her missing, went to her home to begin the search.

What he saw shocked him.

He entered the home of Billie Jean only to find Billie on the couch, watching her favorite soap opera, as if nothing had happened.

He went to talk to Hailey's then 16 year old brother, to console him and have him assist in the search for Hailey. Clint was not the teen's biological father, but had been like a father to him since he was a little boy.

Clint was shocked to see the boy playing a video game, not in the least upset.

What was going on here?

Billie refused to search with him, unwilling to tear herself away from the soap opera. Clint was later to be the one to tell police that although Billie reported Hailey missing shortly after Christmas, she hosted a New Year's Eve party, replete with lots of alcohol.

By this time, Billie had already been making her appearances on the Nancy Grace Show, who now had learned a few interesting facts about the case, including the party. Billie Jean Dunn's language shows the habitual pattern of deception with the ability to change language and change the topic away from what is too touchy for her. Look at the transcripts. Nancy Grace grew impatient as the obvious deception descended upon the live program:

Her pattern of deception includes not only withholding information, but of diversion. You can sense the impatience in Nancy Grace's words, and more so if you see the appearance, via You Tube. As said earlier, Nancy Grace is a television "host" and as such, needs to keep ratings up in order to keep the show on the air, even while attempting to glean information from Billie Jean Dunn.

This is a difficult balance, and although it is not an example of Analytical Interviewing, you will pick up spots where Nancy reflects back to Billie Jean, Billie Jean's own wording.

NANCY GRACE, HOST: Breaking news tonight, live, Texas. A 13-year-old cheerleader, broad daylight, leaves home around lunchtime, heads by foot down the street to a little friend's house for a sleepover. She's never seen again. Bloodhounds scan the neighborhood and the local motel. Police comb that motel surveillance video. No sign of Hailey. Police seize cell phones belonging to Mommy and her live-in boyfriend. They polygraph friends, neighbors. And just hours after we go live with the story, Colorado police, who originally dismiss Hailey's disappearance as a runaway, upgrade the case to missing person, cops searching an abandoned cotton gin, combing creek bottoms and the Colorado River. Searchers zero in on the home of Mommy's boyfriend. As police take DNA samples from Hailey's parents, bombshell tonight. Did Mommy and the boyfriend actually throw a New Year's Eve party? That's just 72 hours after Hailey goes missing. We learn turmoil in the home before with the boyfriend, Shawn Adkins, with him threatening to kill the mom and Hailey. And oddly, during his police interviews, after cops ask to see his cell phone, he starts deleting numbers. Why?Then he says he's sure Hailey can be found a few counties over. In those same interviews, Adkins starts out saying, quote, what a "good girl" Hailey is. But then he does a 180, claiming the little girl -- she's 13, people -- claiming she's promiscuous. And did the boyfriend lie about his job and his whereabouts that day?Tonight, we learn multiple polygraphs gone wrong, including Mommy showing up high, both her and boyfriend refusing to take polygraphs, even walking out. In the weeks before Hailey's disappearance, did Hailey's own mother stockpile research on serial murders, family murders, motive for murders and sexual sadism? She is with us tonight to answer these questions live. Where is 13-year-old cheerleader Hailey Dunn?

GRACE: Good evening. I'm Nancy Grace. I want to thank you for being with us. Bombshell tonight. Did Mommy and the live-in boyfriend **actually throw a New Year's Eve party just 72 hours after they report Hailey missing**? We learn turmoil in that home before, with Shawn Adkins, the boyfriend, threatening to kill the mom and Hailey. And in the weeks before Hailey's disappearance, did Hailey's mother stockpile research on serial murders, family murders, motive for murders, and sexual sadism?JEAN CASAREZ, "IN SESSION": And Nancy, let's remember where this comes from. This is the search warrant affidavit for cell phones and also for a vehicle. And that is what gives a judge probable cause that a crime has been committed to issue a warrant. And it says in this search warrant affidavit that Shawn Adkins and Billie Dunn hosted a New Year's Eve party at their home.And it goes on to say many things. Let's look at the polygraph. It says that Shawn Adkins actually walked out the first time, walked out the second time. The third time, he sat down for it. And when he was asked, Do you know the whereabouts of Ashley (SIC) Dunn -- you know, Hailey Dunn, you know what he said? He said he didn't, and deception was indicated.

It may be that Adkins did not tell Dunn where the remains were dumped.

GRACE: You know, Jean, also in that interview and in some of his police interviews -- everybody, we're talking about the live-in boyfriend of the mom, Billie Dunn, who with us live tonight and taking your call calls. At some point, he starts talking about what a great little girl, a good girl, as he says, the little girl is. She's only 13. Of course she's good.But then he goes on within that same interview, does a 180, Jean, starts talking about, she is promiscuous, sleeps around, does drugs. You know, take a look at these pictures. This is not a drug-head. Look at this little girl. She's an all-American little cheerleader. She didn't even have a boyfriend.GRACE: And he compares Hailey's possible death to, OK, cutting a deer up. (INAUDIBLE) wrong --

OK, got it. I want to go to Billie Dunn. Billie Dunn is Hailey's mother, and it speaks to her credibility that she is here taking our calls and taking my questions tonight. First thing I want to clear up, Ms. Dunn, I have in these documents that I've with me and I've read them very carefully, that you did, in fact, have a New Year's Eve party at your home. That would have been within 72 hours of reporting Hailey missing.

To Billie Dunn: Did you have a New Year's Eve party? Do we need to define what "New Year's Eve party means?" This became apparent as Nancy Grace questioned her. Follow the pronouns: BILLIE DUNN: *Well, we did not. I know it wasn't on my mind* at *all* that it was even New Year's Eve. *I* had an uncle and aunt, and they brought their grandbaby from out of town. They came up. They stayed at my house Friday during the day. They spent the night at my brother's. They were back over here Saturday. I think they went home on Sunday. *We* had family over here. *I've* had a lot of fat of family here. But that weekend, an aunt, an uncle and their grandbaby and my two brothers came over. **Note that she began with "well", which is a pause, making the question, "Did you have a New Year's Eve party" sensitive to her.**
Note next she begins with "we"

Note next that she says "we did not" but did not complete what they did not.

A truthful person will tell us what happened, what the person thought and not what did not happen or what was not thought:
Note next she reports what was not on her mind.
Dunn only owns that some family came over to her home. Grace takes her through a series of baby steps to learn if she had a party or not. Her denial is, "no we didn't" but Nancy Grace now probes to see if it is reliable or not:

GRACE: And when they were there that night...

BILLIE DUNN: There was definitely no...

GRACE: ... New Year's Eve night. What were you guys doing in the home that night

?BILLIE DUNN: *We* were visiting. *We* were talking about Hailey. *We* were *pretty* upset.

 She starts with "we" and not with "I";
Note the order:
1. We were visiting
2. We were talking about Hailey
3. We were "pretty" upset

Dealing
With Deception

Please note that "visiting" came first in her order. This was not lost on Nancy Grace. She also said that "we were pretty upset" which expresses the emotions of others ,instead of "i was upset". Please note that she did not say she was upset, but only that they were "pretty" upset, qualifying being upset.

72 hours after her daughter is reported missing they visited, talked and were only "pretty" upset. Most people would be more than just "pretty" upset.

GRACE: Did you have out food for them? Was anybody having drinks?

Since she began with "we were visiting" as her priority, Nancy Grace seeks to define what a New Year's Eve party looked like. She asked a compound question which should be avoided, as it allows the subject to pick and choose which to answer.

BILLIE DUNN: I know that there was a lot of food out, and I think Shawn had some drinks. Nobody else. Nobody was <u>worried</u> about having a New Year`s Eve party.

Here is how she lies: She "knows" there was "a lot of food out". Didn't she serve it? Did someone bring it in for her? Wasn't she there? If she was there, she would know that food was there. This is a type of avoidance due to the high sensitivity.
Next, she "thinks" Shawn had "some drinks" but will not commit to it. She saw the food, and "knows" it was a "lot" for her uncle, aunt and their baby, her and Shawn.
"nobody else" is a broken sentence. She did not say that "nobody else was drinking."
Clint reported a large volume of empties. It gets worse for her:
"Nobody was worried about having a New Year's Eve party." She was not asked if people or even "nobody" was worried about the party.

Nancy Grace smelled the lie:

GRACE: Did you have the TV on?BILLIE DUNN: Yes.GRACE: Were you watching the ball drop?

A yes or no question

BILLIE DUNN: We were <u>just</u> watching news.
The question is avoided.

GRACE: Are you sure?

This is actually insulting, rather than just a straight question. She was giving Billie Dunn

an opportunity to look a bit less foolish and just come clean.

BILLIE DUNN: Yes.

GRACE: So you`re telling me that you have people over, you had food out, alcohol was being served, but it was not a party.BILLIE DUNN: There was no party, and we weren`t serving alcohol. I think Shawn had a beer.GRACE: So it was just him.BILLIE DUNN: Nobody was trying to have a party. that was -- right. That was on nobody`s mind.

This is how she lies and the pattern is repeated enough to follow.

"we weren't serving alcohol" denies the act of "serving" and not that they were drinking. Note the change about Shawn having some drinks to "a" beer. It is difficult to keep track of lies because they do not originate from memory.

More examples of diversion and splintering of words:

GRACE: To Billie Dunn. This is Hailey`s mother joining us live there in her home. Billie, what did cops tell you about taking Hailey`s bed sheets?
This is a simple question, "What did the cops tell you?" about the sheets.DUNN: *I just know when they came in and searched the house, they took a few things, which they`re more than welcome to take any and everything they need. I didn`t notice the sheet was missing for a couple of days. I did tell them to take it for the hounds, but, yes, they kept it and they can keep it, get anything they need.*

Note that Dunn avoids answering the question, "what did the cops tell you...?" indicating that the question of the cops telling her something is sensitive. This is consistent with the police not sharing information with a suspect. She could have said, "they haven't told me anything" which would have been truthful. Instead, she goes beyond the boundary of the question and gives us vital information:
"I just know" is I "only" know, as "just" is a comparison (downward) word. What does she "just" know?
"When they came in, they took a few things": She was NOT asked "what did they take?" but "what did they say?". This is her pattern of going beyond the boundary of the question.
"*which they're more than welcome*" is an attempt to persuade that she is cooperative.
Question: Who has the need to persuade people into believing that she is cooperative?
Answer: The uncooperative.

This is the same woman who walked out of the interrogation, had played 'cat and mouse' chase games over the polygraph, and who finally showed up under the influence. That they are not just welcome but "more than welcome" has Dunn attempting to persuade Nancy Grace (and audience) that she is cooperating because she is uncooperative. This is why she lied to the police to protect Adkins. To protect Adkins is to protect herself.

"*I did tell them to take it for the hounds*" presupposes that she is smarter than the police and that Billie Dunn was advising the police on what to do, and how to do it. This is the narcissism and arrogance of narcissism so evident in her language. She, Billie Dunn, taught the Texas Rangers how to do a proper search.

"But <u>yes, they kept it</u>" is a clever device as it would appear that she is in the affirmative ("yes") but it is not what she was asked.

"What did the police tell you?" is completely avoided, but Billie Dunn does not want anyone to think she is a suspect, so she goes far beyond the question, avoiding it, and giving lots of additional information.
She turned the table on Nancy Grace, avoiding giving an answer, and began an entirely new topic.

Nancy Grace follows up after noticing she avoided the question with a tangent:

GRACE: Billie, what are they telling **you** about the investigation? DUNN: *Not a whole lot. More than <u>everybody</u> else. They do tell me -- <u>I don`t want them to be too focused on Shawn</u>. I want them to look everywhere, which they reassure me they are. They have different people looking at different areas. I just -- as long as <u>I can believe that Hailey`s alive, I`m going to choose to believe that</u>. But they do tell me they`re looking everywhere.*

"Not a whole lot" is her answer; yet, she is not satisfied with answering the question. She has a need to now rehabilitate herself, now seen as not being given information, with an answer with more information: "more than everybody else" (which is not true).
It looks bad for her, but she will make sure that it appears that it is not just she and Adkins being not told, it is "everybody" else.

She then goes on to report in the negative: "I don't want them to be 'too' focused on Shawn." This is very important to the narcissist: focus on Shawn will lead to her. This is why she lied about him hiding in her house: she thought it was arrest time. She knows that Shawn Adkins will bring her down with him.

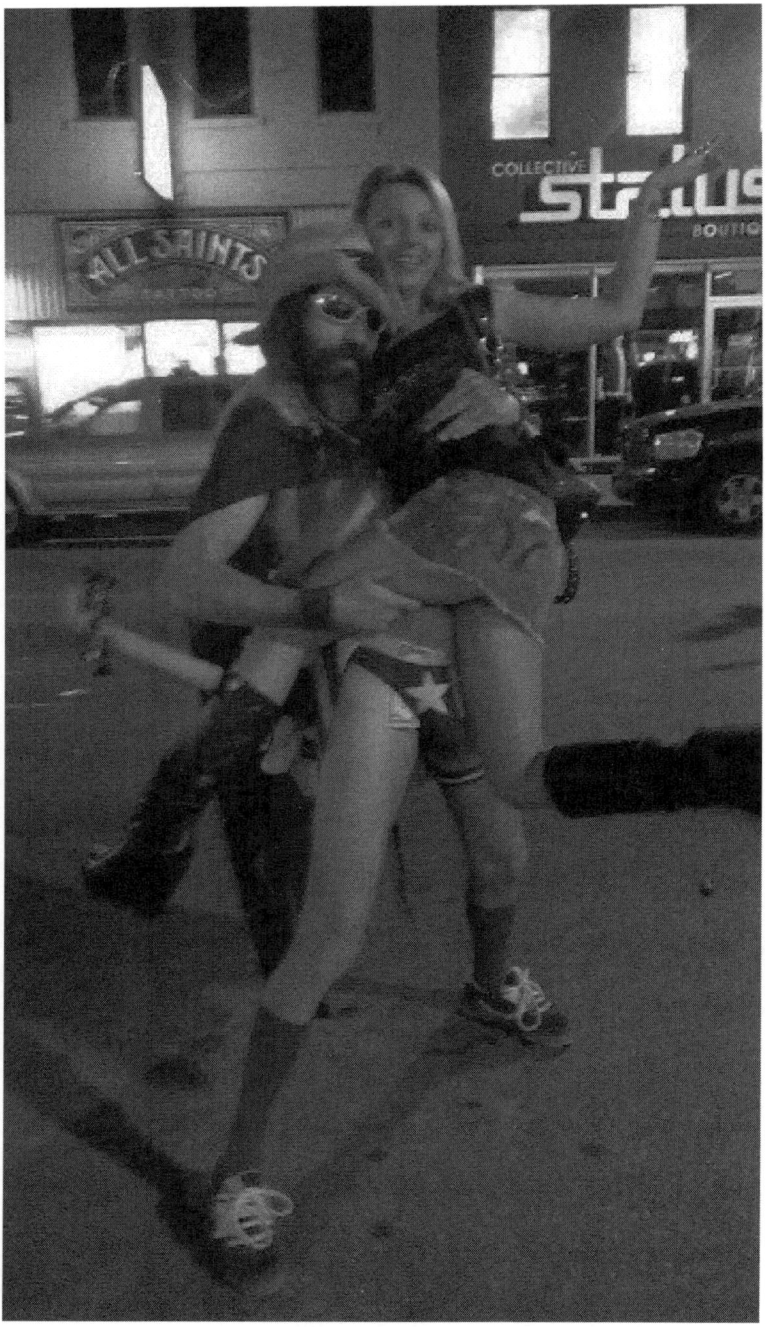
ALL SAINTS
COLLECTIVE
BOUTIQ

A hurting mother searching for missing daughter?

They are in this together.

The question was "what are police telling you?" Her answer is "as long as I can believe..." is a different topic altogether. This is habitual, by the seat of your pants deception, something that only comes with many years of practice.

Here is another example: Hailey's grandmother came on the show and talked about Shawn possibly raping Hailey. Nancy Grace pointed out that Shawn drove to work at 6:00 AM and left a few minutes later, and lied about where he went and then asked Billie Jean Dunn about her daughter being "raped" as posed by the grandmother.
The expectation is that Billie Dunn will address the rape allegation. Her answer?
BILLIE DUNN: *Why didn`t nobody tell me?*

Instead of talking about rape, she turns the table on others, and blames others for not telling her. This completely avoids the topic, "rape", which makes the question of "rape" very sensitive to Billie Dunn, who, instead of answering the allegation, turns the tables on others.
Another example of deception **by Billie Dunn:**

GRACE: OK, you want to talk about the boyfriend. First, out to Billie Dunn. This is Hailey`s mother joining us tonight live from Colorado City, Texas. She`s there at the home. Ms. Dunn, thank you for being with us. Let`s just address those issues right now. Let`s talk about your boyfriend.
The audience and host want to know about the boyfriend as suspicions arose and reports have surfaced that may have contradicted the mother's statements.

Dealing
With Deception

BILLIE DUNN: OK.GRACE: *Last night, you told me he was on his way home from work, but now I'm learning he was on his way home from his mother's home?*

It is very simple: explain the contradiction. She has forgotten that Billie knew of this already and on the previous night used the "either/or" method of deception. This is not the point now, however. The point is going beyond the boundary of the question: BILLIE DUNN: *Yes. He had been at his mother's house all day Monday. Police have confirmed that <u>he got home about 3:00 o'clock,</u> and Hailey left shortly after.*

She said that police confirmed "a" and "b" in the same sentence; "a" being what time Shawn got home, but she added "b", "Hailey left shortly after."
Not only is this beyond the boundary, but it is also a lie. Police did not confirm that Hailey left at 3:00 o'clock.

"3" is the liar's number (Mark McClish) and it is not confirmed by police. In fact, police knew that Hailey did not leave the house at 3:00 o'clock; at least, she did not, as Nancy Grace said above, leave that house alive.
Even as you listen to Billie Dunn continuing to speak out, notice how often she regularly goes beyond the boundary of the question. This is indicative of her method of deception. She does it almost every time she answers a question. She seeks to control the information because she has a need to control the information.

Regarding the number "Three being the liar's number", retired US Federal Marshall and Statement Analyst Mark McClish felt that there was something unusual about the number three, and speculated, based upon years of law enforcement interviewing, that when a deceptive person is going to have to choose a number between one and nine, the deceptive person often chooses the number three.

Finding this in his own work, he asked other students of his course, as well as other analysts, to join him in this study and send any examples that support his hypothesis.

He was correct.

Now, this does not mean that 3 men can't rob someone at 3 o'clock, on the 3rd floor, over on Third Street and steal $3,000.

It can happen.

It just means that if you hear the number three, red-flag it for possible deception.

The only exception?

Officer: "How many drinks did you have?"

Driver: "Only two, officer."

When pulled over, this is the number one answer: "only two." The number one answer is not "two", but "only two."

The word "only" is vital. It is used in comparison, downward. "Would you like to buy this car? It is $10,000!" "No? It's too much? Well, you might like this one, it is only $7500. " The word "only " indicates a comparison exists in the mind of the driver. "Only two" means that he is owning that he had two, but in his brain, he knows he had more than two, therefore, the word "only" is produced, in less than a microsecond, as a form of "leakage", where information inadvertently 'leaks' out through the mouth.

Heather said that she feels that when one is deceptive, the number two sounds "too small" but the number four sounds "too big" and "three is just right."

When we come to the case of "Fake Hate", carefully note how many men she reported attacked her.

In the internet explosion that was this case, "psychics" came out of the woodwork to "opine" or "reveal" the location of Hailey.

They are, as in the words of Marc Klass, "vultures" who prey upon parents, in particular, who could not be more vulnerable than in the case of a missing child.

Psychics have never found a missing person, and their language reveals that it does not come from experiential memory. They are deliberately vague, and Face Book, and social media in general, has given new audience to such nonsense.

In the radio interview of Billie Jean Dunn of which I participated after being requested by the District Attorney's investigator, one of the "psychics" went into an embarrassing crying jag, which, for someone like me attempting to get information, felt like an eternity.

Desperate parents fall prey to the venom of psychics who will often work "pro bono", which, meaning without pay, is done to associate with the case. One even claimed to have "spoken" with Hailey, who was "crying out" from her kidnapper's prison.

Hailey did not leave her home alive.

Clint Dunn, heartbroken, referenced Hailey in the past tense while still missing. He said, "I just said it. Oh my God. I believe my little girl is dead."

He said he had read my analysis and agreed, especially after the shocking revelation of what Billie's home life was like after reporting Hailey to be "missing." He also saw how the case attracted the "Billie Jean groupies" who swore allegiance to her, promising (and even threatening) retaliation to anyone who did not have 'hope' for Hailey. My "hope" for Hailey was in justice, which continues to slumber.

But I still believe that justice will be awakened and that, given all the abundance of information taken from the Nancy Grace Show itself, justice will be realized.

When it comes, perhaps Nancy Grace, herself, should be thanked.

But what of Casey Anthony?

Billie Jean Dunn was no brilliant liar, but an accomplished one in her world where she was able to control information.

Chapter Eight: "Tot Mom"

What would be a book on deception without "Tot Mom" Casey Anthony? I don't know if I ever saw more "tabloid fatigue" is what I saw in the public's reaction to Casey Anthony recently. People are just sick of hearing of her.

She held a nation spell bound as photos of her 'dirty dancing' while Caylee was 'kidnapped' by the fake 'nanny', with Casey unconcerned about her family questioning her…

George and Cindy Anthony.

What a pair! Was he the steroid using, gourmet cook, former cop, now Nigerian Princess investor, or was he Caylee's killer, having drowned her in the swimming pool?

Cindy was a different read altogether. She loved the spotlight and she loved confrontation. She was not stressed by it, as her eyes lit up when she thought of taking a shovel to the head of a protestor outside her home, or when she boldly lied under oath that she, herself, had been researching chloroform instead of Casey.

The apple did not fall far from the tree.

George and Cindy, always in debt, always having to support more and more Nigerian royalty, always falling and filing claims to game the system, suddenly found themselves living the life of Riley with no more financial worries, all since their granddaughter was murdered, allegedly by a Nanny who was watching Caylee full time, but of whom George and Cindy didn't care enough to take the time to meet.

Hmmm.

Here they had a 3 year old granddaughter, who's mother employed a full time Nanny, even while Casey showed up at home to steal quarters from a jar, yet never questioned about "Zanny the Nanny" with such deeply probing questions such as:

"Hey, Casey. Here you are stealing quarters from Caylee's piggy bank. Where do you get the money to pay for a nanny?"

Their beloved grandchild was in the 'hands' of someone they never met, never spoke to, never asked about, never ran a background check, never asked for references, and never...

Well, you get the picture. People show more concern about boarding the family cat than these people showed over their own granddaughter.

Casey was not a good liar, but she was a confident liar.

On one of the Nancy Grace Show's endless "Tot Mom" coverage, a "law enforcement expert" sad, "I know when Casey is lying; her lips are moving!" which caused not only a chuckle from all, but was in the context of dismissal: Since she is lying, there is no purpose in listening to her.

Nothing could be further from the truth.

Even lies come from somewhere, and the words chosen by a liar will often reveal critical information. Here is such an example:

Tim Miller, from Texas Equasearch, spend a small fortune to bring his helicopter and horses from Texas to Florida to search for Caylee.

He did what you would expect a search expert to do: he asked the family where to begin the search.

Cindy Anthony not only refused to let Casey, recently out on bail, answer any questions, or even point on a map, but actually threw Tim out of her home. Tim was shocked as this was the first time a family had refused to help him find their missing loved one.

Cindy took to the microphone, as she soaked up the attention, so much so, in fact, that while in jail, Casey cracked about Cindy's "cameo", indicating the obvious envy between mother and daughter for the media's spotlight.

Cindy said to the press, "*George and I don't believe Caylee's in the woods or anything.*"

In Statement Analysis, we look at anything spoken in the negative as important. I did not hear anyone in the media say, "Hey, is Caylee in the woods?"

Instead, Cindy offered this, in the negative, where she did not believe Caylee would be found.

Caylee was found a quarter-mile from the home, in the woods.

Casey wasn't a good liar, but she was bold.

She claimed to have worked for Universal Studios and did not buckle under questioning. She went as far as to drive to Universal, with detectives, even to the point of walking down the hallways to her "office" before finally admitting that she did not work at Universal.

She gave police the following statement which when analyzed, shows deception. It is not the work of a nuclear biologist. It is, however, another such example used in training deception detection.

I got off of work, left Universal driving back to pick up Caylee like a normal day. And I show up to the apartment knock on door nobody answers. So, I call Zeniada cell phone and it's out of service. It says the phone is no longer in service, excuse me. So, I sit down on the steps and wait for a little bit to see if maybe it was just a fluke if something happened and time passed and I didn't hear from anyone. No one showed up to the house so I went over to J. Blanchard Park and checked a couple of other places where maybe possibly they would have gone; couple stores, just regular places that I know Zenida shops at and she's taken Caylee before. And after about 7:00 when I still hadn't heard anything I was getting pretty upset, pretty frantic and I went to a neutral place. I didn't really want to come home. I wasn't sure what I would say about not knowing where Caylee was still hoping that I would get a call or you know find out that Caylee was coming back so that I could go get her. And I ended up going to my boyfriend Anthony's house who lives in Sutton Place.

The statement not only shows linguistic signals of deception, but gives insight into Casey's method of deception.

When someone speaks of an event that has already taken place, a reliable, truthful statement will be in the past tense. "I went to the stores…" not only uses the past tense verb, "went", but uses the pronoun "I", making it a strong statement.

Repeatedly, Casey drifts into present tense verbs, indicating that she may not be working from experiential memory.

Yet, there are lots of signal of deception, so much so, that this statement makes for yet another, howbeit tragic, tool of instruction. Casey loves the word "actually" which is a strong element in her vocabulary. The word "actually" is actually a trigger for the listener to be on alert for deception by Casey.

The word "actually" is used when comparing two or more items.

"Would you like steak tonight, Peter?"

"Why, no, Dear, I would actually like lobster."

The word "actually" sets up a comparison between steak and lobster and if you know me, I actually prefer both, but that's for Heather to argue with me over.

Casey loves to use the word "actually" because she is always being deceptive. Deception flows from her in a way that tells us that it is life long, habitual, lots of early success, and is not likely able to change. It is who she is, and it is engrained in her personality.

She was an "Event Planner" because she heard someone call themselves an "Event Planner."

She worked at Universal Studios because she heard of someone working there.

When she invented a boyfriend, she used a name of someone she had met, gave him a son, fiancé, and a few more details, and off they went on "double dates" and job referrals.

When she invented Zanny the Nanny, she had heard the name Zanaida Gonzelez" and turned her into "Zanny" who happened to be a "nanny" who could be paid "fake money" from a "fake job" to "fake watch" Caylee, and oh, by the way, Zanny is a "10", with perfect teeth.

Liars, as you saw with Billie Jean Dunn, give too much information, belying a need to persuade rather than report honestly.

Casey's interviews are maddening to some; she drives listeners crazy with her semi-Valley Girl/hipster girl with "actually" thrown in for good measure, only to become enraged when she is not believed.

She had nerve, I will give her that.

Some of the "inside scoop" on Casey?

Did she have an inappropriate relationship with Jose Baez, her "swarmy" attorney? (Prosecutors called him "swarmy" and could not abide being in the same court room with him, openly wondering how it is that Baez passed the bar. I don't know how he did it..

Well, did Baez and Casey have an inappropriate relationship during that time when she spent up to six hours a day alone with him in that tiny office?

Fox News wasn't afraid to ask him.

Herein lies principle:

Statement Analysis teaches that people do not like to lie outright. It causes internal stress and is often avoided via withholding information, or changing the topic entirely. Therefore, when we ask someone a question and the subject refuses to answer, the question itself should be considered "sensitive" to the subject.

I wrote an article in 2009 about the topic of possible inappropriate relationship between Jose and Casey.

The simplest answer is, "No", or "No, I didn't have a personal relationship" or "No, I am not having an inappropriate relationship…" It is easy to say and it is often what we see innocent people do. "Peter, I didn't take your wallet."

"Greta, I didn't have an inappropriate relationship with Casey …"

It is the expected response.

But what did Baez have to say?

He knew that cameras had long since followed Casey, day in and day out, back to his office and were timing their "meetings", especially given how difficult it is to get more than an hour with an attorney. The cameras caught them snuggling up, and we even learned that Baez had been rebuked several times by jail officials to keep his hands off her, but he simply either could not, or he refused to follow their orders.

What would he say to the simple question?

November 9, 2009

"...don't sit under the apple tree with anyone else but me..."

Sorry, I could not resist the song. It was popular when my mother was with my father during WWII years.

Dealing
With Deception

Jose Baez had a very tough job. He has to come up with a defense for Casey Anthony, accused of killing her own child, because Casey locked herself into the "Zanny the Nanny kidnapped her" farce.

Even with parents who went along with the charade, in spite of the horrific smell of decomposition that the grandmother attempted to wash out of Casey's clothes and scrub out of the car, Jose Baez has had to hold the family's party line and "search" for a child who was never missing. Since then, George and Cindy Anthony have retired to a life of luxury, going from being behind on the mortgage to George's new diamond earrings and cruises. No job for either.

Since Casey reported that Zanny kidnapped the child and had police search, Jose Baez has been forced to keep to that defense. His endless filing of motions shows one thing:

He does not have any clue as to HOW to defend her.

Ask yourself: would you?? I know I would not. I think the best he can do is seek a plea, but in his position, taking a plea means a loss of fame and fortune. He may not always continue as a lawyer: see below. Attorneys used to take guilty clients and simply protect them from malicious prosecution. It is how they once saw their jobs: preserve justice, not pervert it as if it was a game to win or lose.

On the Geraldo show, Mr. Baez was asked if he was involved in an *"inappropriate relationship with his client."* This was because he had been rebuked by prison officials on 3 occasions because he would not take his hands off of Casey. He was seen holding her very closely in public (on camera) many times and she was in his office, day after day, for up to 6 hours at a time.

When a person is asked a sensitive question, by not answering the question, they are giving you the indication that the question, itself, is sensitive to them. What would make a question like this sensitive?

Ask yourself this: If someone asked you if you had an inappropriate relationship with person A, how would you answer? *"No, I didn't"* is the only truthful answer if no inappropriate relationship took place. It is short, it is easy and it is very low stress. It is what innocent people say when facing an accusation.

People do not like to lie. It causes internal stress. Instead, they edit their account, or deceive by avoidance. When a guilty person is asked a direct question, a positive answer will then result in unbearable stress, including disbarment for Mr. Baez. Yet, a lie causes internal stress so that if proof is later offered, his denial on Television can be entered into disbarrment procedings. His is a lawyer.

Question: There were 4 dogs sitting on the grass. One decided to run off. How many were left?

Answer: we do not know. We know that one decided, but we do not know if he went through with running off after he made his decision. Editing should not be interpreting.

"I tried to complete my work" in the past tense is an admittance that the person did not complete their work, but wants you to think they did. Perhaps they are seeking sympathy or praise.

Question: *"Do you know about my surprise birthday party?"*
Answer: *"who me? I don't know nothin'!"*. This person has been asked a sensitive question and is seeking to avoid the answer.

Question: *Did you smoke pot last night?*
Answer: W*ho me? I am NOT a drug user.*

This person may have smoked pot, and may have now made a vow to no longer use drugs, and is avoiding answering the question. They likely smoked pot last night. By saying "I am not a drug user" they are editing their answer. They may have stayed up late last night, and confessed to their partner, and now is enjoying Day One drug free. Yet, they skillfully avoided the answer.

"*Did you have sex with Amy Fischer?*"

"*Never, Never, NEVER!*" screamed Joey Buttafuouco. Never does not mean "no". Rather, it is something that liars like to use rather than a straight denial. The word "never" has a nice 'vague' feel to it, and is not a reliable denial. It spans lots of time, perhaps "ever" amounts of time, and unless the question is, "Have you ever...?", the word "never" should not be understood to mean "did not." If the person wanted to say "I did not...", he would have.

Think of him before the judge: "100% NOT GUILTY!", rather than, "not guilty". His emphasis told Statement Analyzers (verbal polygraphers)...yep, he did.

When Jose Baez was asked if he was involved in an inappropriate relationship with Casey Anthony, he was asked a very straight forward question. If he did not engage in an inappropriate relationship, a quick 'no' will suffice. It is easy and without stress. Qualifiers are signs of deception.

Baez answered, *"I'm not going to dignify that with an answer. I am not going to even dignify that with an answer."*

So, there you have your answer. (including the additino of the word "even", which is added. Note that not only is it sensitive as seen in avoidance, it is highly sensitive since it is not only avoided, but the answer is repeated.

What your eyes saw on TV and what you read about with the prison officials repeated rebukes of Mr. Baez was not lying to you. When someone walks like a duck, quacks like a duck, and lands in your pond: go ahead and toss it a piece of bread. I don't think it is looking for Prime Rib.

If he (0r you!) did not have an inappropriate relationship then the best and most simple answer is the truthful one: *"No, I didn't"*

When someone does not answer your question, remember: there is a reason why they will not answer a question. If he did not want to "dignify" the question, we might want to learn about all the other salacious topics he did "dignify" with answers, including the "dirty dancing" rather than searching for Caylee: he dignified that question with the answer of "ugly coping."

When someone refuses to answer a question "*based upon my lawyer's advice*" know this:

It is not illegal for an innocent person to say "*No, I didn't*"

It won't mess up their case. It is not against counsel's advice. It breaks no rules and violates no laws.

Richard Jewel is a good example. He said *"no I didn't"*. Why was he hounded?

Because law enforcement was split in two camps:

Statement Analysis: He didn't do it. Period.

Profiling: Yeah, he might have: he was white, mid 30's, lived with Mom.

This was really outdated. The S/A folks knew from his statements that he did not bomb anything. Verbal polygraphy is a science.

Jose Baez can never go against his client, lest she decide to talk. One day, if she sells her story to the media, the romance of being alone in his office, 5 hours a day, may be part of the script.

He was repeatedly seen cuddling and hugging his client.
He was alone with his client in his office for up to six hours per day.
He refused prison guards orders to stop touching Casey; repeatedly.
When asked if he had an inappropriate relationship with Casey he was unwilling or unable to say he did not.
Therefore, we are not willing to say it for him.

As to the original statement and analysis. Here is the statement again, followed by specific analysis principles highlighted: Principles you can be taught to use in statement after statement, no matter what the context is.

I got off of work, left Universal driving back to pick up Caylee like a normal day. And I show up to the apartment knock on door nobody answers. So, I call Zeniada cell phone and it's out of service. It says the phone is no longer in service, excuse me. So, I sit down on the steps and wait for a little bit to see if maybe it was just a fluke if something happened and time passed and I didn't hear from anyone. No one showed up to the house so I went over to J. Blanchard Park and checked a couple of other places where maybe possibly they would have gone; couple stores, just regular places that I know Zenida shops at and she's taken Caylee before. And after about 7:00 when I still hadn't heard anything I was getting pretty upset, pretty frantic and I went to a neutral place. I didn't really want to come home. I wasn't sure what I would say about not knowing where Caylee was still hoping that I would get a call or you know find out that Caylee was coming back so that I could go get her. And I ended up going to my boyfriend Anthony's house who lives in Sutton Place.

---------------------------*analysis*---

This is what police had to work from, initially. Although knowing Casey Anthony's lies, let's see what happens when we apply the same sensitivity signals to her original police statement. The most important thing to see is the color blue:

I got off of work, left *Universal <u>driving back</u> to pick up Caylee like a <u>normal day.</u>*

**The word "left" when used as a connecting verb (departing a place) indicates missing information. This missing information is 70% likely due to rushing, and 30% likely to be critical missing (deliberately withheld) information.
In this case, we know she did not work at Universal.**

**Q. Why was leaving Universal so very sensitive?
A. Because she did not have a job there.**

Other than the leaving or departing of a place as being very sensitive in a statement, the reason why someone does something is the other level of extreme sensitivity. When someone should simply tell us "what happened?" has a need to tell us "why" something happened, it is, along with "left" to be considered the highest level of sensitivity in a statement. It sounds as if the subject anticipates being asked why something was done, so she thinks to herself, "I better tell they why I did this in case they ask me..."

Here we have the 2nd indicator of the highest sensitivity as she tells us the reason why she had to drive "back" :
"to pick up Caylee"

It is, therefore, noted, that "picking up Caylee" is something that is extremely sensitive to Casey.

Q. Why was driving back to pick up Caylee so very sensitive?
A. Because Caylee was dead and not in need of being picked up

Note "normal" day: this enters someone's language when they wish to portray the day as "normal" and is a signal that it was
anything but. It makes for good story telling, as even a young reader knows that it is a signal that something abnormal or extraordinary is about to happen.

And I show up to the apartment knock on door nobody answers.

The word "And" is in the beginning of her sentence: this indicates that there is missing information between the sentences.
"I show up" is deemed "unreliable" because it is in the present tense.

Q. Why is it in the present tense?
A. Because Casey was making it up. There is no connection to experiential memory.

"Nobody answers" is also in the present tense. There was no apartment so it is that she was also making this up, just as the language employed suggests.

As we progress, we see, already, enough indicators of sensitivity to conclude deception. Casey, however, is not finished:

So, I call Zeniada cell phone and it's out of service. It says the phone is no longer in service, excuse me.

Q. Why is calling Zenaida's cell phone given the color blue?

A. Blue is the highest level of sensitivity in SCAN. It is given for only two reasons: 1. the leaving of a place 2. the reason why.

Here, it is extremely sensitive to Casey that she called Zeniada's cell phone.

Q. Why is it so very sensitive to Casey that she called Zenaida's cell phone?

A. Because Zenaida did not exist; therefore, her cell phone did not exist.

Another indicator of sensitivity is repetition. Anything that is repeated is important to the subject. Here we see that the phone is out of service. This is sensitive to Zenaida.

Q. Why is the phone being out of service sensitive?
A. Because it did not exist and she needs to explain to the police why they will not be able to reach the cell. She appears to be burying herself under an avalanche of lies.

The jury, however, will see it otherwise.

So, I sit down on the steps and wait for a little bit to see if maybe it was just a fluke if something happened and time passed and I didn't hear from anyone.

This has now become a "Statement Analysis 101 Sample" for training. It is useful for learning how to discern deception as it is easy to use hindsight and the details after applying principle.

What do you notice first about this portion of her statement?
Even without
training, it is likely that the reader caught this:

1. Casey reported what happened the day her daughter disappeared, and her statement should have been in the past tense. In her first 5 sentences, she is in the present tense. This is a strong indicator that not only is she lying, but she is making it up on "the fly" (the volume suggests this) and not everything is prepared. Later, through analysis, we saw that Casey did operate 'by the seat of her pants' having a high level of confidence in her own ability to deceive, which is what likely led to the controversy where she was examined by psychologists at the end of her trial, for fitness to testify.

It not only shows deception (present tense) but it now allows the analyst to enter into Casey Anthony's psychological profile, howbeit in a small manner: they are dealing with a confident liar; one who works as she goes along. This would give a strong indication to police, having never met Casey Anthony before, that they are dealing with, perhaps, a pathological liar, one who has had a great deal of success in childhood lying. It is a red flag of trouble.

She has been lying since she learned how to
speak.

Remember: a child is "missing" and what is the mother doing? She is lying.

If you continue your analysis, going by principle, you would have highlighted the word "left" for sensitivity.

2. The word "left" when used as a connecting verb is an indication of missing information.

When the word "left" is used as a connecting verb, the analyst recognizes missing information, and percentage wise:

70% is related to time pressure and 30% is sensitive and perhaps critical information.

Here is how:

"I was at work. I left work at 5PM."

The fact that the subject needs to tell us that he "left" is an indication that there is something on his mind. 70% of the time this is about time pressure, or traffic ahead of him, or, perhaps, he left a few minutes early from work. It is likely something due to time pressure and not critical.

But now watch how awkward the word "left" can be.

"I was in the living room. I left the living room and went to the bed room."

Here, the word "left" is highlighted as sensitive, as it is an indication of missing information. Why? Because if he was in the living room and went to the bedroom, he would not have to tell us that he "left"; as he must "leave" in order to reach a new room. Therefore, it is "extra" information; that is, a sentence can work without these words. "Extra" information is doubly important to the analyst. In the above statement, something happened to cause the subject to leave the living room. It could have been an argument, it could have been nefarious, it could have been innocent, but it is something that must be sought because there is missing information there.

3. Repetition. In Statement Analysis, any word repeated is 'sensitive' or important. The analyst would note repetition and ask "why would this word be sensitive to the subject?" Remember, the statement is NOT reality, it is the subject's version of reality. We are attempting to enter into the subject's reality.

If, in reality, the subject lies, we know the subject has a need to lie. This is critical. The word "disconnected" is repeated; it has significance to Casey Anthony and due to the already large number of sensitivity indicators, the analyst should question the veracity of the call.

4. "Normal" The word "normal" is highlighted in all statements. When someone refers to their own selves as "normal" it is an indication that they have been considered not "normal" (by themselves and/or others) in the past. When a day or event is "normal" in the subject's reality, it is an indication that the day (or event) is anything but normal.

5. Negative. Anything reported in the negative is important. It is the analyst's job to learn why something is sensitive. Here, Casey reveals high levels of sensitivity in reporting things in the negative. A truthful statement is not only first person singular, past tense, it tells what happened; not what did not happen, nor what was not thought, felt, etc. When someone tells us what did not happen, or what was not thought, it is to be highlighted as sensitive to the subject.

Note: "nobody answers" is in the negative. We often see this in theft. "I saw nobody run across the lawn..." sounds silly, but it is an indicator that either the subject is in fiction mode OR he did see someone run across the lawn.

She also says, *"I didn't hear from anyone"* is not only in the negative, but Zanaida has now been referenced as *"anyone"*.

6. Change of language should represent reality and if there is no apparent change in

reality, there is likely deception.

7. "Because"   We highlight any words that explain rather than report, as sensitive. "So, since, therefore, because, hence, and hence (Patsy Ramsey), etc" are all highlighted as the subject is no longer telling us what happened, but telling us why something happened. This is sensitive.

8. Body posture: We highlight "sit, stood, stand, sitting, standing, ect" as sensitive because when body posture enters a statement, it is often an indicator of strain or tension.

9. "And" is highlighted as an indicator that the subject has more information about the sentence that has not been revealed.

10. Temporal Lacunae   "time passed" Casey said. A temporal lacunae is sensitive as the subject has jumped over time and is withholding information. Samples: "and the next thing I know..." and so on. They are always flagged for sensitivity.

From just this small portion of her statement to police we have highlighted multiple indicators of sensitivity, and we have only just begun.

 Thus far, we do not have indicators of sexual criminality within her statement. If this was part of a sexual homicide, we may have found an indicator. Had Caylee drowned in a pool, we would have
likely seen indicators, including "leaving" the house where
George Anthony was.

 Had she been drowned, we would expect to see it creep into her langauge since her language is her version of reality, and would have been a dominant theme for her.

<u>No one</u> *showed up to the house so I went over to J. Blanchard Park and checked a couple of other places where maybe possibly they would have gone; ( ) couple stores, just <u>regular</u> places that I know Zenida shops at and she's taken Caylee before.*

"No one showed up" as "no one" and "nobody" does not exist.
Here we have her explaining the reason "why" she went
to the park. She would go on to say "Caylee loved the park." in the past tense, only to correct herself with "Caylee loves the
park."

If you did nothing except color code this statement, you would
find more than 2 "blues" on the paper, which is called a
"cluster of blues" allowing you to see the extreme sensitive

nature of the statement.

And after about 7:00 when I still hadn't heard anything I was getting <u>pretty upset, pretty frantic</u> and I went to a neutral place.

Emotions in a statement.

Emotions in a statement are often an indication that someone is telling the truth; reliving the experience. It is, therefore,
the location of the emotions that indicates to us whether
or not the person is being truthful or deceptive.

Principle: When emotions are placed in the logical or "perfect" part of the story, it is a strong indication that they have been placed there artificially, indicating deception.

Q. Why does placing the emotions in the story, where they appear to belong, make it deceptive?

A. In truthful statements, emotions are found after the main event. Psychologically, it takes humans time to process our emotions. If someone was held up at gunpoint, for example, she may write about the experience, and if from truth, the adrenaline of "survival" hormones means that after the danger has passed, the person considers her emotions. In the above account, a truthful recalling would have three sections:

1. Pre event: what happened just before
2. Main event: the hold up
3. Post event; what happened after the event, calling 911, and the inclusion of emotions.

The account may be counted by either lines, or words used. Truthful accounts have the following breakdown:

25% of the words or lines are what happened just before
50% of the words or lines are what happened
25% of the words or lines are what happened afterwards.

Anything that strongly deviates from this is to be considered "Deceptive on its Form."

Emotions in truthful statements are found in the last portion.
For an easy example of this, search on Tiffany Hartley. She
uses lots of emotions in her description, and the emotions
are placed in the 'perfect' or 'logical' portion of her
statement indicating artificial placement.

*I <u>didn't really</u> want to <u>come</u> home. I wasn't sure what
I would <u>say</u> about not knowing where Caylee was still hoping that I would get a call
or you know find out that Caylee was coming back so that I could
go get her.*

First, notice anything in the negative as important.
Note also that she didn't "really"; indicating that she was
conflicted about going home.
Note "come" home and not "go" home.
Caylee "coming back" so that Casey could pick her up is of the highest sensitivity to Casey.

Q. Why is picking up Caylee of the highest sensitivity?
A. Because Caylee is dead and cannot be picked up.

*And I <u>ended up</u> going to <u>my boyfriend Anthony's</u> house who lives
in Sutton Place.*

"ended up" is passive language. She uses passive language to
conceal identity or responsibility. Here, she does not want to
say that she wanted to go to Tony's while Caylee was missing
so she uses the passive "ended up" as if it was something that
was beyond her control or responsibility.

Social Introductions:

Casey was writing to the police. This is her written statement.
The rule of social introductions is the same in analysis as it is
in life.

"my boyfriend, Anthony" has 3 components:

1. Possessive pronoun: my
2. Title: boyfriend
3. Name: Anthony

This is an indication of a good relationship. This is how she perceives him, even using his full name, "Anthony" rather than the common, "Tony."

Her perception of the relationship was very high according to Statement Analysis.
This was confirmed later when she was in jail she wanted to talk to Tony rather than talk about Caylee or talk to her parents, or even a lawyer. She only wanted to talk to Tony.

This reminds us to look at all the names in a statement. We look at all names, including pets, as some people love their pets more than humans. We also list phones or calls (texts, emails) with names. (Phones don't call people: there is a person behind the phone call, text, email).

We note how each person is introduced indicating the quality of the relationship.
We note the order in which people are introduced as well. When Casey wrote about not "really" wanting to come home it is her parents (and brother) who live there.

They are not mentioned by name.

Yet, she said that she did not know what she would "say"; this is communicative language. In order for her to "say" anything, there must be someone to say something to.
At "home" were her parents. She brings up the fact that she didn't know what she would "say", indicating her parents' presence.

She gives no social introduction to her parents which indicates to us that the relationship with them is a very bad relationship.

As to those who know the story and watched the trial, this is an understatement. She went many months refusing to take a visit or phone call from them.

Later, Cindy Anthony, her mother, would perjure, boldly, and without Florida prosecuting her for it, to set the killer of her granddaughter free.

She did this while making an oath to God, to tell the truth.

Chapter Nine: Confession By Pronoun

Earlier we saw that in the principle of each of us having a personal, internal, subjective dictionary, there were exemptions, including time, articles and pronouns.

Pronouns are a world all unto themselves.

I liken the use of a pronoun to a golf swing.

When Tiger Woods was a little boy, his father had him practice his golf swing over and over and over. Countless thousands upon thousands of times, Tiger Woods took a swipe at an itty-bitty ball in the hopes of sending that itty-bitty ball into an itty-bitty hole, and when done right, would bring him millions of dollars.

Explain that to some distance culture 1,000 years in the future on what we valued in terms of wealth and celebrity!

The point, however, is that when we practice something over and over again, it becomes embedded in our brain and we become rather efficient at it. Experts, in anything, became experts via repetition.

As a young boy, Bobby Fischer did little else but play chess, hour after hour after hour, memorizing openings, middle games, endgames and everything in between. By age 15, he reached the upper echelon of the chess world, and by age 29, single-handedly, he took away from the line of Soviets, their prized chess world championship. He lived, breathed and ate chess, from the time he woke up, until the time he went to sleep.

Yet, if we take all the hours that Tiger Woods took practicing his swing, from childhood up to today, and took all the hours that Bobby Fischer used studying chess, and put them together, they would pale in comparison to the number of times you and I have used the word "I" in our lifetime.

Since you first learned to speak, can you possibly guess how often you have used the pronoun, "I" and the pronoun "we" in your life?

Me, neither.

But I can tell you that you and I are so good at knowing whether to choose the word "I" or the word "we" via the sheer volume of repetition of use, that the brain does not need to 'pause' to consider which one is appropriate over the other.

Therefore, as said in an earlier chapter, it is instinctive for us to use a pronoun. In fact, if you and I take the next step, we must admit that we are possessive creatures who just love to say "my" when we want something, and to avoid saying "my" when we don't.

We often find "confession by pronoun" as someone takes ownership of guilt, instinctively, by using the word "my" when, perhaps, they wished they had not.

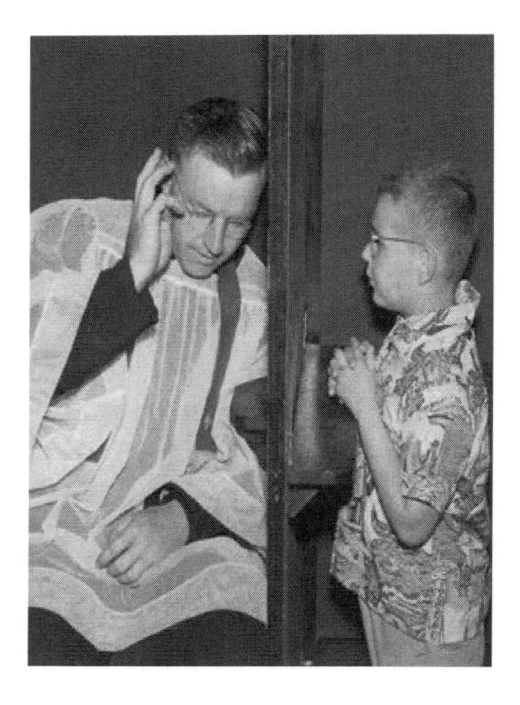

In Statement Analysis, the first thing we do when we receive a written statement is photocopy it and file the original. I often make several copies and like to check my work with others. When work is shared, we only submit the statement and the allegation to the analyst. We do not share suspicions, evidence, history, or anything else. We want the analysis to not be influenced by anything. We should see similar analysis done anywhere; though some may be deeper than others.

With the copy of the statement, before I read it, I circle the pronouns. Avinoam Sapir teaches this and it is something I have done so many times, that I can almost see circles around pronouns when people speak. I instantly 'grab' them 'out of the air' and take careful note.

Pronouns solve many crimes. Pronouns answer many questions. It is estimated that as much as 70% of murders are due to the pronoun "mine". (That is, people clashing about what is perceived to be "theirs").

Pronouns are understood by children at a very early age. Even for children who cannot speak, the concept of "mine" is strong. Adults and children with developmental disabilities understand "mine". It is one of the earliest of ideas communicated by humans.

At an early age, children will use the pronoun "my" and "mine" for everything from food, to toys, parents, siblings, to even attention. The **pronoun** is the single most focused indicator in Statement Analysis.

If someone used the past tense in a verb, we acknowledge that they used past tense. We don't accept, "that's not what I meant" as an excuse; we are content to make a report knowing that later the subject will deny its meaning. If a staff says "I hit the consumer on the head" but later says, "that's not what I meant. I meant to say "I didn't hit the consumer on the head", we don't argue with them.

Why do we insist that the words a person chose are to be taken at face value?

Because the words chosen by the brain are communicated to the tongue in less than a micro second; Statement Analysis listens, it does not interpret. The more freely the subject speaks, the more information we have. When in an interview, the interviewer must be careful NOT to introduce new words or new topics: the best interview is when the subject of the interview introduces his own words. When the subject introduces a new word, or a new topic, then and only then should the interviewer reflect the words (or topic) back in the form of a question.

As one practices Statement Analysis, (media provides us with more examples per day than we could ever have time to cover) things such as verb tenses and pronoun alerts become second nature. (I circle them in my mind as I hear someone speak). This is more accurately called "Verbal Polygraphy". It is the natural result of practicing Statement Analysis.

Pronouns jump out at us. This leads to an important principle:

Pronouns show ownership.

"Mine!"

"My daddy!" "My cookie!" or how about, "my money!"?

It is something ingrained within the human mind from the first moments of language. Most parents recognize it as something they need to monitor and control otherwise it will lead to narcissistic like behavior as an adult. Left unchecked a child will believe everything is "mine" (except disagreeable things).

"My" and "Mine" are exhibited by preverbal children, using their hands and arms to indicate ownership. We recognize pronoun ownership in life and therefore, we recognize it in verbal and written communications.

It is something we do not suddenly dismiss in Statement Analysis. We recognize it in 2 year olds, in 10 year olds, as well as in adults who may be, cognitively, 2 or 10 years old. It is common to all of us. It is among the first words uttered by a human.

If someone *does not* take ownership of something, we do not ascribe ownership of it to them.

If someone takes ownership of something, we do not argue with them.

When an arguing parent says, *"maybe if you controlled your daughter more, we wouldn't be in this situation!"*, one parent is not owning responsibility for the current crisis, but is casting blame on the other.

"Oh, that's not my clean up. It's your dog, not mine It is likely that this subject is not going to clean up after the dog.

"Woke up, made the bed..." is different than "*Woke up, made my bed*"

What is the difference?

The pronoun "my" tells me that the person is either single, or is about to be single. Couples normally say "the" bed, but do not feel a need to say "my" bed. Singles sometimes do, but married couples when having marital trouble will sometimes say "my" bed, especially if they are headed towards divorce. As you conduct an interview, and you have picked up on this word, it may suggest a follow up question, especially if a person claimed to be alone. This was useful to me in child protective interviews where an allegation was made that a sex offender had moved in with a mother of an infant.

"I have to go and pick up our daughter" is different than "*I have to go pick up my daughter*". For most biological parents, if they are together, they use "my", but if there is step parenting involved, the pronoun "our" is likely to slip in. (Foster children and adopted children's parents often say "our" but when a married person says "our" and there are no step parents involved, it is a sign of marital trouble).

On a domestic violence report, a married mother had used the word "we" when describing an ex boyfriend, in the affidavit. Because I had circled the pronoun, it helped guide my questions which later revealed that the ex boyfriend was likely the father of the child, which was why he would not leave the family alone.

When someone says *"I have to take care of the dog"* instead of saying "I have to take care of my dog" it tells me that the subject is likely part of a family and the dog is a family pet. Relevant? Maybe. In child protective, we would observe and ask about pet care as it may relate to abuse or neglect of children. In a recent investigation of an allegation of sexual abuse lodged against an adoptive parent, we made note to view the family's dogs; how they were cared for, who was responsible, etc. Why? Because some cognitively limited adults (this man was 18) *may* have acting out behavior towards pets, if being sexually or physically abused. (It was a false allegation and the consumer was gentle and appropriate with the dogs; responsible for feeding and walking).

Pronouns show cooperation.

"He threw me in his car. We drove to the woods. He raped me and threw me out of the car."

The young woman was dirty, clothes disheveled, and crying hysterically. She was obviously upset and maybe even traumatized.

She was also lying.

*"He threw me in his car. **We** drove to the woods. He raped me and threw me out of the car."*

You may have already noted that "his" car became "the" car, as we note change in language as we check articles. But in Statement Analysis, the first thing you do (after photocopying) is **circle the pronouns**. This is done before the statement is read.

The investigators on the scene believed her but one, trained in Statement Analysis, knew better. He caught the pronoun "on the fly" (live) and took her aside, and while she was sobbing, gently confronted her. She admitted being out with a young man her father disapproved of and confessed the false accusation. Because this detective had practiced Statement Analysis in writing, Discourse or Verbal Analysis developed naturally.

The pronoun, "We", solved the case because "we" denotes cooperation and there is never a "we" involved in sexual assault. The victim's disdain for the perpetrator precludes her from using the pronoun "we". The investigator in this case had training which served him well.

However, pronouns go even deeper than just cooperation.

Within a pronoun, we find **ownership**. When we see ownership of an allegation, we have a confession.

Innocent people will not take ownership of guilt. They have been using possessive pronouns since they could talk, and likely even before. It is decided in less than a micro second and if there is one thing a person will not make a mistake over, it is something they learned before they could even walk, and have practiced it every single day of their lives up to now:

"my".

Pronouns show ownership, even of guilt.

"For those of you who believe in **my** guilt, I want to say to you..." OJ Simpson.

Innocent people will not take ownership of something they did not do. When a person is guilty of a crime, they will use the possessive pronoun to lay claim to the guilt. Picture a child walking around the room, claiming everything they see as their own. That same child, when asked if they made the mess that their brother or sister made, will not label the mess with the same declaration of "mine!" that they have given everything else in the room.

In the murder of 6 year old Jonbenet Ramsey, in at least 3 interviews, as well as in her book, Patsy Ramsey said "our guilt" in her statements.

Scott Peterson used the phrase "my guilt" when he thought he was cleverly asking the public to wait for his trial before making a decision about him. He was convicted of murdering his wife, Lacy Peterson, and preborn child, Conner.

It is a powerful habit, deeply embedded within us, to recognize what belongs to us. If it is guilt that belongs to us, the pronoun will be used to frame a sentence, in less than a micro second, which will give its indication.

Politicians from all persuasions are generous to those of us who wish to sharpen our skills. Celebrities are too. All it takes is a bit of listening.

Last week, I saw actress Lindsay Lohan on television as her probation violation hearing from her DWI was covered live. Ms. Lohan had not complied with what the judge had told her to do. When she responded as to why she was unable to complete counseling she said she was "working mostly". She had previously said she missed counseling due to her uncle's death. She was then asked if she attended the funeral, of which she shook her head "no". She had also informed the court that she was unable to make it back to California for counseling due to the volcanic ash in Europe. She told the court her passport was stolen or lost. When cocaine had been found in her pants pocket, she denied ownership of the pants.

Was she holding the judge in contempt?

Body language experts speculated that her demeanor and posture spoke of her personal disrespect of the judge.

Was she disrespectful?

We don't need to speculate. We only need to listen.

Lindsay Lohan said to the judge, "I don't want you to think I don't respect you" to the judge.

"I don't want you to think *I disrespect you*".

She told us that she disrespecting the judge. (Ms. Lohan also had vile language painted on her nails when she arrived in court.

The judge sentenced Ms. Lohan to 90 days in jail.

Outside the court, Ms. Lohan was recording calling the judge a "f***ing bit**".

Note: the judge is female.

By circling the pronouns in Ms. Lohan's open statement to the judge, we would have picked up on the disrespect for two reasons:

1. Pronoun usage
2. Introduction of the word, "disrespect"

The pronouns told us who held disrespect and towards whom.

Within the language itself, we find wording, that when it is unprompted by a direct question, will reveal itself. At the center of this, is the pronoun, then followed by verb tense.

Pronouns are central to every investigation; whether or not we are working from a statement, a transcript, a recording, or in live conversation. Our attention must be focused upon the pronoun.

In a recent Investigation, a pronoun told us much.

Missing money is common. Because we face many such cases where the date of the missing money is in question, it may be a pattern of unsolved cases. This ought not be.

When an allegation like this is entered we see two traits:

       1. Money went missing on an unknown date
       2. Several employees had access to the money

With these two characteristics, many of these may remain unsolved.

No longer for those trained in Statement Analysis.

Depending upon the number of potential interviews we may have to conduct, if the number is large, we may screen by the means of the Investigative Questionnaire.

(This will be discussed elsewhere)

In the case above, there were 7 staff workers who had access to the money, and it went missing over a time period of several days.

All staff were asked to write a statement describing what they did, from the time they arrived, until the time they left, each day of the daily spread of when the money went missing.

One statement showed multiple indicators of withholding information as well as deception. The interviews were arranged accordingly, with the staff who had tested for deception scheduled last.

During her interview, while freely speaking, staff said "it went missing on **my** shift".

Although she did not realize that it implicated her (she continued speaking past this sentence) she told us that the money went missing on her shift, and the investigation continued and bore this fact out.

One word gave answered the question: "On who's shift did the money go missing?"

Pronouns show ownership. Pronouns show cooperation.

Stephen Truscott, 14, was convicted, in 1959, of murdering raping and murdering his 12 year old neighbor. He sparked national outrage in Canada and had a large following, especially among politicians, who demanded his release. 10 years later, he was paroled and eventually wrote a book to show his alleged innocence.

In 2000, he agreed to appear on a Canadian TV program which investigated the crime, which would spike book sales for him.

His book shows many indicators of guilt, as well as deception, but for the sake of time, I focus upon only some pronoun usage:

"I gave her a lift on my bicycle."

"She wanted a lift to the highway and I gave it to her."

"I hardly knew the girl, I kept trying to tell them. We were classmates but she was <u>not</u> <u>among my friends</u>. What she did outside school (and inside it, too, for that matter) had never interested me."

Truscott down plays his relationship with Lynne Harper. Twice he states that he was just giving her a "lift." He further distances himself from her when he says "I hardly knew the girl" and "she was not among my friends."

It was important for Truscott to show that they weren't friends, even though her family had said otherwise. But much later, forgetting what he had said previously, he said,

"The first knowledge I had that something unusual had happened to Lynne was the morning after <u>our</u> bicycle ride."

Oops!

The pronoun "our" shows cooperation. This usage is in line with what Lynn's family testified about them playing together.

Truscott went on to ask the public to answer the question "why" he would kill her.

He said "She was my neighbor. I wasn't friends with <u>my</u> victim, but I didn't hate her."

Pronouns show ownership, from the time you first began to speak, you claimed things for yourself. Here is Stephen Truscott's verbal confession.

She was my neighbor. I wasn't friends with **my** victim, but I didn't hate her."

Even more than verb tenses, pronouns are critical in an investigation.

Why is it necessary to know the difference between "the bed" and "my bed"?

Truth is always necessary. In Statement Analysis, when information that appears to be unnecessary is given by a subject, we deem it "doubly" important.

In cases where staff is romantically involved with a consumer, just the seemingly innocuous "I made the bed" instead of "I made my bed" may cause you to slow down your questioning, and revisit the bedroom. If the staff is claiming to live alone, we would expect to hear staff say "I made my bed". Even the most basic of terms can make a difference for us, as we listen carefully.

Pronouns give us cooperation and possession.

Staff has been accused of leaving consumer home alone while going with other staff to the store. Consumer reported that Staff A and Staff B walked to the store and left him home alone.

Staff said, "*I* walked down to the store alone. Staff B stayed at the house with consumer. *I* bought a scratch ticket and **we** got some chips and soda, and *I* walked home alone and got back to Staff B and consumer."

Pronouns tell us much. Pronouns tell us about cooperation and about ownership.

Ask yourself: What does the subject claim to own?

Since possessive pronouns have been used since childhood, the subject will say exactly what is meant to say.

What does the subject claim to own?

If it is guilt, then we have a **confession** that will likely be born out in the complete investigative process of collecting information.

Chapter Ten: The Reliable Denial

I really need to get to this, as I am stumbling over it as I press through cases. Why the delay? Why wait this far in the book to get to the strongly referenced principle that I have mentioned throughout the book thus far?

I think the delay comes from within me, and the years that I have spent considerable energy in trainings attempting to convince attendees (mostly investigators) just how reliable the reliable denial is.

It is difficult, especially for law enforcement. They struggle to accept that such simple words as "I didn't do it" could signal truthfulness by a subject. "Hey, anyone can just say that and you're telling me that that's all it takes?" This is a common objection. You've likely read some of the statistics that show that police officers often score poorly on deception detection tests due to the fact that they have seen so many liars over the years that they feel most everyone is lying. This, of course, is not only incorrect, but it wastes precious resources, specifically the officer's valuable time, when it is not embraced nor understood.

I once had a pressing case in which I had to cover another investigator's geographical territory, when I received a call from a police officer. He was upset. He had called the local office about a sexual assault case and learned that I was covering for an investigator out on medical leave and I was more than 2 hours a way.

The officer insisted that I leave my location immediately, and I understood why. As an officer in a small department, there was no room for overtime. Once he started the case, he needed to see it through, otherwise he goes off shift for several days and precious time is lost.

"Please just get into your car now, and tell the subject we will meet him at my headquarters…" he said. "This is a tight case. We've got a neighbor who heard the whole terrible thing."

I assured him that I would call the accused subject and call him right back and get moving quickly, as I understood the pressure he was under.

When I called the subject, I was surprised to learn that he already knew the allegation. He said that he overheard a secretary tell his supervisor that they needed a replacement for him since the client had accused him of sexual assault.

"I did not assault him!", he said. "They are saying I sexually assaulted him. I didn't sexually assault him or even touch him!"

He said all of this without a single prompt from me.

He gave a "Reliable Denial."

A Reliable Denial" (RD) consists of three components. If it has two, it is not reliable, just as if it has four components. An "Unreliable Denial" does not necessarily mean guilt; it means that he has yet to give a reliable response, one that, statistically, is likely to be truthful.

I. The pronoun "I" must be present.
II. The past tense verb "did not" or "didn't" must be present
III. The allegation must be answered accurately

If someone has only these three components, statistically, the subject is likely to be innocent of the allegation.

What is difficult to convince law enforcement trainees is to listen carefully enough to hear if the denial had any changes or alterations to it.

The subject must produce these words, unprompted from the Interviewer. If so, they are highly reliable.

Examples of "Unreliable Denials":

Q. "Did you take that woman's wallet out of her purse and steal it?"

A. "I didn't take that woman's wallet out of her purse and steal it, no."

In this sample, the subject parroted the Interviewer's own words. He did not, in the Free Editing Process (FEP) produce these words on his own. Conclusion: Unreliable: He may be innocent, but we cannot be certain from this response.

"I would never molest that client" avoids saying "did not" or "didn't", and is not reliable.

"Did not touch or molest anyone!" This one drops the pronoun "I", which is critical.

How about this one?

"I did not harm that client in any way at all."

This is actually a bit frightening. He does not deny molesting or touching inappropriately, but he denies "harming" and is something that we hear from pedophiles. It is minimizing language and violates component number III. It does not match the allegation.

Here is a bit trickier:

"I did not steal that missing money."

Investigators, whether in Human Resources, or in law enforcement, should always avoid morally charged language. Too often, someone has stolen, but personally believed that the company or client "owed" them money and can pass a polygraph when asked, "Did you steal?" but would fail the same polygraph if asked, "Did you take…?"

Remember our Presidential example, "I did not have sexual relations with that woman, Ms. Lewinsky" could have passed a polygraph.

I once had a repeat molester pass a polygraph because he was asked if he had "molested" the child.

He doesn't "molest" children, he "tickles" them. This is his internal, subjective and very personal dictionary. A good polygraph examination must flow from the pre-screening interview where the polygrapher learns the internal language "code" of the subject, and "breaks the code" by asking the right questions, based upon the subject's own language.

Back to our story.

I asked the man, "What are you talking about?" I did so to avoid me giving him any information or any language of which to use. He immediately repeated his denial, based upon what he was accused of.

He agreed to be interviewed and offered a polygraph. I told him, "Stay put. I will call you back."

I called the officer and before I could get a word across, he demanded to know if I had left yet.

I told him that I had not, and that the subject didn't do it.

"How do you know?" he demanded.

"Because he told me", I answered.

The officer fumed. He threatened to "report me" to my supervisor and have me drawn and quartered. I told him that I knew he was under time constraint, but that if he just waits a little bit, I would wager him a nice cup of coffee that the alleged victim either is found in the hospital exam to have no signs of assault, or, more likely, that he refuses to be examined by a doctor.

He begrudgingly accepted the bet.

Less than 30 minutes later, the phone rang. "He confessed. He didn't want to even go inside the hospital and be examined. He was angry at the worker and the "ear witness" is now being taken to the hospital herself. She's been hearing voices."

He then said, "How did you know? How were you so certain? You seemed incredibly confident."

I told him that we would speak again, and I would get him an invitation to a training. "It's not easy work, and it is not for the faint of heart. It takes a high level of concentration, and a lot of practice but look at the results."

Think of the time wasted, or even the harm that can come from attempting to bully a confession out of an innocent person.

Thus was the case of Kevin Fox.

Chapter 14: Failure to Train Means Trouble

Police officers, for the amount of trainng they receive, are grossly underpaid. Having said this, it presupposes that the trainings have not simply been completed, but the subject has become proficient at whatever it is he or she has been trained in.

Police officers are trained in a wide variety of skills, including interviewing, car safety, target practice, special weapons, crowd control, k-9, and on and on it goes.

I watched one officer approach a suspect and bellow at him, intimidating the subject into silence. He smirked at me. "Your methods don't work in the street."

Not so.

I have received, over the years, a high percentage of confessions (or admissions; an admission is a confession without acknowledgment of guilt, or penitence. A confession not only acknowledges what was done, but owns the moral failure involved. Either way, getting an admission is key to prosecution and a well-trained officer, Human Resources professional, insurance investigator, arbitrator, attorney, therapist, junior high principal, and so on, can use the principles of Analytical Interviewing (the legally sound interview based upon Statement Analysis) to get to the truth, and, in doing so, use the subject's own language to elicit a confession. I will cover this more on the chapter on "Why no justice?"

Here is a case of blistering ignorance.

Previously, we learned that a Reliable Denial is north of 90% accurate. When one is able to, on his own, produce the pronoun "I", the past tense, "did not", and directly answer the charge, without adding anything, nor subtracting from it, it is very likely that the subject "did not do it."

Attendees are often amazed as I make my way through the list of celebrities who issue all forms of persuasive denials, only to learn that the simple, 3 pronged denial, is missing. Some will give news conferences and go on and on without actually denying the act. Some will deny the guilt of the act, skillfully avoiding denying the act. (Hey, everyone is judicially innocent until proven guilty in a court of law, so for someone to say "I am innocent" is not a lie.)

Lance Armstrong, in all the interviews he gave on television and in print, avoided saying "I did not take PEDs…" including using diversion, or employing the word "never", so as to make the accusation vague, over an indeterminate amount of time, and often said "would not", father than "did not."

Michael Jackson did not deny making a reliable denial.

Even in some famous cases where you thought you heard a reliable denial when you review it, you will find that some will minimize their action, violating component number three (addressing the specific accusation). "I did not harm that child" when, in fact, the child was deceased. Another 'close' denial happened when a drug addict denied killing a sheriff's daughter: " I did not kill her", he said. No, he did not "kill" her, the drugs he supplied her with killed her.

This is why our interview must be precise. More on this in the chapter on "Analytical Interviewing", which, if investigative journalists take the course, will produce "old school" like information that will revolutionize the news industry on the heels of us going from printed paper to internet news.

Back to Mr. Fox.

When I was in my early 20's, I was already a father, working two jobs, and doing whatever I could to be the kind of father and provider I had always wanted to be. By 23, I had a son, and by 27, I had three sons.

I loved walking into places with my three little men following behind me, particularly since the youngest of the three, Jonathan Edwards, was by far the earliest walker, with dreams of being the next "Rocky Balboa." When church was over, he would run home, take off his tie he wore to imitate me, put on shorts and sneakers, display a bare chest, and wrap a towel around his neck, like the Sylvester Stallone character in Rocky. He would then put on his little boxing gloves and, with head done, would feign practicing punching and pulling punches. At only three years old, he was a bit too far advanced in speech and having caught one of the few curse words in the Rocky series (I love the first and the last of the series), he would mutter one particular line that unnerved his mother. I generally hoped that if I did not tell the toddler that it was not appropriate, he would forget it.

One day he came running back into church, in his special Rocky Balboa "uniform", including towel and gloves, and while following me, he continued to mutter lines from the movies under his breath. "Jab, jab, slip the jab" was one of his favorites.

A very conservative couple had visited the church, and as little Jonathan Edwards made his way over to me (to challenge me to a fight), I heard his little mutterings and said a silent prayer,

"Please, Lord, don't let him say that, don't let him say that now, not in front of this couple…oh, please, Lord.."

The couple were well dressed and quite formal in their manners, and here they are looking down saying, "What a cute little boy!"

Rocky, I mean, Jonathan, simply ignored them and kept his air-punches going along with his muttering.

Mrs. Very Conservative bent over and said, "What did you say, little boy?"

Jonathan did not answer. I said a short prayer of "thanks" under my breath, but the Mrs. was not discouraged from the lack of reaction. She asked again, but I answered and said, "Jonathan seems to have some attention deficit (which was just becoming popular to say and sound intelligent back then), yet she was determined to hear the cute little monkey dressed like the Italian Stallion speak.

"What is your name?", she asked.

"Jon-a-shun Ed-words Hi it", he said.. "They call me Rocky", he added, and returned to muttering.

Mr. Conservative, seeing how cute the little fellow was said, "What is it that you are saying, "Rocky?"

Uh oh. I knew once they had addressed him as "Rocky" that he was going to speak.

He looked up at them, and fell down at their feet, even as a crowd watched, pretending that he was Rocky Balboa, knocked down in the final round, and just about to be counted out for the match.

He then jumped up, pretending to be Rocky's crusty old manager, Burgess Meredith's character, "Mickey" and in a 3 year old's imitation of a gruffy voice said, clear as can be, to the fallen "Rocky" character.

"Get up! Get up you son of a bitch! 'Cause Mickey loves you!"

No longer embarrassed I belly laughed and swooped my little love into my arms and kissed him, not concerned if the visiting couple would now walk out, 'deeply concerned at the spectacle' they had just witnessed.

He was my "Rocky" and my "Jon-a-shun" and no one else's. He might struggle pronouncing his own name, but he certain got "son of a bitch" clear as can be!

Mr. and Mrs. Conservative then broke out laughing, and ended up proving to be a kind, gracious and loving family and a friendship developed.

Yes, I had the Brothers Hyatt, and they stuck together, thick and thin, took corrections like "men" (Jonathan would say "that spanking didn't hurt dad, but I won't run into the street again", just to make sure I knew how tough he was. By 5, he was skating, getting cut and stitched up, and proudly returning to the ice to keep skating and show off his stitches, just like "those guys in Canada like to do. I'm as tough as them!"

No surprise that his favorite hockey player, even more than Wayne Gretzsky, was Mark Messier, who, as "The Captain" could freeze a younger player in camp with just a glare, or, in the case of discipline, could deliver an elbow to the kisser of his own wayward team mate, just to make sure maximum effort was given.

Jonathan eventually gave up boxing for hockey.

So with my three men, I had Little League, hockey and chess and wondered if life could get any better for a father.

I did wonder, however, what it would be like having a daughter, but knew, from having 7 sisters, that girls are far more complex than boys and eventually they "betray" dads and go out and marry.

In spite of the feeling of contentment, I did see other men fawn over their daughters, but I also wanted to cultivate a young lady, and not have a junior "Rocky" on my hands, but as life so throws its curveballs, in 1990, my little girl, Sarah Anne was born.

Her mother said, "this one is mine! You have your boys. They just want you all the time. This one is mine."

Of course, I had seen too many hours of Sesame Street to let that one go: "Share, share, that's fair!"

We had a good laugh.

Sarah loved me, as only a little girl can love her daddy. I dressed her (with wildly encouraging approval from Sarah's mother), in little pretty dresses. I adored her.

She sat on my lap, even as an infant, as I read book after book after book. (Today, the well developed brain is serving others in life as a Registered Nurse, with plans of higher education ahead).

When I played ice hockey, she came to all of my games and would run to the glass when she saw me go down (note "go down" avoids telling you whether I was checked to the ice, or if I embarrassingly slipped while trying to speed up skating backwards. Let those of you with the most Statement Analysis training throw the largest Statement Analysis stone at me).

Her brothers, far from jealous, found her to be wonderful, with Jonathan, in particular, loving being bounced from the role of "baby" in the family. He, at just 5 years old, would be his 3 year old's little sister, from that time forward, right through high school.

Her brothers protected her, held doors for her, included her in any games in which there would be "no rough stuff", as the old school, "do no harm to female" thinking was noble for me growing up, learning early that only "cowardly men strike women." *When Jonathan eventually played high school hockey, he continued to get into hot water by refusing to check a female opponent.

Terry Elvis had his Heather.

Clinton Dunn has his Hailey.

I had my Sarah, my little doll, of whom I eagerly invested myself into, watching her succeed at dance recitals, while also noticing her gift of mercy upon other children.

I saw this, in no uncertain terms, when 2 foster siblings stayed over for a week or so. Severely sexually abused, they not only wet the beds, but one, in particular, tore to shreds Sarah's favorite doll.

Sarah knew, instinctively, that something was wrong, and did not cry, but found the one doll that the foster child had not yet destroyed and said, "Here, she is yours. She needs you to take care of her now. She is all alone."

The troubled child was expecting a violent reaction from the adults, including me, which, itself, tore at my heart. Instead, she found only love and compassion. She tore up those dolls in rage, and expected, and perhaps even wanted, punishment.

She received warmth and love, from a very young girl, herself, and Sarah's family.

Little girls are magically different than little boys.

Little boys say "look at me hit the ball!" or "look how I build my lego…"

Little girls say, "Daddy, look at me." "Look and see me…" as if to say "Daddy, know me. Know my heart. Know when I am crying on the inside, while there are no tears. Know my pain, my fear, my joy, my love, Daddy…look not at what I have done, but look at *me*."

There is nothing like the "Butterfly Kisses" song to touch a father's heart when it comes to his little girl.

What must had Terry felt when he read some illogical and nasty posts about him while Heather was missing?

What did Clint feel when Billie Jean tried to, even subtly, cast a shadow of doubt upon him?

What must Kevin Fox had felt when he learned that not only was his precious little girl taken from him, but that police believe he did awful, unspeakable things to her?

The Story of Riley Fox

Kevin Fox was arrested for the sexual assault and murder of his 3 year old daughter. I saw the case and immediately decided to analyze it.

Statement Analysis yields far more than a polygraph. Statement Analysis can indicate where the withheld information is, and, at times, what is not being said, and how this may be relevant to a given case. This is why Avinoam Sapir rightfully calls it "Scientific Content Analysis", that is, "scientific" meaning that the same even handed application should yield the same results, and that "content" indicates far more information than just "truth or lie" results in a lie detector test.

Kevin Fox was not only left bereft of his little girl, but now he could lose his life. What was the cause of this?

Yes, parents must be eliminated as suspects, but police officers must not only respect the rights of citizens, but learn:

The most volume of information comes when you shut your mouth and listen. It matters not that an attorney is present. Let the subject speak and let his words guide you to the truth, even if he is being deceptive.

Too often, police encounter so many deceptive people that they become jaded. It is not sabbatical or time off that is needed, or even a 'desk job.' They are cops because it is who they are, within themselves.

They need training. They need a lot more training then is currently provided around our country.

Police Departments need politicians to stay out of their work and allow Departments to simply hire the "best and brightest" without regard to anything else: just get the best and give them the best equipment, including the best training.

I once had a shaken baby case where the officer was screaming in the face of the father, at 2 o'clock in the morning, in a room in the basement of a hospital, where his daughter lay upstairs, her tongue hanging out, and her pretty blue eyes staring dead ahead of her; no recognition of life other than being kept alive by a breathing apparatus.

While the officer screamed, I saw the suspect disassociate, with ease, giving no reaction to the officer.

I went and bought the officer coffee, and said ,"take a few minutes break, you've been on this all night. Let me take a crack at him."

Relieved, he took the coffee and went for a walk.

I said, "You military?"

He said, "Yeah, ex."

Ah, I thought, that's why he was able to tone out the screaming.

I remained silent for a few minutes and offered him coffee. "No thank you." I noted his polite response.

"Tell me what happened", I said, in a quite voice.

"...And what happened next" followed.

The baby would not stop crying and in a moment of panic, thinking the mother would arrive and say, "See? I knew I could not trust you with the baby!" and he would not see his little girl again."

"So, I didn't mean to, but I just lost it. I shook her and she, she...she stopped crying."

Indeed.

His admission meant that not only had he lost his daughter, but will now pay for taking her life. By the way, he was also on drugs, something that further desensitizes the soul. It was not just being in the military and being used to yelling, it was the drugs, too.

I went upstairs, handed the written confession to a most shocked detective, and went to say my last good bye to the little girl. She was just as I saw her last, tongue out to one side (oh, how I wanted the nurse to push it back in!), eyes straight forward without signal, but there was one thing else about the baby that to this date I cannot forget:

Someone had put a pretty pink bow in her young hair, tying it upwards, in what our day would call "Pebbles Flintstone style."

She was so beautiful, and had the promise of life taken from her in a moment of unrestrained temper.

Imagine, as we do in Statement Analysis, that you are Kevin Fox and you have not only lost your little girl, but are falsely accused of her murder.

You are now to ask yourself, "What would I say?"

This is the actual practice we follow, often making notes of not only the questions that we have prepared, but a separate sheet of "honest, innocent" answers that are expected.

We then compare the actual answers with the ones we wrote out. We teach investigators to literally "enter into the statement or language" of the person and learn, as it were, from the "camera lens" of words chosen to learn what happened. I will show you precisely how this works in the case of murdered young boy, Dylan Redwine, later. Empathy, presupposed truth, and projection, is so important in analytical interviewing because it allows for a show down between "The Expected" and "The Unexpected" in the wording.

We are confronted by "the unexpected" and that is where we begin our analysis.

In what follows, Statement Analysis is in **bold** type. We now look at an example of a Reliable Denial.

Kevin Fox claimed that he did not murder his daughter.

Is Kevin Fox telling the truth?

Statement Analysis gets to the truth and this interview highlights principle well.

Statement Of Kevin Fox Regarding His Interrogation by The Will County Sheriff's Office. Portions of the interrogation have surfaced on video. In the video, Fox is seen repeatedly saying "I did not kill my daughter."

The video is disturbing (on so many levels) but none as great as the ignorance of the interviewers who ask questions, but will not listen to the answers.

Two principles to be covered:

1. The Reliable Denial Exists of Three Simple Components
2. The "Daughter" in Analysis.

Mr. Fox went to the news camera and said,

"I want the public to know that <u>I did not kill my daughter</u>. I have always cooperated with the authorities in the investigation of <u>my</u> daughter's death."

This is a powerful denial and although in such a case we expect to see sensitivity indicators this is something we do not find in guilty statements. The denial itself, is first person singular, past tense, without qualifiers. It is to be considered *very strong* if it was spoken freely, and not reflective language. This Reliable Denial now puts him in an "above 90%" category.

We do not discount that the 10% of deceivers who can say "I didn't do it" when, in fact they did, have other linguistic signals and even tests that we can give, to find out the truth.

What would you say if I falsely accused you of killing your little girl?

"I didn't kill my daughter. I don't care what you do to me. I didn't do it. No, I don't need to wait for a lawyer, and no, you don't have to wait for me to tell the truth. I am telling the truth now, as I say, "I did not kill my daughter."

I would feel no need to say "on advice of counsel…" or "please be patient, this is a complicated case" or anything other than "shut up! I did not kill my daughter! You need a new job! You don't know what you are doing! My daughter's killer is out there because I didn't kill her!" and rage would likely pour from your heart.

"I did not kill my daughter" was something he said, repeatedly, in the video-taped interview, and he then said it to the media.

If this came from him in the free editing process, we can conclude, in spite of any sensitivity indicators, that he did not kill his daughter.

There may be other issues, as sensitivity indicators may show guilt of neglect, or of other crimes, but not homicide.

On Oct. 26, I went to the Will County Sheriff's Department at the request of the investigators. I tried to cooperate and answer their questions, however, they became very abusive -- yelling and screaming at me <u>that I had killed her</u>."

Dealing
With Deception

"tried" means attempted and failed yet here he tells us why this attempt failed. Embedded admission? No.

Note *"I had killed my daughter"* is within his statement. He is directly quoting his interrogators and has no possessive pronoun attached to it. This means that he entered into the language of his accusers and has not spoken from the FEP (Free Editing Process) We note it just the same, to see if there are enough indicators of deception to overthrow the powerful denial that he began his statement with. We look to see if, even in a denial, he frames his own guilt, or is if it is a direct quote of the deputies (the interrogators). Note that present tense language (things/topics/issues in motion) indicating that at the time of this statement, the yelling and screaming is something that continues to this date and is sensitive to him. It is not an indicator of deception, but follow up questions should be around the yelling, sleeping, nightmares, etc. At the time of the statement, it is still "active" to the subject.

"For hours, I told the investigators that I did not kill my daughter.

I asked them repeatedly to call my father so that he could get me a lawyer.

I was told that I did not need to speak to my father or a lawyer."

After four hours of not being heard, I would ask for a lawyer too.

Note the strong denial is his own quote, not that of someone else.

Note that the word "told" is fitting: strong affirmation in communicative language.

Confusing "said" and "told" is indicative of deception. Here he is consistent with the setting.

Communicative language: he "told" them he did not kill her. This use of "told" is authoritative and strong.

Note that I "asked them..." is softer language. He demanded that they know he did not kill Riley, but only asked, as a request (soft) that his father be called. This is an example of ignorance in interviewing by police as well as a violation of his rights. He was young and wanted 'counsel', which, in his mind, was his father.

"I was kept in a locked area for approximately 14 ½ hours. I was told by the investigators that if I did not give a statement saying I was involved in my daughter's death that they "knew inmates at the jail" that would make sure that I was (expletive) every day I was there."

The ignorant investigators even threatened the once heart-broke, but now terrified young father.

Note the heavy use of the pronoun, "I" showing ownership of his sentences.

Note the absence of qualifiers. His language is straight forward. The time period is important because it is likely that in reviewing the tape of 14 1/2 hours, he said, "I did not kill my daughter" early, often, and late in the tape. He has no need to persuade because he didn't do it.

Note "approximately" is appropriate to measure large amount of time. Note first person singular, past tense indicating reliability and confident connection.

"I was involved in my daughter's death" is the language of the interviewers/interrogators and not his own. He entered their language; this is not an embedded confession.

It should be noted that it is not his language but that he is repeating and quoting the direct language of the deputies.

He enters into their language: it is not his own.

"One of the investigators got 6 inches from my face screaming at me that I was a (expletive) for not talking and that my wife was going to divorce me if I didn't cooperate."

This is not how to get information.

"do unto others as you would have them do unto you" is a good principle in interviewing. Would you like someone to treat your son this way? Is this any way to learn the truth?

In fact, it suppresses the truth by putting the subject on the defensive. I get far more information, including many confessions, from trained listening, and reflecting back the subject's own words, working diligently to NOT introduce language to the subject.

Note personal pronouns and consistency of pronoun usage (I, me, my, me) is an indicator of truth.

Note that the "screaming" is not "screamed" and likely continues to date of the statement. Note the absence of qualifiers.

This is another indication that his initial denial is trustworthy and reliable. He framed "*I killed her*" within his denial, by entering into the language of the ignorant interrogators and has no personal pronoun connecting him to the murder.

This is significant. He is quoting them directly.

*"I was told that I would be in jail for 30 years unless I talked. At one point the investigators threw a picture of **my** deceased daughter on the table in front of me. They screamed that I had duct taped her mouth and hands.*

Note "deceased daughter" is softer and respectful. This is an indicator of innocence. Even while dead, the language shows "my daughter" (see chapter on Father-Daughter molestation in Statement Analysis).

Note "told" continues as appropriate indicating it came from memory.

Note appropriate "told" versus "said" which would have been inconsistent with screaming. Note again that he is quoting what they said to him with their language, not his.

This was the first time I learned that she had been bound.

This is critical: Here, he says "she had been bound" which is passive language. Passivity in language is often used to conceal identity or responsibility.

Question: *Is passivity appropriate here?*

Answer: *Yes, because he does not know the identity of who bound her.*

There is no sensitivity within his sentence.

Can you imagine the pain in his heart, learning that his little girl had been bound, helpless, unable to fight back? Can you imagine her terror? I cannot. Can you imagine Kevin's terror? I can only try.

"They wanted me to say that there had been an accident at home and that she had hit her head -- that was the first time I learned that <u>she had lumps on her head.</u>"

"She had lumps on her head" is passive and without knowing who is responsible (from the reliable denial), passivity is appropriately used. Passivity avoids responsibility. Since Kevin did not do it, his speech, chosen in less than a micro-second, employed passivity because he was not responsible, and did not know to whom the responsibility was to be placed. This is a strong signal of veracity in speech.

Note that he quotes others and thus far, has not owned anything for his own, in his own language. Note that "first time" is repeated, which would indicate sensitivity, but it must be noted that it is not a repetition: it was the first time he learned she had lumps, which is different than the first time he learned she had been bound; different items

"<u>They said</u> if I said that she fell and I panicked and tried to cover up the accident I could only be charged with involuntary manslaughter and would immediately go home on bond and could not get more than 3-5 years. They <u>told</u> me to say that I duct taped her mouth and hands."

"they said" now is different than "told" so we must learn if the change is justified.

Here, it is with more details and appears to have come, likely at the suggestion of the "good cop" who was 'befriended' Fox, and the softer language indicates that this came from memory.

They "told" him, (above) short, harsh statements.

They "said" to him the entire story of accidental death and cover up.

Veracity indicated.

This is not embedded: he enters into their language and is straight forward. This means that when they "said" it was an accident, they were being 'nice' to him, but when he did not go along with them, they returned to authoritative. This was their amateur version of "good cop bad cop" used on a young man.

Kevin then says authorities told him to say that he performed an act on his daughter to make it *"look like a sexual attack."*

*"I have never been under this kind of pressure in my life. I was isolated, alone and terrified. As soon as I saw my brother and lawyer I told them **I did not do this**. I love my wife, daughter and son more than anything in this world. I trusted the authorities and they betrayed me and my family. I can only hope the truth will come out."*

Note: First person singular, past tense, and "this", after being issuing reliable denials above. Consistent use of pronouns Note lack of qualfiiers Note that no personal pronouns were used to own the statements of the interrogators. Without knowing any evidence whatsoever, we would have concluded that he did not kill his daughter. There aren't even indicators of sensitivity outside the photo. This is an example of a truthful statement and boorish untrained, ignorant interviewers who thought they didn't need Interview Training but could bully their way into a confession. They are not the norm and shouldn't be viewed as such. Many investigators have taken Statement Analysis training and don't need to berate someone while attempting to learn the truth.

It is very difficult to believe that the interrogation even needed to go beyond 5 minutes after "I didn't do it." Kevin Fox used consistent language throughout. Note no confusion of "I" and "we" that are often in weak and/or deceptive statements. No qualifiers, and no hedging of language.

This is his statement and he owns it.

He "wants" to tell, is weaker than just telling; but in context, it shows a slight sensitivity due to having <u>not been believed</u> by police and the district attorney's office. This is why it is something he "wants" to tell, but what he tells is as straight forward as it can be: "I did not kill my daughter".Note that there is no change in "daughter" anywhere. A change would have been significant (we would have looked at the context). He is straight forward and does not go from her name to the possessive pronoun, or back and forth with change; something we see in deceptive statements.Kevin Fox told them, from the start, that *he did not kill Riley*.It is a tragic shame that they didn't listen.

This is a result of either poor training, or officers' inability to retain the training, or a refusal on the part of those entrusted with enforcing our laws, to utilize the greatest weapon against crime we have: our brains.

What of False Confessions?

False confessions do not come from experiential memory. I once saw a program in which a teenager was berated into police, force fed details, into confessing to a murder in which he did not commit.

While he spoke, he slipped into present tense language. Why? It indicated that he was making it up, as he went along, using the words of the police officers! Later, his father produced dental x-rays that show that on the day of the murder, his son was not even in the country, but was traveling south of the border, and had emergency root canal.

The interviewers objected saying "How did he know all the facts?"

The morons fed the facts to him.

In Analytical Interviewing the Interviewer attempts to say as little as possible, perhaps 10% of all the words spoken, only, while the subject of the interview does 90% of the talking.

We do not introduce words, which only teach the guilty how to lie, and cloud the innocent to make them appear guilty!

So after sleep deprivation, what of a confession? Like a 'psychic' revelation, the language of a false confession will show deception because it did not come from experiential memory. It may come from memory: memory of a TV show, or memory of what a cop just told him, or a memory from another case ('psychics' use this quite often), but it does not come from experiential memory.

Fox' confession showed deception. He parroted back to investigators their own words and avoided the Free Editing Process (FEP) which would have allowed him to speak and choose his own words freely.

The Reliable Denial has three components:

1. **The Pronoun "I"**
2. The past tense verb
3. The specific allegation

If a denial has less than three, or has additional words beyond the three components, it is not to be deemed "reliable."

The actual innocent will tell you so, early and often, if needed.

Eventually, Kevin Fox was released but not before the second worst period of time in his own young life; being incarcerated is only second to the pain of losing his little girl.

Kevin Fox was initially charged in the young girl's murder, based almost solely on a videotaped confession that he had killed Riley. He spent eight months in prison before he was cleared of all charges due to DNA evidence and the confession was ruled out based on coercion. The killer left a pair of mud-covered shoes at Forsythe Woods County Forest Preserve, which were collected by police. But the police never followed up on this piece of evidence. The shoes had the name Eby written on the inside, the last name of the actual culprit. They overlooked many other important case facts as well. The same night as Riley's abduction another house on the same block was burglarized. The Fox family later sued the state of Illinois and won $15 million in a federal civil rights lawsuit, which was later reduced to $8.5 million.

Scott Eby was later charged on five counts of first-degree murder and one count of predatory sexual assault after DNA evidence linked him to Riley. By the time the police caught up with Eby to charge him in connection with Riley's murder, he was serving two consecutive seven-year sentences. Eby later confessed to killing Riley after first breaking into another home on the same block as the Foxes'. Eby said he cut through the back screen door of the home and then pushed the door in. He found Riley lying on the couch and decided to kidnap her when he saw that her father was asleep. He said that he put Riley into his car and drove her to the park where he assaulted her on the floor of a restroom in the park. Then he killed her by drowning her in a nearby creek within the park. He subsequently pled guilty to Riley's murder and received a life sentence without the possibility of parole. Scott Eby was on parole and lived only about a mile from the Foxes' home at the time of Riley's murder.

No amount of money will ever give Kevin Fox his little girl, Riley, back to him. As the years have passed, Kevin has missed all the wonderful milestones if Riley's life that I have had the privilege of celebrating with Sarah, including graduation high school, college, and passing the nursing boards. Kevin will never have these wonderful moments with his beloved Riley.

He was likely left with nightmares, depression, anxiety and hopelessness when he considers not only what was done to Riley, but of the months he spent incarcerated, as the public thought he had assaulted and killed his own daughter.

At least, perhaps, the suit money can be used for any mental health services that he and his family may have needed over the years, and may still need for the rest of their lives. I hope not, but I do not know how a man can cope with such heartache and miscarriage of justice on top of it.

Perhaps Terry Elvis' faith could speak to the broken heart of Kevin Fox.

Chapter Eleven: Fathers Molesting Daughters

Here is an interesting twist in Statement Analysis: It is near impossible for a father to molest his own daughter in Statement Analysis.

When I say this in a training, the look of incredulity that falls over the faces of the attendees is, often, blunted by those who know, "something's up here."

Avinoam Sapir teaches, "The Statement is Alive; the Subject is Dead."

The wisdom in this simple statement is far beyond any boundary I have been able to place upon it, in its applicability to cases I have worked on, assisted others on, or covered for the Statement Analysis blog.

The Statement, itself, is alive to us, but the subject, that is, the person, does not exist to us.

A good example of this is when reviewing a police statement about a stolen car. Did the husband falsely report his car stolen so that he could cash in on the insurance, or was it actually stolen.

It was reported on Wednesday night, so the insurance investigator, now working with local law enforcement, had solid training.

"Mr. Smith, I'd like you to write out a statement of what happened, from the time you woke up, until the time you went to sleepWednesday."

Mr. Smith objected. "I already told you guys, I was out and it had to be stolen sometime after 10PM, so what's the purpose in wasting my time. Why aren't you out there finding my car?"

Insurance companies sometimes poach law enforcement's best and brightest to do investigations for them, similar to when District Attorneys, or Attorney Generals use their own detectives; they are hand chosen. Insurance companies pay more, and offer more opportunities for trainings such as Statement Analysis and Analytical Interviewing. Often, these insurance investigators are good at what they do.

In this case, the insurance investigator noted the reluctance upon the part of the man to write out his entire day, so he insisted upon it. He was careful to say little other than "from the time you woke up, unto the time you went to sleep Wednesday" even when the man said, "you mean from the time I woke up until the time I reported it missing at 10?"

The insurance investigator said, "Mr. Smith, please write out what you did from the time you wok up, until the time you went to sleepWednesday."

Already, the insurance investigator thought to himself: the subject did not go to sleep Wednesday night.

But this was just a thought.

"Everything?", Mr. Smith nervously asked?

"Yes."

"Do you mean like what I had for breakfast, kind of everything?" Mr. Smith asked.

The insurance investigator was not taking the bait. He wisely avoided introducing any words into the subject's vocabulary. This statement must be his own.

When the Statement was received, it was read back to Mr. Smith, and asked, in the presence of the police officer, if this was his statement, his handwriting, and had anyone added anything to it. The man said, "no."

He then went to leave when the man said, "I thought you were going to question me?" to which he was told, "Later."

The investigators took the statement to the police office, made photocopies, put the original in his file, and began the work.

First, they counted the words.

Next, they noted the passage of time, beginning early in the morning (about 6AM) ending after 10PM.

They then counted the number of lines that were written and divided that number by the number of hours that "passed" in the statement.

They found the average.

Mr. Smith wrote a detailed statement about his day (including what he had for breakfast) and the statement spanned from 6AM all the way to at least 11PM.

They found that the writing came in at approximately 3 lines per hour. This was the norm for him.

Then, they took the statement and counted the number of words that he used before the theft of the car, the number of words used to report the theft itself, and the number of words dedicated to what happened after the reported theft.

They now had two mathematical equations even before "reading" the statement.

Next, they literally circled all the pronouns.

Then, they wrote down the names of everyone who appeared in the statement, in the order of appearance, and noted any change in any names.

The insurance investigator began to read the statement:

"At 6AM, I woke up. Got coffee. I got dressed and had to leave, as I was late for an appointment. Sue got dressed, and she was also in a hurry..."

It was an "aha!" moment.

At 6AM, I woke up. <u>Got</u> coffee. I got dressed and had to leave, as I was late for an appointment. <u>Sue</u> got dressed, and she was also in a hurry..."

The insurance investigator said, "he is not married."

The police officer countered, "oh, yes he is. Sue, he mentioned her, right there, is his wife. I have his file, too."

"No", said the other. "According to the statement, he is not married. This is critical. The man, that is, the "subject" himself, is not married according to the statement. The statement is alive, but the man is not. The subject is "dead" to us, and that is how we must think."

The well trained insurance investigator was referring to two important points:

1. Incomplete Social Introduction
2. Social drink

He explained that by mentioning "Sue" without saying "my wife Sue", he not only deprived her of the title of "wife" but he dropped the pronoun "my" from introducing her. We are, all of us, social and possessive creatures, and we like to take ownership of what is ours. Since he is

Dealing
With Deception

writing this to two men he does not know, he should have said, "my wife, Sue" but in terms of the statement being alive, Sue is deprived from the status of being his wife.

"This is indicative of a problem in the relationship. In fact, there is more"

He then pointed out the word "coffee" in the Statement.

Most of us in the United States like to drink coffee. I drink 3cups a day, black, no sugar, and try not to drink a 4th. However, not everyone feels it necessary to include this detail in their statements and generally, ("generally", meaning most of the time) when one mentions it, I like to ask, "Were you with someone else?" because coffee, in a statement, is often a social drink and lots of times it is a signal that a conversation took place that the subject is thinking of when he wrote the statement.

He might mention coffee, but not butter on his toast, for example. "Coffee" in Statement Analysis, should signal to the Interviewer that another person may have been present.

Here, we have two signals that something is up:

1. Incomplete Social Introduction equaling poor relationship
2. Mention of coffee, but without a pronoun!

Did you notice, "got coffee" had no pronoun?

Who got coffee?

Deceptive people are counting on you and I to interpret their words rather than listen. Statement Analysis is all about listening.

I cannot say who "got coffee" because the subject did not tell me who got coffee.

I cannot say that he is married because he has refused to tell me he is married.

I believe, word by word, what one tells me, unless they prove to me that I ought not to.

I know he knows how to write pronouns, thy are circled everywhere. The dropped pronoun, therefore, stands out.

He is not married. He did not "get" coffee. These two things are "according to the principle that the Statement, itself, is alive and speaking to me", while the subject, himself, is "but dead to me."

His statement proved to be deceptive.

He was in a world of credit card debt, and the car had been acting up so badly that he felt it was "worth more dead than alive."

His wife refused to go along with his story.

She was, indeed, up with him and is the one who brought him coffee. He "removed" her from the status as "wife" because he felt that she was betraying him by "not trusting his judgment" and it was during coffee, together, that they argued.

He was arrested and she was able to get immunity from prosecution by testifying against him. Her lack of "trust" in him was wise.

This shows us why we say "the subject is not married" because we are not reading his record, but are entering in his statement's portrayal of reality. To him, at that moment in time, she was not "my wife", but was a trouble-maker ruining his plans. Psychologically, when he was writing out his statement, he was recreating the scene in his mind. The time of coffee was very unpleasant and stressful to him, as he considered her "betrayal" of him, and a "real wife" would have gone along with his illegal scheme.

We may intend to deceive, but our words give us away.

In the case of a father molesting his own daughter: it is almost impossible, that is, in Statement Analysis.

For years I investigated child abuse cases, including many where a father had, indeed, molested his own daughter or step daughter, but in Statement Analysis, we recognize that in order to do so; that is, in order for a man to molest his own daughter, he must "change her", in his mind, from his "daughter", into something else, in order to satisfy his perverse urge.

Here is a statement of a man who wished to "deny" the allegation of molesting his own daughter. First, we will note what he said, without emphasis. Then, we will see how many principles of Statement Analysis are exampled in this short statement.

1. Look for Reliable Denial
2. Look for any change in language as a change in reality.
3. Look for missing information as seen via "left" or "departing" a scene.
4. Look for any subtle blaming of the victim or someone else.
5. Any words repeated are sensitive

6. "this" is close; "that" is distant

These are all principles applied to all statements. All the analyst needs to know:

What is the purpose of the statement ? That is, what is the allegation?

The allegation is that he molested his little girl, who told her mother, who immediately called the police. This short statement is rich in content.

I. First, lets look at it as is, and then
II. II. look at it with emphasis added by me.

This is a load of crap. You people should be disgusted with yourselves. Do you think that I am disgusted? This is a bunch of lies and you people know it.

What I did is this. I got home from a friend's at 10AM and my wife and my daughter were home. She was ticked that I was out early because she

wanted to go shopping. She left. I was busy and the girl had homework anyway.

The next thing I know she gets home from shopping, wants me

to carry in the groceries and my daughter is crying like there's

something wrong. you get called. Cops get called and here

I am with this crap."

II Now we look at the statement again, with emphasis added for clarity, and Statement Analysis added.

<u>This</u> is a load of crap. You people should be <u>disgusted</u> with yourselves. Do you think that I am <u>disgusted</u>? This is <u>a bunch of lies</u> and you people know it.

Let's begin with "this" and "that." The word "this" indicates closeness, while the word "that" shows distancing language. "I don't want 'that' book, but give me 'this' one (closer)."

"I did not have sexual relations with <u>that</u> woman, Ms. Lewinsky."

Whatever it is that this man is thinking of when his brain chose these words, it is "close" to him.

Next, we note that the word "disgust" enters his vocabulary. Had he heard the allegation when the wife called 911? I don't know, but I do know that not only is "disgust" in his brain, but it is repeated. Statement Analysis: anything that is repeated is important or sensitive. He has disgust not only thrown to them "with yourselves" but he associates disgust with himself. Remember, the brain knows what it knows.

Now note that "this" is a "load of crap", whatever "this" is in his personal, subjective internal dictionary, and that there is also something that is also close, but it is identified as a "bunch of lies", which the word "bunch" indicating more than one. "Lies" are a bunch. Bananas are a bunch, and "bunch" seems to be a lot. As far as we know, the allegation is singular.

<u>What I did</u> is this.

Here, he acknowledges that he did, indeed, do something. This is different than "I didn't do anything."

Speaking of which, when you read the statement, did you find a reliable denial? Did you find an attempt at a reliable denial?

Did he make any denial?

He did not. Remember principle: If he is unwilling or unable to say that he didn't do it, we are not permitted to say it for him.

He did something. We need his words to guide us to what he did.

*I got home from a friend's at 10AM and my wife and **my daughter** were home. She was ticked*

Note here that he does not use his wife's name, but he does give title. This is an Incomplete Social introduction indicating that he has a problem with her, at this point in the statement, not as wife, but with her, as a person (missing name).

Note what he calls the alleged victim: "my daughter." Remember: In Statement Analysis, a man cannot sexually abuse his own daughter (it's extremely rare; I have yet to see it). Here, she is "daughter' and she is safe.

When he got home from "a friend's house" (note "a" friend, not "my friend", which provoked suspicious thoughts of a girlfriend, but it was not so. It was a male friend of whom his wife did not approve, as she felt his male friend was often behaving like a pedophile, and was a sexual pervert. She had no proof other than a mother's instinct. Hence, "a" friend, since the topic of his friendship with the creepy friend is uncomfortable to him.

that I was out early because she

wanted to go shopping.

When asked to tell us "what happened?" and someone says or writes "why" something happened, it is very sensitive information. It indicates that the subject is worried about being asked "well, why did you…?" so he anticipates being asked, and answers it before hand. It is very sensitive, as is the word "left" in Statement Analysis, when it is used as a connecting verb.

The word "Because" (or "so, since, therefore, etc") is one of two words that is given the color coding of BLUE as being the highest level of sensitivity in a Statement. When we have "two or more BLUES" we often have solved the statement or crime.

"Left" (or "departed")

"I was at home and went to the doctor's" shows the mind 'moving forward' to the doctor's office.

"I left home and went to the doctor's office" shows that the mind is stalled at the leaving, with the word "left" telling us that there is missing information that the subject is keeping from us. LSI says that it is "70% likely missing information about rushing, traffic, being late, etc" but also that the remaining 30% is deliberately suppressed information that the subject does not want you to know.

We highlight this in "BLUE" as the highest level of sensitivity in a Statement. IN this one portion, we have two BLUES close together making it a very sensitive portion of the statement.

Question for Analysis: Why is the wife leaving the home so very sensitive to the accused suspect?

We continue:

*She left. I was busy and **the girl** had homework anyway.*

We now find a change in language.

A change in language should represent a change in reality, within the statement. If no change in reality is evident, it may be a signal that the subject has lost memory of his words chosen, and is lying, making things up as he goes along. But if there is justification for the change, it is a signal that experiential memory is working, and a change in reality exists.

"The officer pulled his gun, and fired his weapon, and re-holstered his gun."

The "gun" became a "weapon" when it was fired, but after it was finished being fired, the brain turned it back into a "gun" again.

"My car sputtered and died along the side of the road. I left the vehicle there until the tow truck could arrive."

This is a truthful statement. It was a "car" while it drove, even roughly, but abandoned, it became a "vehicle."

When it is repaired, it will turn back into a "car" again!

The man has changed his "Daughter" into a "girl" (gender specific). We now need to learn:

Found only within the statement: What caused the change of language? What caused the "daughter" to turn into a "girl"?

The answer is in the statement's context. It is in there. You have to listen to him.

The next thing I know she gets home from shopping,

This is called a "Temporal Lacunae" or a passing over of time. It is a signal that his brain is thining about what happened during the timespan, but he wants to skip over it.

When you find a Temporal Lancunae" (TI), flag it and concentrate your interview there.

wants me

to carry in the groceries

Here he gives us a touch of insight into his personality. He says, in a statement about being accused of child molestation, that his wife wants him to lend a hand and help carry in some groceries. He reveals a bit of his character in this short statement.

*and **my daughter** is crying like there's*

Did you now notice that the "girl" has changed back into his "daughter" again? What has caused the change of language? Remember, something has to do it.

something wrong. you get called. Cops get called and here

"something's wrong" is an admission just like "here's what I did" and "something's wrong" as he comes closer to an admission of sorts, if not a confession.

I am with this crap."

"This" is indeed close, and it is different than the "bunch of lies" that he never identified.

He did not deny molesting his own daughter. Her statement and his statement agreed:

1. She was "daughter" when her mother was home. It was the mother's presence that kept her safe.
2. She became "girl" when her mother left.
3. When the mother came home, she was "safe" again, and was "daughter."
4. The blaming of the wife is evident!

He is not only lazy, but claimed that "she knew of my little problem" and "shouldn't have left me alone with her."

He literally is blaming his wife's grocery shopping for the molestation. The sensitivity about his "friend" was well justified. "Birds of a feather…"

The mother, sadly, miscalculated and thought that she would just rush down to the market and her daughter would be okay and had homework, and so forth. Though she originally insisted that her daughter come with her, the daughter protested due to the amount of homework she had. This was the tragic mistake.

The statement is deceptive; he molested her, but line upon line, there is no direct lie found in it. This is the case of liars: they rarely, if ever, lie outright. Those that do are rare, and dangerous, indeed.

The daughter will now suffer for a lifetime, along with others that love her. The mother will never be comforted, knowing that for a momentary lapse of judgment, and yielding, her daughter was molested. By his reaction in blaming his wife, you may know that he is not likely to ever take responsibility for his evil action.

Change of language is critical.

I once worked with a pretty co-worker who told a new employee to go out "with Peter. He's a good man to go with…" in orientation.

Months later, I heard her say something similar to another new hire: "Yeah, go with Peter for training. He is a good person to go with…"

I caught up to her and said, "Hey, did you used to have a crush on me?" She said, "Yeah, I used to but not any more. Why, how did you know?"

I asked, "What changed? You once called me a "man" and today, in telling that new worker to go on orientation with me, you said I was a "person." What happened just a few months ago?

Without missing a beat, she said, "Oh, I met your wife, Heather."

It was Heather's presence that caused the change in reality that caused the change in language.

While sharing this anecdote with a Rotary Club, a man asked, "I noticed you said she was a "very pretty co worker" and am wondering why you felt the need to add that she was "very pretty."

I said "Vanity."

The audience chuckled, but I pointed out that that type of question is what I teach: getting people to listen carefully, especially to additional language and ask questions about the use of language.

In fact, I'd love to have him in my next training.

Chapter Twelve: Small Business Theft

In a small business, theft can really hurt. In the trainings conducted in small business, sometimes it is but 3 or 4 individuals, often family members, who want some assistance in reducing theft among employees.

We conduct very specific training in this manner, and as stated elsewhere, it begins in the Interview process.

Once you have learned (even if "you" is just "you", the CEO, driver, janitor, and everything in between in your business) how to spot deception, it not only applies in the daily sales transactions that you face but in hiring help.

Remember the expression, "Good help is hard to find"? It think that honest help is a lot harder to find.

I once knew a man who got a job with "the phone company" way back when. He seemed very glad to get it, as he had a wife, and two small sons. His wife worked full time in the same business, but the husband, well, he was a different story. He bounced around a lot. He seemed to go from small business to small business and something usually went wrong.

When an friend who had union connections got him a job with the local phone company, for the first time, his wife and children had good medical benefits, and he, for the first time, had a good wage. His wife was relieved and felt like, finally, the man she loved got a "break" in life.

Suddenly, he quit.

His friends and family were stunned.

"You quit? You know how hard it was to get you in there? Do you know the strings I pulled and the favors I called in? Are you kidding me? Why did you quit?"

He said, "It was in a bad neighborhood."

He was a giant of a man, married to the tiniest of wives, with two strong sons who looked up to their father.

His friends still supported him and helped him apply here, there, and everywhere. As these things sometimes go, it is hard to get a good paying job without a college education, of which he lacked.

Yet, roll the dice, he got hired by another huge company: the Rail Road!

This was another much coveted job where he made an even better wage with still the stellar medical, dental and vision benefits that the phone company had, along with a great retirement that would be in effect in just 20 years. He would be a young man on full retirement before his 50th birthday!

A few weeks after training for the Rail Road began, he "fell" between cars and hurt his knee. The man working with him, seeing him on the ground, said, "get up; you're fine." He said, "No, I can't get up. You'll have to call for help. "

He told his superiors that he would have to go on medical leave.

The RR responded with, "No, you're on probation. Show up for work if you still want your job! If not, you're no longer employed with us."

His wife begged him to go, but when his friends begged him, she said, "His health is more important. His knee will only get worse." She stood up for him, and got more hours at her job, along with food stamps.

Months later, he "knee healed."

He was now ready to go back to work.

Discouraged, his friends helped him fill out applications but the jobs were all very low paying, and he had not only a lack of education, but a lack of marketable skill to offer.

The Post Office hired him.

His friends could not believe it.

He would be paid good money for a job that required no skill: just drop an envelop off at the right house. No critical thinking necessary. Unskilled labor at Federal government money. Perfect.

Life seemed to finally turn out with some sunshine for him.

Then, one day, while delivering the mail, he fell through a step at a door. The home owner apologized and asked him to get off his porch. He refused.

The home owner had to call the local post office to get him off the porch because he was standing in a broken slot, 12" in depth, claiming to be "stuck."

This time, however, he was past the probation period.

He was helped out of the porch and as he left, he threatened the home owner with a law suit.

The Post Office did not fire him, and after getting enough medical leave to make sure his leg was okay, he returned to work.

Lo, and behold, he claimed to have been bitten by a dog, and, although he was 6' 4" tall, the bite (not discernable to friends) left him with too much fear to go back to work.

His long suffering wife worked two jobs, and his older son eventually dropped out of sports in order to get part time work. Back then, disability wasn't quite so easy to game, and he was turned down for it, so he did what he thought best:

He stayed home and watched television.

Ah, the great American dream.

Today, employers find it difficult to find anyone who wishes to work, and when one is found, depending upon the age, the employer finds himself up against an array of "worker rights", including the alleged right to "bring my dog, Fluffy to work, as he is a "Service Dog" and I suffer from anxiety and he is better than medicine, therefore, you have to offer me a reasonable accommodation so that I can work with Fluffy by my side!"

Yeah, that happened to me recently. I was threatened with a discrimination suit but my defense was, "My clients are allergic to dogs!"

You should hear the stories reported by the welfare workers! They hear incredible reasons why people cannot work today. One woman claimed that her cat saved her life, therefore, she owed it to her cat to stay home (on government assistance) for as long as the kitty lived.

Some workers have their portable smart phones hooked up to video games against their buddies and each time an employer turns his head, the worker is frantically slamming the thumbs into the machine, scoring "points" of some sort, or killing zombies, or something of value to somebody, but not to the employer.

When someone is finally hired, the fear now is that the new employee might just employ the "five finger discount" to merchandise and in a small business, this can be quite painful.

Business after business has complained to me that "law enforcement can't keep up! They do not have time to investigate and we do not get back our stolen money or merchandize and are afraid to put in claims because our insurance goes up and up! What can we do?"

My answer:

Fight back against deception.

First, learn how to conduct an Analytical Interview. Learn how to get to the truth before you hire them.

Set up methods for the truthful to pass with flying colors, and leave behind the deceptive ones. Statistically speaking, it is the deceptive ones that are going to fall, trip, stumble and file claim.

Think back to the man with all those comfy union jobs, one after the next.

Do you believe that he was truthful about what happened to him? Or, do you believe that deception, even self deception, existed at the center of all of this?

Deceptive people steal.

Deceptive people steal time.

Deceptive people take that which does not belong to them and deceptive people go after money that their own hands have not earned.

Deceptive people "game the system."

There are still honest workers out there, who are still willing to give an honest day's work for an honest day's wage. They may have become a lot more difficult now that we have become the land of the entitled but they are out there.

Analytical Interview Training teaches even small companies to get written samples before the interview process and then how to interview off of the analysis.

How "fair" is this?

Consider that the interview is based upon open ended questions and is then based upon the subject's own words, rather than an interpretation of words.

It is as fair as can be and will help small and big companies, alike, weed out deceivers in the interview process who will only end up hurting you in the short and long term, if hired.

Let's move on.

You've not used this process to weed out the deceptive applicants and in your company you've had a theft.

Your client, "Bob" has had his "hoodie" stolen and has accused staff.

Bob's mother is so angry that she is thinking of moving him to another agency. It would be a terrible loss of revenue, far worse than a simple theft.

Yet, you do not want to falsely accuse anyone, either.

In this case, the company sought intervention. I had them have the accused staff write out a statement of his day and would guide them on how to interview him based upon analysis of the statement. Instead, they asked me to interview him. See if you can spot the deception:

"*Saturday March 23rd, Bob had a small get*

together at his house. Bob had a monster

~~jacket~~ sweater that matched my Jacket.

I asked Bob if I could try the sweater

on with my Jacket. Bob complied. I only

had the hoody for about 20 minutes. I

then took off the hoody and laid it

on the back of the recliner. When I

left the hoody was still on the chair.

On Tuesday, March 26th, at about 1250pm, Bob's

mom found me down town and accused me of stealing his hoody. I told her as politely

as possible what I knew about the hoody

and where I last saw it. She went on

about what would happen if the hoody wasn't found..."

I interviewed the worker from this statement which he had in front of him. At first, he was hiding it from me, but I said to him, "Is this your statement?" and "has anyone changed it in any way?" and finally, "Would you like a lawyer or anyone else present for the interview?"

I do not violate anyone's rights, nor do I need to. I am there for information.

The interview began with a lengthy sermon by the subject, about the evils of theft. He went on and on about how his father and his uncle were both in jail for theft and that to him, thieves were lower than drug dealers.

Yet, in his statement, there is a change of language that must be addressed. In fact, there are two changes that are significant:

1. Hoody and Sweater
2. Chair and Recliner

Now, remember the principle: When language changes, there should be a justification for the change found within the statement. If no justification is found, it may be that the subject is not working from memory and has "lost track" of his wording. Yet, if there is a change

"Saturday March 23rd, Bob had a small get together at his house. Bob had a monster ~~jacket~~ <u>sweater</u> that matched my Jacket. I asked Bob if I could try <u>the sweater</u> on with my Jacket. Bob complied. I only had the hoody for about 20 minutes. I then took off the <u>hoody</u> and laid it on the back of the<u> recliner</u>. When I left the <u>hoody</u> was still on the chair. On Tuesday, March 26th, at about 1250pm, Bob's mom found me down town and accused me of stealing his <u>hoody</u>. I told her as politely as possible what I knew about the <u>hoody</u> and where I last saw it. She went on about what would happen if the hoody wasn't found…"

We will not do a full analysis here, nor show how to develop the proper questions, suffice for now: Did you notice that sometimes it was a 'hoody' and sometimes it was a "sweater"?

Did you also see the "chair" change to "recliner"?

Let's deal with these two changes primarily before the conclusion of the account.

In the "Chair" versus "Recliner", there isn't anything in the context that would cause it to change; therefore, the analyst should be on guard for deception.

But the hoody is different. Which is more desirable for a young person, a "hoody" or a "sweater"?

I am a grandfather and I wear a sweater.

The owner was young and the accused was young.

Did you notice that when the owner had it, it was only a "sweater", but when the staff person had it, it changed into the more 'cool' item of a "hoody."

The staff person was deeply embittered with Bob. He and Bob went to high school and he and Bob had similar grades, were cut ups, never-do-well class clowns, who barely graduated.

Bob, however, had an IQ just below the cut off level for "social services" and "disability" while the staff person had to now work, "supporting" or "waiting on" Bob, while Bob got a free apartment, internet, and enough money to buy a "monster hoody", while the staff person got minimum wage and could not afford an apartment. Seeing Bob have the nice and well fitting hoody was all too much.

He joined his father and uncle in their professional calling.

This may seem very small and insignificant to some, but to the small business owner, he knew police did not have the time nor resource to solve this case, but he also knew that the parent of the young male in his charge could have taken her son to another agency, costing them a major loss.

They were grateful to learn the truth.

Chapter Thirteen: Mid Size Business Theft

In small businesses, deception and theft can have a major impact on the bottom line. Just as "the little foxes spoil the vine", so it is that even in larger businesses, small thefts can add up. Such was the case of a friend who owned a chain of stores where small theft was common, incessant, and at the end of each fiscal year, ranged from $40,000 up to $80,000. These losses were in the form of cash, product and lottery tickets that were to be sold. A few years ago, I had this conversation with him about the losses.

I asked him how much money, on average, did he recover after reporting the thefts to the police.

"Recovered? Are you kidding?" (See how sensitive my question was to him, causing him to answer a question with a question?)

$40,000 to $80,000 is a lot of money. It could be someone's salary, college tuition, car, mortgage, and so on.

He was not bitter about police. He said that they did what they could, but usually just expressed gratitude that "no one was injured."

One winter day, I said to him, "The next time one of your stores is robbed, follow these directions: Do not talk to the employee other than to say, "Write down what happened, from the time you go to work until the time you went home."

I said, "If he asks you any questions, write down his questions for me, but politely decline. Whatever you do, do NOT influence his writing sample."

Then I instructed him to scan the statement and email it to me. If there are multiple employees during a theft, have them all write out the same statement.

He said, "What will you do?"

I said, "Let's save money goes missing and 7 employees had access to it, and one of the seven took it. I will analyze each of the statements and I will tell you who did it, what time he did it, and maybe even how he did it."

He was amazed and began to laugh, uncertain if I was having a bit of fun with him.

I was not.

A few weeks later, one of his employees was held up at gun point. He instructed the manager to do exactly as I said to do.

I received the statement, made a copy of it, and immediately went to work.

It does not matter if this is an email, a text, a statement about arson, robbery, rape, kidnapping, or a sales pitch: it is words and the words are designed to communicate. Where there is communication, if there is deception intended, the words will show themselves.

It took me only 4 or so hours and I called him back:

"There is no thief. He has the money."

He asked if I would be willing to share my analysis with the two investigating police officers. One blew me off, "oh yeah, nouns, verbs, I had that training. My partner is a word nerd, talk to him."

A "word nerd" is my kind of cop. Soft spoken, a good listener, this was going to work out just fine.

I carefully took him through the analysis and showed him how the description of the armed assailant was really the subject himself, and how I believed that if he was arrested, he would talk.

Well, he was arrested but he refused to talk!

This surprised me because of the analysis suggested that this was not the brightest criminal mind, but he seemed to have enough ego to be pushed into a confession. I told the officer that I believed the other worker mentioned in the statement is his girlfriend. He said, "no, I checked that already. They have to disclose personal relationships and they denied it. " I said, "pronouns don't lie, and although I don't think she knew about his scheme, she is his girlfriend. She is not a "person" to him.

He was released on bail and the officer returned to his apartment for a follow up interview. I had advised that follow up interviews are the best for confessions. There, the non-girlfriend co-worker just happened to be there, doing the smoochies, and offering her support.

I still was surprised that he did not give it up.

Weeks went by and his attorney called and asked if I was going to testify. I agreed to testify. Statement Analysis is not an "court witness" of sorts, but I can testify as to my opinion of the written statement, with the chance to explain why I believed it pointed to him.

After learning that the statement and the statement analyst would be in court, he decided to talk.

He pled guilty and was ordered to pay restitution.

Restitution!

This was music to the owner's ears!

Finally, someone was going to be responsible for stealing and not get away with it. I told him, "let this spread from employee to employee, and from store to store."

Next, we set up trainings for the Interview process so that as new workers are hired, the deceptive ones can be eliminated from contention.

The results came through in just a few years: Theft dropped every year, from the high of $80,000, down to just a recent $800 theft.

I was, however, angry at the $800 theft.

"How did she get through the interview process?", I asked.

"Oh, I was on vacation that week and there was no one here with the training when she was processed and hired…"

That wouldn't happen again, he assured me.

Batting 1.000 is a tall order, but whether your company is small, mid sized, or large, it should be your goal.

Statement Analysis, and the subsequent interview, "Analytical Interviewing" are the keys to success.

Chapter Fourteen: Fake Hate

This was a fascinating case.

Here, a young woman reports a horrific crime, and the nation responds to her televised appearance of 462 words in less than 5 minutes, with a tremendous outpouring of love and support.

From all over the country, people sent money to Charlie Rogers, the alleged victim of three violent attackers.

Schools held protests, candle light vigils, people got tattoos in honor of the victim, and an entire new civil rights movement was on the cusp of beginning.

In fact, as I reported earlier, not a single article, in a single news paper, news blog, or commentary, could we find anyone daring to question the veracity of the story.

Mayor So and So called for a special day of hating hate, and an array of well educated, intelligent people spoke loudly about condemning hate and supporting Ms. Rogers.

I watched the same broadcast that the rest watched and I said, "Uh, oh. She is not telling the truth."

Smarter people than me said she was.

What was the difference?

Training, practice, more practice, more training and more practice.

I liken a two day seminar to learning all the major chords of the guitar. In fact, you can learn, in just two days, all the chords of a guitar that a rock group might use, in its entirety, over the course of an entire concert.

You will know where your fingers go, and which strings to pluck, just as the rock and roll stars do.

The only difference?

You'll sound like nails across a blackboard.

Statement Analysis principles can be learned in 2 or 3 days. It is the application and practice, over the upcoming years, that makes the analyst.

This is why Statement Analysis Services offers one full year of follow up support, including updates, samples, and actually getting involved in cases to assist.

Yet, when you have at least one person in your company who has become adept at Analytical Interviewing, you are at a great advantage over your competitors.

Union negotiations? Need to find the other side's willingness to negotiate?

I work for attorneys who are bitterly contesting millions of dollars: they want to know: "Is the other side bluffing?"

Statement Analysis can give these answers.

Here, in this chapter on "Fake Hate", anyone with training would have said, "well, I think I will keep my donation, or give it to another cause, such as…Ben & Jerry's, I've been wanting some Cherry Garcia for quite some time now, and.."

No one wants to play the fool and give money to a huckster and Ms. Charlie Rogers was just that: a huckster.

I use her video tape in my training and it is an emotionally powerful exercise, where I tell her story and have the class write out all the painful words they expect to hear from a truthful victim.

Then, as they watch the video, I have them write down all the words that they hear.

Then, I turn on the lights and have them compare the lists.

It is a "wow!" moment for most everyone. It is something else.

I then say, "You have written out "the expected", that is, the words you expected a truthful, hurt, wounded victim to say, but you are now confronted with words that do not seem to fit the pain of the assault.

We then apply principle after principle until our conclusion suggests itself.

Deception indicated.

Interestingly enough, word by word, Charlie did not tell a lie. Each sentence is truthful. Lies are found within the withheld information.

A 33 year old female had reported a vicious attack by three masked men. Initially, state and federal law enforcement did not release the victim's name, as they reported it as a "hate crime" and wanted to protect her identity.

The subject willingly gave an interview to television to assert her account as truthful. In this appearance, she spoke for about 5 minutes.

Following this appearance, support came in from around the nation including candle light vigils, protests, and fund raising. Tattoos were sold in her honor.

On August 21, 2012, police arrested the subject for making a false report.

Familiarize yourself with the transcript of her statement and we will do the analysis as a large group exercise.

Follow the principles of analysis, noting any particular indicators of sensitivity.

Below is the transcript of the interview given by Ms. Rogers.

Charlie Rogers reported to police that she was the victim of an assault in which three masked men entered her home, assaulted her, tied her up, and carved slurs into her flesh. She reported that then they spray painted slurs in her basement, poured gasoline around the house, and lit it in fire, making this crime attempted murder. She reportedly escaped, ran naked to a neighbor's house, where she told the neighbor about the attack and called 911.

Analysis is in **bold** type. *Italics* and underlining are added for emphasis in the analysis.

In Analysis, we look for linguistic indicators of veracity, ranging from the most elementary ("*I told the truth*") to the more complex (use of sensory detail) in order to discern truth from deception.

Many people feel intuitively that someone is either truthful or deceptive. Each person, upon hearing (and watching) the televised appearance, makes a decision to believe the account, or to question it. With analysis, we are able to not only give an opinion, but are able to express the specific reasons why we believe the statement to be truthful or deceptive.

The horrific nature of the reported crime is one that has caught the nation's attention. Analysis dates back to the time of King Solomon and is based upon the very language that one uses, presupposing that someone is truthful and a truthful response or reaction is expected.

With this presupposition, we are then to move forward, from word to word, with an expectation of truth. If we are 'surprised' by what is not expected, we note this carefully, allowing the subject (speaker) to guide us along the way.

Eventually, the analyst will draw a conclusion: Truthful, Deceptive, or Inconclusive. Given the length of the sample here, an analyst should be able to rule out "Inconclusive" in the conclusion.

First we have the statement in its entirety, as aired by media, followed by its repetition with emphasis and analysis in **bold** type. In the color coding schematic of Scientific Content Analysis, blue is the highest on the sensitivity scale.

"Being a victim in a situation like this, or a survivor, um, and then having your, uh, integrity questioned I guess, it feels very victimizing again. It feels very, uh, saddening, uh, it makes an already difficult situation more difficult. Um. Because you know my world, has been changed forever by these events and and uh, so that the idea that that people think its a lie so, uh, it's hurtful.

It's understandable, I mean, intellectually, I understand that people sort of have a hard time wrapping their heads around the events that have happened as do I.

Um, but I'm a person, you know. With feelings, with concerns and just so uh, it feels like I don't know, like a punch in the stomach, kinda. Like a betrayal.
Instead of the focus being on safety and healing and the investigation the whole things turned into a defense and it starts to feel like, oh, you know like, you know it doesn't even become about the situation. It becomes something about all together different and then I started to feel like a pawn in a game. That isn't my game, you know. This isn't, you know, I didn't ask for this, I don't want this, and so you know the, I , whatever peoples intentions are or are not, um, it is important to me that they understand, for myself and future victims, hopefully there will be none but.

People are people. Agendas are agendas and I think that this is so important that we distinguish between those two things. Um. I was hurt. And, like what matters is the story. You know?
That's awful. It feels awful to me. This is an investigation. This is a crime. This is not, it deserves a level of respect. I know when these sorts of things happen, it, it ignites fires and that's a good thing, in some ways, um, it can also be a very bad thing. Um.

I'm not a pawn in a game, you know. I'm a person and it very much feels like I'm being used as a pawn. I want people to know I'm not afraid. I want other victims to know that it is important to come forward. I also wanted some control over what was happening in the media. Um. And I

though that the best way to do that was to do it myself. I want people to understand. Maybe you don't know me.
But you probably know somebody that something like this has happened to. So, for people to think that this doesn't happen here; it does. It did.

Everyone is worthy of safety, of justice and of fairness and I'm not hiding from this anymore. There is fear, but there is resilience, you know, there is, forward."

(end of statement)

I.   Presuppositional Expectations
II.   Line by Line Analysis
III.   Analysis Conclusion

The subject reported a horrific attack. We expect her to assert that she was attacked.
Since the attack was very violent, we have an expectation of sensory description. Victims of violent attacks often talk about things they sensed, through sight, smell, or touch. This is a signal that someone is entering into experiential memory and being truthful. Some examples include: "the smell of motor oil on his hands", "his breath smelled like beer", "his hands were cold..." or the feel of the knife used to cut, the sound of the gunshot, and so on. We all have a connection with the past through our senses which firms the events in our memory.

We expect rage at anyone who questions the account. When someone is the victim of an attack, there is no possible acceptance that it did not happen: it is too real, too painful, too close. Anyone who says otherwise will be met with a harsh reaction.

We expect to hear fear. The three attackers are on the loose, and even when someone wishes to conceal fear, it is evident.

Because she reportedly came forward and gave her name due to her veracity being challenged, we have an easy expectation that she will connect herself to the attack. This is done simply, without qualification, by the single most used word in the English language: "I." We expect to hear, "I was attacked" and "I told the truth." We would not expect her to not say these things, nor to qualify with "I think I told the truth..." or, "I think it happened," Both the absence and the qualification would be flagged for deception on such a plainly horrific violent attack. The statement here is in italics, as we break it down for signals of truth or deception. We seek to learn; Is memory playing? Does she speak from experiential memory?

We let the subject guide us.

People do not like to lie; therefore, they simply leave out information rather than directly lie and cause internal stress.

I. Presuppositional Expectations

The following is 464 Words.
Because this is not an account of the attack, we are unable to measure the statement on its form.

Of the 464 words, we now count commonly expected words in a violent crime situation

1. The word "attack" is used: 0 Times
2. The word "crime" is used: 1 Time
3. The word "truth" is used: 0 Times
4. The word "assault" is used: 0 Times
5. The word "danger" is used: 0 Times
6. The word "pain" is used: 0 Times
7. The word "cut" is used 0 Times
8. The word "violated" is used 0 Times
9. The word "blood", (in any form) 0 Times
10. The word "arrest" is used 0 Times
11. The word "violent" is used: 0 Times
12. The word "pain" 0 Times
13. The word "cruel" 0 Times
14. The word "hurt" is used 2 Times (emotional, not physical)
15. The word "pawn" is used 3 times.
16. The word "agenda" is used 2 times.
17. The word "people" is used 8 times.
18. The word "person" is used 2 times.

These are all terms expected in reporting such a violent, sadistic crime. Their absence is noted as is their frequency of use.

II. Line by Line Analysis

"Being a victim in a situation like this, or a survivor, um,

It should be noted that deception is often indicated in statements that begin without a pronoun.

Where a subject begins a statement is always important. Here, the statement does not begin with what happened, or an assertion that the subject has told the truth, but rather a classification:

"*Being a victim*" is then changed to "*survivor.*"

There is no pronoun connecting her to being either.

She does not tell us that she is a victim, nor does she say she is a survivor. This is why we listen, and do not interpret. We need a pronoun to connect her and it is absent. This is an example of <u>passivity</u> in language. Passivity is often used when concealing identity or responsibility. She does not tell us who is a victim nor who is a survivor.

We should also note that "*survivor*" is a status that is desirable. Since she is speaking for herself, this may be an attempt to portray herself as a "*survivor*" in a complimentary form, without making a direct statement. This should lead the analyst to question if the subject is making a truthful report, or is attempting to persuade. Since she does not connect herself to the crime, we cannot connect her to the crime. Because of this, the analyst should be on the outlook for language that distances the subject from the crime, but instead ties the subject to a motive for making a false report.

<u>Question for analyst</u>: Since the absence of words describing the crime is noted, and an attempt to portray the subject as a "survivor", is there other language that supports or refutes the notion of having another motive?

and then having <u>your</u>, uh, integrity questioned <u>I guess,</u> it feels very victimizing <u>again.</u>

Note that the subject distances herself from having her integrity questioned by using the pronoun "your" instead of "my integrity"; and weakens it even further by reducing this to a "guess."

The subject has not told us that her integrity was questioned.
In reading the online accounts of the attack, this analyst did not find a single article questioning the subject's integrity.
That she uses the second person "your" and reduces it (or its impact) to only a "guess", the reader should wonder if the subject, herself, has fabricated the notion of having her integrity questioned in public, especially since television is a public medium for her refutation.

Please note that the subject does not tell us who feels "victimized again", noting that the word "again" may indicate that if it is not her, than she was not "victimized" the first time.

When someone is deceptive, they wish to avoid the internal stress of lying so they withhold information instead, allowing the reader/listener to simply believe the subject is talking of herself. Later she can say she did not lie: she did not say she was a victim, nor was she victimized again. This is how deception is discerned.

Since she does not tell us she is being victimized "again", we cannot say it for her, but we can also conclude that if the "again" is deceptive, the original is also not about her, but is deceptive. <u>She cannot be victimized "again" if she wasn't victimized.</u> The distancing language of the use of the second person affirms this.

It feels very, uh, saddening,

Note the passivity. Previously I stated that passivity in language is used to conceal identity or responsibility. "*The gun went off*" is an example of passivity. It is truthful, the gun was fired, but it conceals the identity (and responsibility of the shooter).

Note that she speaks of emotions, not of physical pain from a horrific assault. Physical pain, especially from the up close and personal carving of flesh, is something we would expect to hear about, not emotions of sadness. We expect anger at such a terrible intrusion and invasion into her personal body.

We continue to note that she does not say that she is feeling sad, only "it" feels "saddening" (rather than "sad"). This distances her from "sad" twice; once by the absence of a pronoun linking her, and the other from being "sad" directly, as it is only "saddening", or that which causes sadness. This distancing language is noted for deception.

uh, it makes an already difficult situation more difficult.

Note that she reported a horrific attack, but here it is reduced to a *"situation."* We do not expect someone to call a vicious and violent attack a "*situation*." this is called soft language. Soft language is an indication that there is no linguistic connection to the assault.

Note that she does not say for whom an already difficult situation exists. If she cannot use a simple pronoun to connect herself, we cannot do it for her. Now, we find that she uses a first person pronoun:

Um. Because you know <u>my</u> world, has been changed forever by these <u>events</u> and and uh, <u>so</u> that the <u>idea</u> that that people think <u>its a lie</u> so, uh, it's <u>hurtful</u>.

Here she uses "my world", in the present, has been changed. By what? She says "these events", with "events" being plural. What events? The attack? The TV appearance?

1. Note that "event" is not a word linking to the "attack" as it is softening language.
2. Note that "events" is plural indicating other "events" have "changed" her world.
Now note what is so "*hurtful*": it is not the vicious attack with knives and gasoline, it is only the *"idea"* that *"people"* think. It is not even the questioning of her account which is

hurtful, it is only the "*idea*" of it. This distancing language indicates that the questioning of her account may not be real, but only an "idea"; which is buttressed by the fact that I have not found any news agency questioning her account.

Please note "*it's a lie*" may be an <u>embedded</u> admission. This is especially note worthy because we have not heard any interviewer say to her, "*people say it's a lie*", or, to match her language, "people have an idea that it may be a lie"; both of which would have been excused as entering into the language of another. Therefore, this appears to be an embedded admission of lying.

It's <u>understandable</u>, I mean, intellectually, <u>I understand</u> that people sort of have a hard time wrapping their heads around the events that have happened as do I.

Truthful people do not accept the possibility that they are lying, but when it comes to experiencing trauma, personal and violent, but when it comes to physical assault, there is no allowance for someone to question the veracity. Any questioning brings anger and biting words. This is similar to the report of violent crime: "the SOB stole my life!" and not "the gentleman caused me discomfort." Language must match reality. Here, the subject allows for others to not believe her. Her allowance is wise. Psychologically, liars sometimes do not want to be in the position of defending their lies; they do not wish to be linguistic adversaries, therefore, they "understand" or allow for doubt. When someone allows for doubt, it is wise to believe them.

The most important word in the English language is "I." It is used more than any other word, and it is a word that humans are perfect at using. They do not say "we" when they mean "I", as they know if they were alone, or were with others. Here, she finally ties herself, via the important pronoun, "I" to something, making it a very important sentence.

"*I understand...*" Since this is the first entrance of the word "I" into her statement, it is an important sentence and it is something she links herself to: understanding that she will not be believed.

She does not use the word "I" to tie herself to "attack"
She does not use the word "I" to tie herself to "truth."
She does use the word "I" to tie herself to disbelieving her story.

This is called allowing the subject to guide us.

Even she, herself ("") has trouble believing it. If it happened, why the trouble?

If the subject allows for even herself not to believe or "wrap her head around", while bearing the physical scars of a violent, sadistic attack, we should allow ourselves room not to believe it, either.

Um, but I'm a person, you know.

She declares herself to be a "person", which is gender neutral, instead of a "*woman*." We now have "*person"* introduced and will note its further use in the singular or plural form. We seek to learn how she identifies herself. She did not call herself a "victim" nor a "survivor" as the pronouns were absent. Here, the pronoun "I" is used. Why the need to declare that she is a "person"?

With feelings, with concerns and just so uh, it feels like I don't know, like a punch in the stomach, kinda. Like a betrayal.

"She is a "*person*" with feelings. This indicates that she may believe there are others without "feelings" and is a focus upon the emotional. She then describes her feelings like "a punch in the stomach". This is unusual since we learned that her stomach was reportedly carved with a knife, a terribly painful and humiliating experience. Yet, there is no mention of it, only a "punch" related to emotions and not a physical attack.

Instead of the focus being on safety and healing and the investigation the whole things turned into a defense and it starts to feel like, oh, you know like, you know it doesn't even become about the situation.

The subject introduces the word "focus" here and then tells us what the focus is not on:
1. safety
2. healing
3. investigation

1. Safety. There are 3 violent, sadistic, hateful men on the loose who "found" her (as reportedly written in her basement) of whom we would expect her to be in terror of.
2. Healing. By the time of this interview, the wounds are fresh.
3. The investigation is mentioned last.

Note "*starts to feel*" is emotions and not physical.

Note the word "situation." Why is it that she cannot bring herself to call it an "attack"? Why is it reduced to a "situation."? This is a linguistic disconnect and another signal that she is not linking herself to a violent crime.

In order for us to link her to the violent crime reported, she must tell us so.

If she cannot bring herself to link herself to a violent assault, we cannot do it for her.
If she cannot bring herself to say "I told the truth" while interviewing over her veracity, we are not allowed to do it for her.

It becomes something about all together different

"*It becomes*" is also passive language. Who made it become something? This is an indication of deception as she does not want to say who it is that is making it become something. When a deceptive person employs passive language to avoid being recognized or responsible, it is often the subject, herself, who is responsible but does not wish to be revealed. Without a pronoun, there is no strong statement made. Next, the pronoun reemerges:

and then I started to feel like a pawn in a game.

We always note when someone reports something as having begun, but not completed. She "*started*" to feel, which uses "*feel*", another emotion, instead of physical or sensory descriptions of the attack.

She introduces two important words to the reader:

"pawn" and "game."

A "pawn" is a small piece used in a larger scheme.
A "game" is not a word we would expect to hear over a vicious attack. She has introduced to the audience the notion that a "game" is being played out before them, and she is a part of the game. This is a strong disconnect from a violent crime.

That isn't my game, you know.

Analysis takes note of anything reported in the negative as highly important. Here, she tells us "this" isn't "my game." This affirms that it is a "game" but only that she does not want ownership of it. This is evidenced not only by the negative denial, but also by the word "that".

The word "this" indicates closeness; while the word "that" shows distance. "Please pass my that book. No, not that one, but this one..." showing closeness and distance. She denies that the game, of which she feels like a pawn, is hers, and uses the distancing word "that". With "that" there is a "this", just as with "this" there is a "that" in language. When someone says, *"I didn't do that"* the follow up question should be, *"What did you do?"* (Parents know this instinctively)

Since it was she who was physically attacked and it is she who is talking so that people will believe her, why is she employing distancing language? Why is it "that"? Why is she distancing herself from the report, linguistically?

This isn't, you know, I didn't ask for this, I don't want this, and so you know the, I, whatever peoples' intentions are or are not, um, it is important to me that they understand, for myself and future victims, hopefully there will be none but.

Here we have broken sentences, which indicate incomplete thoughts, or self censoring. She began with telling us what "*this*" is not, but then stops and tells us that she didn't "ask" for "*this*" and that she does not want "*this.*"
She then began her sentence with the strong pronoun, "I", but quickly changed to "*whatever peoples'...*"

She introduces "*pawn*", "game" and "*intentions*" into the statement. This is very important in understanding what it is she is doing.

By now, it is evident that she is not asserting that her police report was truthful.
She does not link herself, linguistically, with a violent crime.
She introduced "game" and "intentions" to the statement, telling us that something else is going on, and it is not about a physical, violent, sadistic and cruel assault.

We also take notice of "*people*" being used; the plural of "*person*" which was something that she called herself. The link is not lost upon us: intentions, game, pawn, are all related, just as "person" is related to "people."

Investigators should see to learn if she acted alone.

She then tells us what is important to her: it is not that the three assailants are caught before they return to finish what they started, but that people *"understand."*

In a truthful account, we expect to hear terror, physical descriptions, and harsh language of a harsh attack. We expect of upmost importance that the three attackers be caught so that she, and others, can be safe from such horror.

People are people. Agendas are agendas

She introduced the word "agenda", and repeated it, making "people" and "agenda" two things that are sensitive to her.

She does not speak of the attack, nor does she affirm truth, but speaks of agendas, games, pawns, understanding and feelings.

and I think that this is so important that we distinguish between those two things.

It is important that "we" distinguish between "those" (distance) two things: "people" (of which the single is "person") and "agendas", that is, a reason that someone has for another purpose, like a pawn being sacrificed tactically, in an overall strategy to fulfill an agenda (checkmate) in a chess "game."

Um. <u>I was</u> hurt.

The "um's" are added as spoken, as they show pauses, which indicate sensitivity or time to think. For some, it is a habit of speech. Habits of speech are noted for when they appear and when they do not appear. Here we have a strong statement:

"*I was hurt.*"

The problem for the analyst is that in a horrific attack as described, including attempted murder and mutilation, the words "*I was hurt*" are needless. In Analysis, whenever we have unnecessary words, or "unimportant" information, we deem it "doubly important" to the analysis being done. That she was hurt in such a brutal attack does not need to be said; in fact, simply saying "I was hurt" is an understatement. What caused her "hurt"? We follow the context for answers. Just prior to this sentence she spoke of being a pawn in a game that is not hers. This is emotional and not physical. We rely, then, upon the next sentences to help us understand what "hurt" she experienced:

And, like what matters is the <u>story</u>. You know? That's awful. It <u>feels</u> awful to me.

She does not make us wait long to find out: emotional. She now introduces another new word to her account. It is a word that truthful people who have experienced violence against them do not like to use; "story."

She introduced her audience to the themes of "games" and "agendas" and now tells us what matters.

What matters is not the three dangerous men on the loose, or who they may harm next. What matters is the "story."

This is a very strong indication that Ms. Rogers is telling a "story" as part of a "pawn" in a "game" because she has an "agenda."

The subject, Ms. Rogers, is leading us to understanding.

Note the emotional description of the hurt: "it feels."

This is an investigation.

Yes it is. It is now not only a local investigation, but a federal one, as well. If it is a hoax, it has just gone from misdemeanor status, to felony status in which she could face prison time like her university's professor who reported a fake hate crime as well. (Kerry Dunn case)

This is a crime.

This is also a truthful statement, as seen in its plain language. "This" is close and may refer to the false reporting.

This is not, it deserves a level of respect.

Note the call for "respect" and not for "fear" or for catching the three violent perpetrators who can get to her again. Instead, she begins with what this is "not", stops herself, (missing information) only to introduce a new word, "respect."

Why would the respect enter this? She has spoken of her feelings and now speaks of not only respect but a "level" of respect.

The broken sentence shows an incomplete thought. Here she tells us what "this" is "not", which shows the closeness of the word "this" and the importance of the "negative"; which she then self-censors. What she was about to say is important and would be learned in a follow up interview.

"This is not a hoax" If this is a direct lie, it would be difficult for her to complete the sentence. It is very difficult to make a direct statement against reality. Recently, a subject yelled at me, *"I didn't do..."* and stopped. I did not respond but just listened and took notes. In the entire lengthy interview, the subject was unable to put together a complete simple sentence of "*I didn't do it*" in spite of many opportunities.

A brutal and horrific attack does not need to be said to need "*respect*" as it either happened or it did not happen, as reported, regardless of sexuality. It needs to be investigated and prosecuted. The level of brutality described, including the attempt to burn down the house, is attempted murder. Yet, she wants "*a level of respect.*" This is an indication that she is not speaking of the crime, but of her story. (Note: At this point in the analysis, my emotions are engaged. It is something I needed to be aware of: I feel sorrow for the subject who seems to crave respect and relevancy. It is important for an analyst to gauge emotions.)

For the subject, the vicious attack deserves only a "*level*" of respect: why the need to qualify "respect" by level? That "this" only deserves a "level" of respect brings doubt upon her story. She allows for understanding of doubters and instead of being scarred from the assault "demanding" justice, she speaks of a "level of respect".

This is a strong indication that she feels in life, that she is not being given a "*level of respect*" and it is likely attached to her advocacy. These are indications of motive.

Should her story prove to be a story and a hoax, people will speak of her mental health and excuse her behavior, yet here she may be signaling her intentions, which she understands and is purposeful. If it is a hoax, she is not "insane"; in that she does not understand what she is attempting to do with regard to her advocacy.

I know when these sorts of things happen, it, it ignites fires and that's a good thing, in some ways, um, it can also be a very bad thing. Um.

What are "these" short of things? Breaking into a home and carving someone's flesh? Please note that "these sorts of things" are rare. Carving into flesh? When was the last time we heard of assailants carving slurs into someone's flesh? To reduce it to commonality is a red flag for deceptive hoax.

Note the reference to igniting fire. Did she ignite her own fire, which, in spite of three men with gasoline, did minimal damage to the home?

If she started the fire, it makes sense that it would enter her language.

This shows an attempt to portray this horrific crime as common. It is not. This is very unusual because it downgrades the special status of such a unique victimization and seeks to "share" common ground with others. When did we last hear of someone being brutally attacked and have slurs carved into the skin?

Note that igniting a fire, in "some" ways is a "good thing" but it also can be a "bad" thing, with "good" qualified by "some ways" but "bad" having no qualification. The "bad" here, in her statement, is stronger than "good."

I'm not a pawn in a game, you know. I'm a person and it very much feels like I'm being used as a pawn.

What we hear in the negative is always important. Many times someone says "this is not personal" and you learn: it was personal.
"It's not about the money" is often exactly about money.

Here, she may be signaling that she is playing a "game."

I want people to know I'm not afraid.

With three violent men, who hunted her down and attempted to kill her, on the loose, she wants people to know she is not afraid. This appears to be an attempt to portray herself in the role of "survivor", that is, favorably, rather than report truth. This is status, including "heroine" status she attempts to bestow upon herself, and must be weighed in correlation to people, or a person, having an agenda.

I want other victims to know that it is important to come forward.

She assumes that others who have been attacked, tied down, carved into their flesh and house burned would not come forward. This shows no connection to the reality of what she reported.

I also wanted some control over what was happening in the media.

"Control" and "media" are linked together. This should be understood with the introduction of the word "agenda."

Um. And I thought that the best way to do that was to do it myself.

This is another linguistic indication that the subject may not have acted alone. She "thought" it best may be because someone else thought otherwise and indicates that even in coming to do the televised interview, there may have been some debate.

I want people to understand. Maybe you don't know me.

Here is a perfect place to say that she told the truth. Instead she wants people to "understand" and she recognizes that people do not "know" her. This links "understanding" to "knowing" her. This is very personal. She wants understanding and it is likely that she has felt very misunderstood in her agenda and this may explain what she is doing.

But you probably know somebody that something like this has happened to. So, for people to think that this doesn't happen here; it does. It did.

This sentence may be embarrassing to her as she tells the audience that they may know someone of whom "something like this has happened."

Do you know someone who had his or her flesh carved with slurs?
Do you know someone who had 3 men break in and attempt to burn someone to death in their house?

This shows a disconnect from reality. She did not report a common hate crime of any sorts, but went very far into sadistic details along with reportedly slurs spray painted in her basement. "*We found you ******" as if she was being hunted down.

This is terrorizing and could paralyze someone with fear. No one would be safe until the three monsters are found, yet...she speaks of her feelings, respect, games, and agendas. She does not, even once, reference the horrible nature of the attack.

Everyone is worthy of safety, of justice and of fairness and I'm not hiding from this anymore. There is fear, but there is resilience, you know, there is, forward."

"*Everyone*" is a word related to "*person*" bringing focus, not upon the attack, nor even upon attackers at large, but upon Charlie Rogers, herself. We look at all references to persons within a statement, in all analysis, even in a short interview like this.

"*Victim*" or "*survivor*" appears to be attempt to portray herself in media terms that is favorable to subject.

"*There is fear*" is passive. This is not expected in such a personal vicious attack. Passivity suggests concealment. What is the fear? Who is afraid? What is she afraid of? Being caught and found out as a liar? In a vicious attack, we expect one to be

She was interviewed because she has been accused of lying. This makes the question, "Are you lying?" the non spoken question. It is simple to answer:

"*I did not lie. I was attacked by three masked men.*" She did not say so.

If she cannot bring herself to assert herself as having told the truth, we cannot be expected to do it for her. This is a rule in analysis.

III Analysis Conclusion

Based upon this interview, void of any and all physical evidence:

There is nothing within this short interview that shows that Charlie Rogers is telling the truth about the assault. Not even Rogers, herself, affirms it to be true.

We expect her to say she told the truth but she did not. If this really happened to her, why doesn't she make a simple assertion to say so?

This is indicative of a hoax that she, along with her agenda, has perpetrated upon the public. The public has responded with overwhelming support, rallies, politicians and the raising of money. The subject has a lawyer now, and will likely need one.

Ms. Rogers is deceptive about being the victim and survivor of a horrific attack.

She will likely face charges of lying to law enforcement, locally and federally.

Part Two: After the video was released, a friend of Ms. Rogers spoke to a media outlet, who agreed not to use her name.

Question for Analyst: *Did Charlie Rogers act alone?*

We know that her story was a hoax. What we do not know is if she acted alone, or with someone else.

Were the carvings self inflicted, or did someone help her perpetrate this hoax?

A woman who would only say she is a *"friend"* of Charlie Rogers spoke to a media outlet and described the wound on the stomach. Before we look at the quote from her friend, , we do what we always do with Analysis: Review the expected.

What would you expect to hear from a friend who has just witnessed the horrific carving up of her flesh in order to communicate something so vicious as this?

How would **you** describe such a wound on a friend or loved one?

What words would you use? Angry words? Words that contain forensic descriptions? Words such as "blood, cuts, deep, harsh, painful"? Imagine she is **your** friend and you saw this gruesome barbaric cruelty perpetrated against someone you care about. What words would you choose? We expect anger, disgust, and repulsion, as carving into a friend's flesh is abhorrent and shocking.

Her friend said this about the mutilation of her flesh:

"things carved <u>on</u> her <u>body</u> that can <u>only</u> be described as hate, that <u>somebody</u> can only be taught and <u>we</u> need to stop teaching it."

1. Notice the word "things" is the noun here. It is not that she was cut into, the noun shows us the topic is not the carving into the flesh, but what it was that was cut "on" the flesh which is the topic of interest for the friend. This means that the injury is not of interest, but the message. This is not what is expected. We now see if the rest of the statement agrees with the noun, or does she talk about the brutal attack and barbaric carving, or is it the "things" or messages, that is the friend's focus:

2. Notice the "*things*" carved "*on*" her body. This should lead investigators to learn how deeply cut Rogers actually was. This is an indication that the cuts were not deep "in" the flesh, but were more likely surface cuts "on" the flesh.

I noticed that as I wrote here, I felt the repulsion of such an act, and I have written carved on her "flesh" but in looking at the subject's statement, she uses the more distant word "body" instead of the more detailed "flesh" which I used. This suggests that I, and readership, are more horrified at the thought of this crime than the "friend" of Rogers.

They can "only" be described as "hate"; which causes us to ask, "What limits the subject from describing it other ways? Size? Scarring? Blood shed? No description is given, which is distancing language.

3. Note "somebody" is singular. Rogers reported that it was "3 masked men" who attacked her, but here, the friend instinctively calls the perpetrators "somebody."

a. Does she have knowledge that only one person did it?
b. If only one cut her with a knife, but the other 2 encouraged or did not stop him, it would be that "they" did this.

This "friend" should be investigated as having participated in the hoax in order to get the message of "teaching" hate out to the public.

The friend gave no forensic descriptions of the wounds, instead used it as a platform of the message, echoing Rogers' own words about being a "pawn" in a "game" played by more than one piece ("pawn").

4. That she uses the word "*we*" when it comes to "teaching" suggests that the friend is part of the hoax and likely wishes to be part of the fame in gaining a platform for her and Charlie Rogers' agenda. The pronoun "we" shows unity and cooperation.

That Charlie Rogers did not act alone may come from indications from her own words, but this "friend" appears to have knowledge of the wounds, themselves, yet uses no language to indicate the brutal attack, nor anger towards the attacker (s) whom she identifies in the singular.

Police should seek to learn if Charlie Rogers was assisted by this friend in perpetrating the false hate crime hoax which has stirred the passions of many, and now is soliciting donations.

Question for analyst: Did Charlie Rogers act alone?

Answer: It is likely that Charlie Rogers did not act alone and that this friend may be the one who carved "on" her flesh.

Update: the police affidavit reported the following:

a. No blood stains on the bed where she said the attack took place
b. Location of the store where the knife and gloves and ties were purchased
c. Ms. Rogers denied ownership of the gloves. Police found her DNA inside of them as well as the DNA of another person: female DNA
d. FBI forensic medical doctor said the wounds appears self inflicted, except some appear "passively" inflicted, perhaps by another, and they are superficial and avoid sensitive parts of the body.
e. Ms. Rogers wrote on Face Book, a week before the report that she would be watched and would change the world.
f. Inconsistencies from Ms. Rogers' statements.
g. Implausibility of various aspects of her report.

We also learned that her original attorney did not release funding for her, but withheld the money until the police completed their investigation. She has a new attorney for the criminal charges.

2013 update: Ms. Rogers pleaded guilty to various charges including filing a false report.

Chapter Fifteen: Coping With Deception

What is your area of hurt?

Where was it that deception caused you the most pain?

Were you part of the housing scandal who lost your home and your credit but got a check for 34 bucks? If so, the bitterness can linger for a long time.

Or, was it much worse?

Was it the man you entrusted your precious child to….

Or that man of whom you, yourself, blamed the ex wife. (I always tell women to find a way to interview his ex wife, especially if you have children. Let her tell you every ugly piece of information possible and when she is exhausted and you have listened carefully, and can ask yourself, "Do I still trust him?", you might just be okay.

Maybe you are just a parent who would like to know if your teenager is lying to you. Caution: you may not like learning the truth!

Some of you will take the training and take the practice very seriously and when I warn you, "Do not practice on your friends and relatives, for you will lose them", you will practice on them anyway.

It's rather hard not to.

Or, like me at Sam's Club, with Christina when she was just a little girl, and I said, "Ma'am, is that the only membership you sell? It's expensive!" where she said, "Yes, that is the only membership we sell" immediately covering her mouth with her hand, provoking me to look closer at her and say, "you just lied to me!"

Christina said, "Dad!" as if to rebuke me.

Undaunted, I said, "Look at your hand over your mouth!"

The poor woman almost burst into tears and said, "I'm sorry but my manger is pushing these and you can join for much less and I am sorry…"

I said, "It's okay. You made a mistake. "

Afterwards, Christina, an accomplished lie catcher at age 7 said, "Dad, you always say it is impolite to point out lies in public!"

She was right.

I could get my nose tweaked by doing that.

Another time Christina rebuked me is when we were looking at German Shepherd puppies. The parents of the pups were in kennels in the front yard, while the pups were in kennels in the back yard.

Christina and I noticed that the sire seemed a bit…um, just a bit skittish, not at all like the strong, well bred German imports.

The man said, "$10,000 to sail him to America."

Christina and I exchanged glances. By now, she was an old salt of 11 years old. Two tings bothered her, the first being the obvious "sail" instead of "fly"? But it was the second indicator of deception that I was proud of her for catching: the passivity.

He did not say "I spent $10,000 on this dog…"

So, we had a little fun with him.

We quickly went back to the backyard, where Heather and Sean were playing with the puppies and loudly said to the man's wife, "Wow! $10,000 for the pup's father!"

The man was just walking up behind us, a few paces slow.

She said, "$10,000 for what dog? Who's talking crazy?"

Christina started to suppress her giggle, but was rapidly failing.

"Why, it cost us $10,000 to sail him here from Germany!" the man boasted.

Caught, the wife said, "Uh, dear, he flew here, and it was for less than half that."

Satisfied that we were not going to be buying from a liar, puppies from a skittish male, we all smiled until he looked right at us. "I won't be selling any of my puppies to you!" he said, slamming the door.

He should not have seen us smugly chuckling.

I hate being lied to, but I was not there to "show him up" and although he was the deceptive one, it was not good manners to have gloated over his embarrassment over being caught in a lie, and having a wife who refused to go along with it. I felt badly for the wife.

A few days later, she called me. "Are you still interested? You seemed like a nice family and I am sorry for the way he acted."

Because the father was skittish and because of the lie, I did not want to buy from them, though it might have been that the father was skittish because he had been locked in his kennel so much, but still, I just did not want to take a chance.

CK Dexter Haven is now grateful that we waited until we found an honest breeder in Massachusets.

How did we know she was honest?

We knew by listening.

In fact, I asked her what she thought of the "all natural diet for working dogs" to which she extolled its virtues, longer lives, better health, teeth, coat, less vet bills, and so on.

Christina politely asked her, "How come you don't feed it to your dogs?"

Without pausing, she said, "Because I can't afford it. I have too many dogs, so I buy premium dog food, but I wish I could put them all on the all natural."

Rarely have I met a more honest breeder We bought Dex from her. Her short sentences and blunt truth comforted my pronoun-weary soul.

Every day presents itself as a day where someone will deceive someone else. The young man will ill intentions towards your daughter...

The sales pitch who wishes to accomplish nothing but separate you from your dollar...

The pick up line...

And, of course, the potential for loaning the Nigerian Prince a few bucks in US currency, in return for millions of dollars and multiple wives...well, I will let that run itself out for George Anthony.

Recently, ads have been popping up with rare dog breeds:

"My precious little Coton De Tulear (with gorgeous picture) is in need of adoption. I am going to Kenya, on a mission field to help feed and educate the starving Kenyans. Would you adopt my little Fee Fee? Of course, there is no fee to it, but it does cost me $500 to ship him to you, including the crate and the vet certificate Here is his picture. Please send me $500, with your name, address and phone number and nearest airport. Within 48 hours, I will contact you with the flight information and where you pick him up. I know you will give Fee Fee a wonderful home for the rest of his life."

I wondered how many fell for that one. The same man had 16 different tiny breeds up for adoption, with 16 different African countries to minister to.

Bigger penis? Whiter Teeth? Hmmm, what should I do? Some of these border on the absurd, but consider this: someone must be buying the snake oil, otherwise, they would not be able to pay for air time!

What about doctors?

Doctors need lie detetion training, to best serve their patients.

I have longed to visit a skilled therapist who could unwind the self-deceived, long buried memories from childhood, who, trained in Statement Analsysis, could give me that joy that onl comes when you see that a life worth living is a life worth analyzing! Those $700 per hour Harvard Therapists with their Statement Analysis training!

Lawyers benefit from the training, especially those who go 10 rounds against other attorneys and do not like to lose.

Statement Analysis (and Analytical interviewing) should be used in jury selection, weeding out the narcissist and the ones primed for self gain and self glory, over the cost of justice.

Heck, even the junior high principal who has lost most of his hair from stress and chewing antacids all day would find life's medicine would go down a bit easier with a spoon full of sugar, known as Statement Analysis.

In fact, I cannot think of a vocation where some form of lie detection would not be beneficial.

Toll Booth operator, maybe?

Chapter Sixteen: The Emotional Cost of Lying

Do you remember the tale of the knight who had gone through the land, wounded the reputation of a fair maiden, and had gone to the Queen's court, there, to await sentence, having humbled a maid but not married her he was to lose his head. (tough town).

While in the court of the Queen, many courtiers in attendance took to liking this young knight, even to the point of excusing his misdoing and eventually, they sought for a way for the queen to set him free.

Even the Queen felt the knight's character had within it elements worthy of redemption. She came up with a riddle. Solve the riddle and return with the answer within 1 year, and you shall live. If you are, after one year, unable to solve the riddle, you will surely lose your head.

The riddle is this: *"What is it that every woman wants more than anything else in the world?"*

This sounded good to the knight who said to himself, "Piece of cake!" or something similar in Olde Englishe . This will not be difficult.

He set out on his journeys throughout the kingdom, searching far and wide for the answer. Weeks turned into months, but to no avail. No one knew the answer. Not old men, young men, old women, or young women. No one knew the answer to the question, What do women really want?"

Finally, with head hung low (picture dejected Charlie Brown walking away from the dead Christmas tree and the sad music playing), he walked up to the Queen's gate to enter in, thereof, and face the punishment.

Suddenly, an old, and very ugly woman appeared before him.

"I can solve the riddle" she said. "I will give you the answer."

He said, "Pray tell me, olde loathesome to my eyes woman, what sayest thou?"

The hideously old woman said, "Every woman wants to be in charge. She wants to rule over her husband. She wants to be the boss."

Instantly the fair knight knew that the hideously and scarily ugly creature known as the olde woman was correct. He burst into the court to which all cried out, "Have ye got it? Hae ye got it, young dude?"

He answered and said, "What every woman, everywhere in existence, for all of time, is to be lord over her husband. "

At first a silence fell upon the beautiful courtiers, as they searched the queen's face for a hint of direction and approval, when suddenly, the Queen's beautifully toothy smile burst open and she cried "Yes, Yes! Yes, o noble knight! You have answered wisely!"

With great celebration and a small apology to Geoffrey Chaucer, the newly nobled Knight took to his gorgeous steed, ready to ride off and meet a beautiful wife to call his own.

"Wait, wait, wait just a minute, " the old lady whispered. "What about me?"

The knight said, "You saved my life but are loathesome to me to look at you."

"Yes" she said, it is true. But I will give you a choice. Listen carefully and choose wisely.

You can have me one of two ways, to be your wife.

One: You can have me now. Old, loathesome, wrinkled and hard to look at, yet I will love you faithfully, comfort you each night, cook for you, and be good and kind to you, all the days of my life. I will never even look at another man, but will love you faithfully, even though my appearance is poor, yet I will never even think of another man.

Or, you have a second choice.

You can have me young and beautiful to look upon. Maybe I will love you, but maybe you will be cuckolded by another man's child. There is no greater pain for a man that that, but you choose. You know that with my eternal beauty, you will still age, but I will not. Will I be able to resist other suitors, younger and stronger than yourself?

Choose which you wish to marry.

The brave knight, having once humbled a maid, and made no recompense for his crime, yet had his life spared, and did, in so many ways, wish to be a noble knight, and do that which is right, had come to the place in life where confusion reigned over his heart.

"It is, old scary loathesome lady, too much for me to choose. Therefore, Let me fall into your hand and you choose which I shall have!"

At this, the ugly old woman's eyes suddenly became bright blue, from a distinctly old, gray matter of death, and a smile came across her mouth, not one of cracked and yellowed teeth, but of beauty. She began to stand aright, no longer hunched over, unable to tell if she was wearing stockings that needed to be pulled up, or none at all.

"You have chosen wisely and have let woman have the dominion over you, just as I taught you, and you now shall have:

Me, young, beautiful, stunning, but also loyal, faithful, to love only you, to deliver to you only your progeny, and to dream of only you.

You get me both ways; utterly devoted and beautiful.

And that is precisely what she turned into. The beauty that was within her, flooded from her heart, into her bones, skin, hair and eyes. She became a thing of breathtaking beauty, inside and out, lifting the knight's heart so high, he thought it would explode from the inability to bear such joy and happiness.

He gave her what every woman wanted: control.

Sadly, we aren't faced withs such riddles in life, and there are no guarantees, but we do push back aginst the odds in our favor when we can discern truth from deception.

"Bring me a sword. Cut the baby in half. Give one to her and give the other half to her. Then, bring my a peanut butter and jelly sandwich, for the King hungers for lunch.

Hardly.

King Solomon repeated back each woman's argument naming each baby deliberately first showing who the mother was This was done before the calling of the sword. Lie Detection helped Solomon; lie detection is invaluable for us today.

There are those who are offering trainings today and can avail themselves to help you, your family, your police department, your profession, and your business in learning how to survive and cope with deception.

Deception is everywhere. There are no ancient queens waiting to deliver us life sparing information on the internet, but there is, however, a great army of legions of deceivers waiting to pounce on any weakness we might show.

Be armed.

Be prepared.

Let your communication be known as strong and that "your yeah means yea, and your nay means nay" so there is no ambiguiouity. Be a person of your word.

Be prepared, in the training, to be confronted with some personal issues about yourself that you might wish were different.

I did.

I found myself telling polite lies, right up from childhood. "Golly Gee, Auntie Polly, your blue hair looks great!" This may sound funnny, but it is not true. In fact, it is wrong. Children need to be taught that lying is wrong, and has condquences. Yes, it is hard to teadh tht lying is wrong in our political liamte, but it must be done. It must.

The emotional toll is just too much.

Chapter Seventeen: The Insult of Being Lied To

"Sticks and Stones may break my bones, but names will never hurt me."

That's a lie.

It is not just that one must presuppose you to be of lesser intellect in order to "put one over you", there is also the insult of the negative; a lie travels around the world while the truth is barely getting dressed in the morning.

Once scarred with a lie, the insult can continue.

A reputation can be tarnished for a lifetime by a false accusation. It can impact future employment, and the smaller the town, the greater the impact can be.

The following story illustrates this very point. It not only shows how difficult it can be to shake a lie, but highlights just how the love of money, that is, the ability to shower oneself with the things money can buy, is tantamount to pouring gasoline on fire; the liar is fueled by self, therefore, money can be an explosive motivation.

New York Met fans have long lined the pockets of therapists with their tales of annual woe. The Met owners invested with Bernie Madoff, the infamous fallen Wall Streeter who's hedge fund gymnastics took away the pensions and investments of many, all with the promise of higher returns. The Wilpon family, principle owners of the Mets, have been unable to pay for quality product on the field ever since the money was lost. The name, "Madoff" is now akin to being ripped off, and has turned into a verb, in some circles, such as being "madoffed by that firm!" Big deception, big loss, lots of impact.

Yet, what of it to the common man, that some multimillionaires have to sell off one of their luxury toys? It's in the news, and it has happened to someone else, and it seems all to far-fetched to matter.

Unless, of course, it was your personal retirement account that is not only gone, but will not be replaced.

But what of small town America.

I was knew a man of whom I will call "John Smith."

John struggled in school, never quite able to keep up, and at a young age, enjoyed the feeling of working in the potato fields of northern Maine.

For this culture, school was out and all the kids did it.

Behind in math and science, John flourished working with his hands, delighting in outworking the same kids who, days earlier, had teased him about his grades. In the school classroom, he was at the bottom, but in the potato field, he was not only efficient, but was given 'charge' over some of the other kids, due to his efficiency and serious competitive drive.

But the future did not hold treasures for the young John, in potatoes, as he soon learned. Unable to complete his high school requirements, he drifted from meager job to meager job, always on the edge of survival, part government assistance, part hard work until finally, an opening came at a mill, a mill in which real wages were paid and a real product, paper, was made.

John found his place in life, out-producing others in the mill, and soon met his wife there, also a mill worker, though no where near as proficient as John.

John was proud of his production, but not much of a talker, so a supervisor or manager position was not in the cards. He was, however, content with his wages, and with the feeling of having done a good job.

As is the course of life, kids followed and the family struggled to make ends meet. Embarrassed by food stamps, yet unable to, with his shift work, get a second job, John took any overtime available to him. In spite of best intentions, the mill found itself competing with much cheaper foreign labor, and was pushed into layoffs.

John, in spite of his production, had less years in the mill than his wife, so he received the layoff, rather than her.

The small family, already under financial stress, began to splinter.

John, always used to working hard, now found himself depressed, anxious about bills, and drinking.

As you can imagine, the story now takes a turn for the worst.

John, not feeling like a man, fell deeper into depression, greasing his downward spiral with cheap liquor, so much so, that he was adding it to his coffee in the morning. He went days without showering, and could not look his now teenaged sons in the eyes.

His wife eventually became romantically involved with an older man, at the mill, and moved out on John, leaving him to wallow in his alcohol-fueled misery.

Eventually, John was given disability and had enough government assistance to have a small apartment and a few items of his own, like a television and lap top, which was his connection to the outside world.

The one thing he did not have, however, was his dignity.

Drinking day and night, alone, and not knowing if his own sons had even graduated high school, he reached the endgame. He either was going to end his miserable existence, or give up alcohol and find work. He knew that finding work would nullify his government benefits, particularly since it would prove him capable of work.

He carefully contemplated the future. He could end his pain and suffering now, with a gunshot to the head, and saddle his sons with this horrible legacy for the rest of their lives, or…or he could look at life as if he had nothing left to lose, and give it one more shot.

He humbled himself and went to a fast food restaurant; the only one in town; in fact, the only one within miles, and applied for work.

It was humiliating working next to 16 year old kids who all talked of football games, proms and exciting futures.

He also ached for alcohol.

He gave thought to "one of those meetings" but was concerned with the small town stigma. Instead, he "took matters into his own hands" and in spite of all sorts of medical advice, he said he "weaned myself off, little at a time" and used the only thing he knew how to use, since boyhood, to get through the darkness: hard work.

He volunteered for every over time shift that they could offer. He offered to trade with kids who wanted Saturday off for the big game, or Friday nights off to go out on dates, and volunteered for all holidays and odd hours, anything to keep himself busy.

The hard work began to pay off. He found himself giving himself a home-made hair cut, and began to actually go for walks, rather than sit in front of the TV, where he longed for beer. There were not many workers his age to socialize with, but little by little, he began to make friends, and even accepted an invitation to a barbecue; the first one he had been to in almost a decade.

Now in his forties, John felt that his life had meaning again, and although he was not good at speaking, his talent to take everyone else's shifts did not go unnoticed by management, and they promoted him to manager, since the manager's most pressing challenge was filling shifts by kids who were constantly calling out of work. His productivity was so high that even when he could not find someone to cover a shift, he, himself, could do the work in two stations, covering, for example, French fries, even while taking customer orders.

The regulars liked him, as he was always proud of keeping the place at its cleanest, often coming out with a mop into the dining area, chatting a bit awkwardly with customers, making sure they were comfortable.

He was most proud of what he called his "uniform"; a short sleeved shirt and tie. What others had made fun of, he wore as a badge of honor.

He moved to a nicer apartment and his confidence in life was not lost on his bearing. When his sons saw that "dad has become something", they felt, for the first time in their lives, proud of him.

He enjoyed the status of "father", even loaning his sons a few dollars for a date, or gas money.

Even as his new walk and health was evident to his sons, it was also evident to the pretty, and a bit younger, mother who lived next door with her 13 year old daughter.

Since he walked every night, he was noticed by the next door mom, we will call "Mary", who, herself, was in financial straits, constantly behind in the rent, and always facing the risk of being evicted from her home.

Besides this, her 13 year old daughter liked spending time with John, often joining him for a football game on television, where they shared a common interest in not only football, but of oe of John's sons.

Although John's son was much older than the 13 year old, she had stars in her eyes over the handsome young man, who viewed the young girl as just that, a little girl.

She, however, had different ideas.

She grew up too fast, as some in depressed small towns do, and had been removed from her father's care by the child protective services, and placed with her mother, who, herself, was always on the protective service's radar. She had often left her little girl home alone, had run ins with the local school administrators for truancy, and was, in the words of her teacher, "too advanced for her 13 years."

John did not see this coming.

The young girl not only showed up each time John's son was there, but soon took to John as a father figure.

Several incidents conspired together for the perfect storm in John's life.

John often gave a fatherly hug to the little girl, whenever she cried that she was overweight, or that John's son did not seem to notice that she even existed.

Mary, on the other hand, was glad to have her daughter elsewhere, while she entertained men in her home.

Mary still had quite a figure, which was not unnoticed by John.

One night, Mary's daughter was having another one of her crying episodes, "I'm fat, no man will ever want me, no one likes me…" and so on. John assured her that she was "pretty" and that at her age, she did not need to think about boys. As she was leaving, Mary saw the hug that John gave her daughter and sought one for herself.

In her hands were a bag of chips and a six pack of beer. She was dressed in tight jeans and a t shirt, intending to get John's attention.

Lonely and glad for female attention, they took to the couch and the beer began to have its desired effect.

Mary told John that she was now three months behind in the rent and would be moving soon. "It's a shame I am moving, just as you and I are getting to know each other."

John could not resist.

"Mary, I have a few dollars saved up. It is not much, but it is enough to get you caught up on your rent, and we could work out a way for you to pay me back."

Mary said, "No, I couldn't do that. My social security check is two months late, and I am expecting a child support back check due in any day, but still, I couldn't do that."

John bought the lie. "Oh, I could loan you the money and you could pay me in two payments, the first with the social security check and the second with the child support check. It's perfect. Now you don't have to move. "

After 'resisting' John's generous offer through the night, John finally asked her, "Would you like to go out to dinner with me next week?"

Mary said, "Oh, that would be wonderful! I have not been taken out to dinner by a gentleman in years!" (this was true. She had been taken out to dinner regularly, but not by a gentleman).

"But wait", Mary said. "I won't be here! I was having such a good time tonight I almost forgot about it. You have that affect on woman, I guess."

As you now know, the next morning John's check was cashed, his small savings gone and Mary had to "postpone" the date, as she wasn't feeling well.

John noted that Mary was not only avoiding him, but so was her daughter, who didn't even stop in with her homework, as was her habit.

As the weeks passed, John struggling now with loneliness, the taste of beer, and of his depleted account, decided to take action.

He knocked on Mary's door and said, "It's time to pay back the loan." He said this in a way that made Mary instinctively know that she had over played her hand, and put him off too long. The romance she hoped to use, had slipped from John's mind, and resentment had taken its place. Still, she gave it her best try.

"Oh, John!" she said, putting her arms around him. "I thought that something may have happened to you. You haven't come to see me!"

John had not ever come to "see her" before, she had always come to his home.

It did not work.

"Mary, I need that money. My son is trying to buy his first car."

"Oh, okay, John. I'm sorry. The checks did arrive and I deposited them 3 days ago and am waiting for them to clear, that's all. I'll have your money."

"I'll have your money" sounded prophetic.

Mary told John that in a few days she would come over with the cash in full.

Two days later, a knock came on the door.

Thinking it was Mary, John was relieved to think that he could now be the "hero" to his son, and loan him some money for "that first car" that his son would own. He had worked hard to rebuild the broken relationship with his boys, and this was a great opportunity.

Instead of it being Mary, it was two well dressed women, with brief cases, asking if they could enter his home.

"Of course", said John. "What is this about?"

They introduced themselves as child welfare workers and instead of stating the purpose of the visit, they asked John, "Do you know why we are here?"

He could not think of an answer. His sons lived with their mother, and things have been peaceful the last few years, since he regularly paid child support.

When he was unable to answer, a darkness settled over him like a shocking jolt of electricity.

"Do you know a girl named…? She is "Mary's daughter…"

He had been played.

Mary's daughter has now accused John of child molestation.

It was a lie.

He was now at the mercy of a 13 year old girl who knows how to cry on cue.

Let's stop the story at this point and ask, "What is at stake here? What consequences may arise from this investigation?"

John could be arrested.

John could lose his job.

John could lose his reputation.

John could be incarcerated.

John could face the wrath of inmates as a pedophile.

John's world felt like it was caving in on him, from every angle.

The child protective workers were divided in their opinion of the 13 year old's testimony.

One of the workers was trained in Statement Analysis.

She had the following done:

The child wrote out a statement of the night in question, in which she accused John of sexual molestation.

Mary was to write out a statement about what the child told her, in detail, separate from the child.

John was to write out a statement, first, of the night specifically named in the allegation. Then, due to suspicion that something else was in play, the trained social worker had John write out a statement about his relationship with the child, and his relationship with Mary.

Next, the social worker interviewed:

The child's father;

The child's teachers;

John's two sons, especially the one who was the child's 'love interest.'

She also reviewed the child protective history of Mary, and interviewed Mary's former therapist, doctor, and even found the names of some of Mary's former boyfriends, who were willing to talk about the child's care, safety and wellbeing while in the care of Mary.

Statement Analysis concluded:

1. The child is deceptive
2. The child "entered into the language of the mother", that is, the mother coached the child.
3. The child was emotionally abused by the mother, who had used the girl's crush on John's son as the fuel for her scheme to not pay back the money to John.

The case was closed, officially called, "Unsubstantiated" for child sexual abuse.

The investigation took almost 6 weeks to conclude.

The workers not only felt good about their work, knowing that they protected an innocent man from possibly going to prison, but had counseled John on how to fill out the forms in small claims court to get back his money from Mary.

John was left devastated.

He initially thanked the workers for their diligence, but was soon left with the reality of what just happened.

His ex wife knew it was a scam, and his sons never doubted their father. Beyond that, life quickly fell apart for John.

Although these matters are confidential, small town America sometimes does not allow for such.

Whispers began.

"Why were those women from the State there?"

Also, Mary had a field day with friends and neighbors alike, saying that her little precious child had been sexually molested by that "dark, lonely monster of a man who works at..."

John was stared at while at work. In the dining area, parents pulled their kids closer when he came by.

Some of the regulars still said, "hello" as was their custom; some did not.

The lie of one, due to the desire for money her hands did not earn, was a cancer to the name of an innocent man.

John called the social workers. "Can you call my company and tell them that this was all a lie?"

No, they could not do that, for it would violate the confidentiality of the child, who, by the way, was receiving treatment and in a foster home, and "is doing much better."

John was not comforted. He was unable to see her, now, as a child, but as the offspring of a villainous woman who attempted to destroy his life over a few dollars.

As the months went by, John could tell that his superiors did not show the confidence they once had in him, as they suspected that sales would be down during the hours that John was there. It was not true, but it was something they "felt in the bones", and "didn't need statistics" to prove anything.

They wondered if this man, living alone, was a pervert or not. They could not fire him, lest they face a suit, but they wanted him gone, just the same.

A man who had rebuilt a broken life, and finally made something of himself, was now being torn down by something that did not even exist, except in the minds of the suspicious.

He dared not walk near schools nor Little League games, nor would he ever again jostle the hair of a child, or even comment on how "cute" a baby was in his town.

Fortunately, he was able to "transfer" to another store in the chain, as the management at his present employment were more than willing to give him a glowing recommendation, just to be rid of him.

Older now, and far more cynical, he pulled up roots to start again.

Is there much wonder why the ancient Scripture talks about the lethality of the "lying tongue"?

The liar tears apart families.

The liar tears apart lives.

The liar destroys reputations.

The liar bankrupts.

The liar steals when it benefits the liar.

The liar "falls on the job" when the fall benefits the liar.

The liar has come to steal and to destroy, and the defense remains the same:

"Be as wise as serpents, but as gentle as doves."

We can live life trained to detect deception, without being a slave to a cynical heart, one which cannot, or will not trust.

To live life in a constant state of hyper-vigilance is to destroy one's own immune system, depleting strength year after year.

To not trust is to not be vulnerable and where there is no vulnerability, there is no reception of love.

Without love, there is no life to live.

There are those, so traumatized in life, that they struggle to trust, and struggle to love and be loved. It is easier, they say, to live a shielded protected life, trusting no one.

Hollywood stories generally end well. I would like to say that our fast-food manager became the proud owner of his own eatery, but it is not so.

I would like to say that Marys do not exist, just as I would like to say that Bernie Madoff did not exist.

It is not true.

Pilate, antiquity tells us, was a ruthless politician, at once subject to Caesar, while carefully eliminating his own enemies, and strengthening his power base at home.

He was, as it were, in training for his final test: to condemn the innocent Christ, or, by the warning of his beautiful young wife, set Him free.

It was his ultimate test in life, and he had been trained well in deception and deceit, and would be left powerless, by an unarmed mob, even while trained soldiers surrounded him.

We like to tell ourselves that if we were under a big test of morals in life, that we would pass. We like to believe that if we had to testify in a capital case, where our testimony would save a man's life, but ruin our own, that we would do the right thing.

Yet the answer lies in our training up to the point of testing.

Did we do the right thing, in the fourth grade, when we were caught cheating on a math test, or did we lie, to protect our own self?

Did we tell the truth on that broken date? Or, did we, instead, lie, telling ourselves how moral we were for sparing the pain of another?

When we took the pen from the bank, did we do so inadvertently, indeed, by accident, or did we really like the feel of it in our hand?

Everyone lies, but who are those that learn from such mistakes and grow responsibly, and who are those who, instead of growing responsibly, became even stronger liars?

Their words will give them away.

When caught, the brave own their lie, and are ashamed of it. But those who strengthen themselves with lies, do the most damage in life.

Here is one such powerful example for you to consider.

Let me ask you a question:

Have you ever been in a foreign country? Yes, or No?

It is likely an easy question for you to answer, unless you live smack on the border between two countries and are never really sure where you are at. (Yeah, I can stretch it, too).

Now, what if you were in a foreign country that was, literally, on the other side of the world from where you live…would that be something you could answer, yes or no, with certainty?

What if the liar had the power and authority to put you in prison? Would you want a man who boldly lies to hold such power and authority over the lives of others?

Richard Blumenthal.

Is it possible that a Harvard educated Attorney General could boast about his service in Vietnam even though he never went to Vietnam and secured 5 deferments just to avoid going there?

How can this be?

Answer: Liars, that is, those who fabricate reality, hold the rest of us in contempt.

Instead of saying, "I am sorry. I shamelessly sought to gain votes of veterans and I have insulted their intelligence", he had something else to say.

I'm reasonably sure that if I were to fly in a plane to a foreign country, particularly one in which a war was raging, I would remember being there. It is not something I would forget. But when confronted with a lie, the "Pilate test" occurs and the result will be precisely as life has trained (and predicted) it to be.

Blumenthal talked to Viet Nam vets about himself being in Viet Nam in order to garner support.

The problem? He wasn't in Viet Nam.

When caught, his reply to being seen as a liar will reveal what his life training has been.

In this case, we ask who is the target of his apology? His mea-culpa was a bit light on the "mea" and the "culpa" may be "misdirected."

Here is what his life long training had him say:

"On a few occasions, I have misspoken about my service and I regret that. And I take full responsibility, but I will not allow anyone to take a few misplaced words and impugn my record of service to our country."

That is a comment by Connecticut Attorney General Richard Blumenthal regarding questions surrounding his past statements about his military service in which he claimed, as a young soldier, to have been in Viet Nam.

By now, you have learned to key in on the word "but" in Statement Analysis, to know the important information in a sentence follows this particular word. It means that the information that follows "but" will often refute, or minimize by comparison, what preceded it.

"On a few occasions, I have <u>misspoken</u> about my service and I regret that. <u>And</u> I take full responsibility, but I will not allow anyone to take a few misplaced words and impugn my record of service to our country."

"On a few occasions" remember, the shortest sentence is best. Additional words give us additional information. If a sentence can work without a word, the added word should be noted.

"few" is an attempt to minimize.
"occasions" are instead of formal speeches. Attempt to minimize. What would you have said? Remember, the statements made were in front of not only live audiences, but cameras rolling. Maybe he meant that he said it, off handedly, at a picnic, or something. Would you forget that you didn't go to a country, thousands of miles away, while being shot at with weapons that could have ended your life?

This is why deceptive people, uncovered in Statement Analysis, get caught: they cannot change.

If you study statement analysis in an attempt to become a better liar, **it will not help you**. It is something ingrained within you at childhood; truth or fabrication, and it is habit forming. Even those who read that deceptive people often employ words like "*swear, honest to God, swear to*

God, honestly" and so on, still employ these words, as the brain tells the mouth what words to use processing this information in less than a microsecond.

*"I have **misspoken** about my service "*

No, he did not misspeak. He said he was in Vietnam and research has showed that he worked hard at making sure he was **not** in Vietnam, but safely in Washington, D.C, running "Toys for Tots" in the reserves. I think that if you or I traveled thousands of miles and stood in a country that had bullets firing all around, we would, with certainty, know whether or not we were there.

Note that "misspoken" , past tense, is a word used to soften or minimize (neutralize) the word "lied". Misspoken conjures up thoughts of an innocent mistake, rather than an intention to deceive. It sounds like a simple mistake. Hey, who hasn't said the wrong word once in a while?

*"and I regret **that**"*

"*that*" means distance, "*this*" means closer.

"regret"is an emotion. He has not owned, nor asked for forgiveness. I think anyone who said that they were in another country only to be caught lying would likely regret being caught. I believe his regret is genuine, but it is not linked to deception, but rather to having been caught.

*"And I take **full** responsibility"*

at first glance, this sounds strong. But remember, the shortest sentence is best. "And I take responsibility" is shorter. "full" is the emphasis that he feels he needs to add, thus weakening the statement, however, this wasn't the end of the sentence. The word "but" now employs the most important part of his message:

"but"

"but I will not allow <u>anyone</u> to take a few misplaced words and impugn my record of service to our country."

he will "not allow"; forbid, control. How can he "not allow"
"anyone" (neutral gender)

This shows the arrogance of a liar. He now expresses himself in terms of divinity; controller over destiny, and over the minds and hearts of Americans who will hear these words. He will not "allow"; language that deludes himself and shows how far from reality he is.

When you read this you can now see why someone with his intellect and place in life can be so utterly void of common sense. This is a warning to you and to me, about how liars think.

In your life, could you go to your job, or to your family, and simply announce that you were in, for instance, "war-torn Bosnia" during the height of conflict? You know, when they thought you were home, or at school, all that time, you were really dodging bullets in the streets of Bosnia. Your family might look at you and call the doctor.

It is equally absurd; showing how out of touch a deceptive person can become over the years. A young liar may be good, but a liar who reaches the age of a grandparent has a lifetime of practice at deception but ego overrides and causes them to look foolish.

Who is "anyone"? The reporter that decided to check the facts? Shoot the messenger?

I'm thinking...he, himself, doesn't seem to be the "anyone." When something feels awkward to you, it is because, well, it is awkward and it should be.

"to take a few misplaced words"

Here we have a change in language, from misspoken to misplaced. A change of language represents a change in reality. When the girl kissed the man, the man fell in love with the woman. Notice the change? She was a girl, but once they kissed, she became a woman.

Where there is no justification for the change, it is likely deception.

"The car ran roughly. I ran out of gas. I left the vehicle on the side of the road."

It was a car when it went, but now that it cannot transport, it is a vehicle.

Here, we have a change. His words were "*misspoken*" but now, are not " misspoken at all, but were "misplaced", meaning, put into the wrong place.

This means that he stands behind his lies and reveals what his regret is:

That he spoke his lies in the wrong settings. Had there been no cameras running, he could have used his "Vietnam" experiences to persuade vets to vote for him and if called on the carpet, he could easily deny.

But because the cameras were rolling, it is hard for him to watch and listen to the lies he told.

He takes "full responsibility", **but** he has provided service to his counrty. The use of the word **but** suggests that he doesn't take responsibility at all, because he feels that he has a record of service to his country after all. "But" is often used to refute, or at least minimize that which preceded it. It is used in comparison.

"I like steak but I love lobster.

This politicians statement regarding the lies he told about his service in Vietnam reveal that he is a chronic, long term liar, who thought he was above being questioned, and is still in denial about his own mortality.

There is much talk about "pathological liars" who "can't even tell when they are lying."

Be careful with that one. The "pathological liars", when confronted, wiggle uncomfortably, and use lies in attempt to justifiy themselves. Guilt aside, we count on the internal stress that lies cause to flush out the language for us.

How is it that politicians can demand that we, the public, trust them, when they who are closet to them, their own families, can not trust them?

The arrogance and deceptive nature of the statement issued by Blumenthal tells me that this is a man who has long lied without much consequence and that he has been a man of power, who has had much success in exerting authority over others. I'd hate to be a defendant up against one who is not afraid to invent his own reality. One can only imagine orders passed down from him that impacted the lives he was in contact with.

It is frightening.

Imagine what stories his own family could tell!

Statement Analysis teaches that liars hold the rest of us in contempt. This is a perfect example. Could you imagine me being falsely arrested and facing one of this man's prosecutors? Can you picture a fair trial?

Yes, closer to home is Mr. Smith and the lie told to gain money, but what if you, in your company had hired Mary? What if you had hired the obviously well educated and intelligent Blumenthal?

Bernie Madoff was not unqualified, educationally, or intellectually, in his position. Many liars are well educated and talented, but do not learn from, nor repent from, their lies.

Dealing with deception is not easy, but the training is worth it. Courses, seminars, and self study are all available to you, the father, mother, business owner, consumer, and anyone and everyone else who must rely upon the currency of human communication to survive.

Deceptive people pass counterfeit currency. By taking the "poisoned pawn" from the chess player, the tactic to follow can be brutal.

Businesses, like families, like hearts, must be protected.

Are you bitter?

There's a simple test you can administer to yourself, to see if you are bitter towards one who has used deception to harm you.

It is one thing to be hurt, but it is quite another thing to have that hurt linger to the point where it dominates your thinking, and holds you, in a type of prison, where your heart is not free to love and live.

For some, even years has not helped ease the bitterness.

But first, are you bitter? It is more than just a sickening memory of a lie told to you? Is it something that has a hold of your heart and your mind, and will not release itself?

Have you prayed for forgiveness, yet still long to see the other person get "what's coming to him"?

The Bitter Test is simple:

If you answer "yes" to any of these questions, You've got bitterness.

   a. Do you lose sleep over it?
   b. Do you have imaginary conversations about it?
   c. Do you regret not 'telling them off' when you had the chance?
   d. Do you fantasize about revenge?
   e. Is it all but impossible to pray for them, unless you are praying for vengeance?
   f. Does it consume you, leaving you feeling empty?
   g. Do you wish you could stop thinking about it?
   h. Can you recall each and every word, with startling clarity?
   i. Do you wish you were free from the bitterness?

j. Or, has the bitterness become 'comfortable', that is, something you are used to using to keep vulnerability away from you?
k. Do you remember what it was like to trust?
l. Do you long to trust again?

The bitterness can run deep. It is a noxious weed that grows through the cracks of cement, while tender fruit plants seem to die the first sign of drought. The weed is ugly, and it seems to survive all weather conditions, but it is so because it has deep roots. The roots must be dug out. Simply clipping off the surface may look nice, or feel good for awhile, but when the above symptoms return, you'll know the weed has been busy growing back.

There is help, however, that you might consider:

Journaling through your pain.

I've referenced it before, but it bears repeating: There are healthy therapeutic benefits to writing about your pain. Experts seem unified in this and many recommend what I have also found to be helpful in moving past a bitterness:

1. Write out what happened. Give lots and lots of detail, but only write out the actual facts of what took place, deliberately avoiding emotional content; that is, how you felt about what happened.
2. Now that you have written a full account (hopefully you've exhausted your mind in recalling facts) you are to write specifically about the emotions you felt, each and every step of the way, and how you feel at the time of your writing.

I have found this helpful in relieving psychological pain and highly recommend it. If you have been on the receiving end of deception, you already know what it is like to have your entire life blown apart by a liar.

Perhaps it is time to prayerfully consider having your life put back together again.

Chapter Eighteen: The Trap

At the conclusion of a training, a woman approached me and said, "I work for a liar. What do I do?"

Because of the training she had just attended, I knew what she meant, just as I knew what she did not mean.

She did not mean that her superior comes in and says "I'm 43 years old" when he is really 51. She is not talking about casual lies, "Geez, Miss Plum, you look dandy today!", nor polite flattery.

She did not mean he exaggerates his self importance, or that he is even unreliable in scheduling meetings, or other annoying, but tolerable events. I knew exactly what she meant, and I did not miss the distinct look of pain upon her face; a pain that comes from prolonged exposure to stress, instability and unpredictability: things that liars impose upon us.

She meant "lies"; the kind of deception in this book, the kind that ruins relationships and ruins lives and companies.

She could take comfort in knowing that, perhaps finally, she was speaking to someone who knew, instantly, what she was talking about.

Sometimes knowing can be dangerous if you do not know what to do with the knowledge.

One man said, *"My boss has just graduated from speed to cocaine. She is burning through dollars as fast as she is burning a hole in her nose. Her behavior is erratic, and her judgment is going to destroy the company. What do I do?"*

Addicts lie.

Addicts lie constantly, and struggle to tell the truth. Everything about them is to protect their addiction, and it is a powerful force to reckon with. Psychologically called "denial", it often cannot be overcome without tragic circumstances driving the addict to the most dangerous levels of despair. Some look into the abyss and return, and some do not. Even as marijuana has become popular today, few seem willing to grasp what impact this has upon teenagers, who not only have their natural drive impeded, but learn to cope with life's stressors chemically. Others may fight over the notion of "gateway" drug or not, but teachers know.

Drugs destroy lives. Drugs desensitize the soul, even as the user attempts to numb the deep psychological pain. The bait and switch is powerful: the initial user does, indeed, gain psychological relief just as chronic pain patients receive relief from their physical pain.

Tolerance sets in, along with both physical dependence, as is the case of opiates, and psychological dependence.

The body goes through a procedure of sorts, first finding relief at a certain dosage, only to, in short order, find the need for more for the same relief. Fascinating to me is the similarity within language.

As we have seen previously, a school teacher notices that the normal, happy little boy in her class, who needs daily prompts to wash his hands, suddenly washes his hands several times during the day, causing her to be concerned about sexual abuse. She ties together "water" and the possibility of sexual abuse. In statement analysis, we find the same thing: "water", in various forms, enters the subject's language.

In the issue of denial, we are dealing with deception; first self deception and then the deception of others. I once spoke to a well respected substance abuse therapist who, after more than twenty years experience, told me she was unable to tell if an addict was lying. Smart as she was, she acknowledged how deep the denial ran, in the brain of the addict, and appeared, much like the working of physical tolerance, the subject develops a "linguistic tolerance" to lying.

This is a fancy way of saying that lying becomes comfortable over time, even for one who was not raised as a liar, and increases over time.

The addict, unlike the habitual liar, may not have been raised this way. Since all children lie, parental correction (or negligence) makes all the difference in life. The addict may be a "habitual liar", but not necessarily from childhood.

What's the difference? Really, what is the point?

Habitual liars from childhood have this engrained within their personality. It is their nature. For the addict, who was not a liar from childhood, there is a critical difference in terms of hope: the addict, upon becoming free or "clean", will generally not only recover the truthful nature of personality, but, in the upcoming years (yes, years), will have an increase in clarity and understanding. Therefore, I am fascinated (and inspired) by those who have maintained sobriety over many years: often their emotional intelligence and self awareness is amazing.

In the business world, pressure upon those who are "at the top of the food chain" can erode away resistance to the lure of numbing pressure with chemical relief. Even worrying about the myriad of lives dependent upon their own business acumen can wear down, with incessant stress, the will of the addict, regardless of whether one believes this to be a genetic predisposition or not.

Once given into, the addiction, and subsequent lying to protect it, slowly and steadfastly eats away at the judgment of the addict, impacting business and personal decisions.

The lies begin.

Like the opiate addict, the tolerance increases and the addict finds that the lies spread, finally landing into the realm of "inconsequential", the worst of all classifications. This is where the liar is deceptive when there is no reason nor call to lie. It is now "second nature" and habitual.

One woman told me that she worked for a liar for five years and it almost destroyed her life. He lied when no lie was necessary and, like most accomplished liars, it took quite a while to catch on to his tall tales. Eventually, it came down to what so often happens between supervisor and worker; his failures were blamed on her.

For the woman who approached me after the training, what should she do?

It is easy to say "blow the whistle!" or "be courageous and do the right thing", but one must consider some variables to this all-in-one answer. Life is complex; communication is complex, and lying, itself, breeds confusion.

She was in deep pain, and this pain resulted from:

1. Being falsely blamed for his mistakes
2. Having credit stolen from her
3. Being victimized by not only his selfishness, but his insecurity, which would be then piled upon her subordinate, leaving her depressed, anxious, and open to illness, with her compromised immune system.

The liar puts himself and his own needs, even his own emotional needs, above the material needs of his company, as well as the needs of others, including family.

I once interviewed a man who had recently been released from prison after serving seven years for the murder of his aunt.

He was a cocaine addict who could not afford cocaine, so he switched to the lethal and much cheaper alternative, "crack cocaine", which he described to me as a high that was instantaneous and so pleasurable that he said he was unable to adequately describe other than to say "The moment it is gone, every fiber of my being screamed for it again."

His addiction started with marijuana in high school, where when he felt stressed, he "relaxed" with it. It was popular among friends and, at least in his account, it did not impact his education. (this is something I disagree with). Having some college, he entered the work force and found that the stresses of the working world were actually more intense than those of a term paper due in high school.

He sought relief where he had sought relief in high school: chemical relief.

This tie, however, he met with someone who offered him a 'taste' of cocaine. He was instantly hooked.

In short order, it, the drug, became his 'god', that is, his principle passion in life. He lived only to make enough money to buy cocaine, running up credit cards, borrowing from friends, lying, being caught in lies (he was not a habitual liar from childhood), until he was eventually fired. His "full time job" was the drug. He spent his days scavenging for anything he could pawn, and cared little for food or shelter, fell behind on his rent and was eventually evicted.

He moved in with his elderly aunt.

He did his best to hide his addiction, but she noticed that his behavior became more and more erratic. He borrowed money from her, and eventually, began to steal from her.

One morning, he felt "at peace" with himself, making the firm decision to get help and straighten out his life. In just a few short years, he had aged right before his eyes, scarcely able to recognize the young man, who looked at least 10 years older, in the mirror.

He spoke kindly to his auntie, and told her he was turning over a new leaf.

She, burned time and time again, expressed doubt.

Within him, something snapped.

He reached over the table, grabbed a steak knife and plunged it repeatedly into his aunt's chest.

He was sentenced to 15 years in prison, but was released at 7. He was a young man in his early 30's, who looked closer to 50.

He spoke, with stark clarity, at not only the lies he told others, but the lies he told himself. He explained to me an angle of "denial" that is very difficult to embrace:

It is as if the sun is shining, and the liar claims it is pouring rain. He said that this is how his brain worked: what was bad was good, down was up, and left was right. His judgment was not only mistaken, but it was bizarre and the only thing that was consistent was that he needed to protect himself from all threats,

Real,

Perceived,

And fake.

This is where the "paranoia like behavior" comes in with addicts and it is that they see, and say things that do not exist.

They lie outright, in that they are able to fabricate reality.

What do you do?

I often question those who, once they understand the nature of a liar, if they recognize any signs of substance abuse, for this is critical in strategizing what can, or what should be done.

However, the very first thing I advise clients who are certain that someone over them, in authority, is lying, is to be silent. I ask them to "wait" and begin to unravel things slowly. In terms of "doing the right thing" and "blowing the whistle", consider the following:

1. You may not be believed.

You may know the subject (in this case, the superior) is lying, but others may not believe you. I always advise clients not only move slowly but document everything; date, time and exact quotes.

2. Even if believed, consider that "nothing" may be done about it. This is especially true if you work for a bureaucracy, or if you work in a position where the liar has enough authority to frighten the others around you, into silence.

I have seen cases where all the witnesses were on payroll! When it came down to backing the whistleblower, or paying their mortgage, fear often ruled the day.

3. I also ask clients to consider what may or may not be accomplished. If, for example, there is a board of directors, the destruction of a liar may be brought to their attention, but again, it is a risk.

4. Is the liar abusing substances? This will add the level of denial, and it is not likely that any kind of intervention will take place with the subject's own subordinates.

   At times, the liar may put you in the position of stretching you, ethically. It is critical that you have someone to 'debrief' with, that is, a trusted friend to whom you may share information, prioritize and seek clarity.

   Lies can confuse and at times, some clients have found that by going through the lies, the situation was not as "intolerable" as it first seemed, this being because of the personal insult and pain that a liar causes. One woman concluded that she thought things were worse because of the personal stress the lying boss caused her, but productivity continued.

5. Sadly, if the liar is an addict, it may be that "waiting him out" is the best strategy. Even where there is personal care and empathy, once denial hits, you may be stunned to learn how quickly the liar will turn on you, employing lies against you and saying (and doing) things would could have scarcely predicted.

Liars will go a long way to protect themselves and if coupled with substance abuse, it sometimes does take "rock bottom" to be reached before action is taken.

This is when your documentation can best serve you.

But when the liar has taken his lies to the realm of criminal, it is time to call an attorney. The liar may seek to do things that are ethically questionable, but eventually, this could lead to criminal behavior and here is where you must draw the line: you cannot allow the liar to get you to forge, to lie, or to do anything illegal, even at the threat of your job.

Losing your job is a lot better than losing your freedom.

Sometimes just "knowing", can bring pain.

It may be, at least, initially "exciting" to catch the liar, but you must consider:

The wrath of the liar.

Lance Armstrong was not happy with his unreliable denials. He thought he would appear truthful if he attacked his accusers.

Lance Armstrong is not stupid. He is, however, a pathological liar who, even while "confessing" to Oprah, continued his deception. He showed his need to deceive by, among other things, accusing his accusers. This is always a failed strategy, though still employed.

Alex Rodriguez did this with Major League Baseball, either suing, or threatening to sue anyone, and everyone, who did not believe him. He made enemies everywhere and it only highlighted that he was lying.

Even Ryan Braun's who's comically deceptive "denial" could not stop himself from attacking an innocent man who's only job was to schedule a pick up with Fedex.

Braun had tested positive for Performance Enhancing Drugs and had been suspended. He appealed his suspension on the basis that the sample sat for a day in someone's fridge, rather than having Fedex come on a Saturday.

Braun's statement was read, by an ESPN reporter, out loud to various other major league ballplayers, for the camera, and it brought chuckles.

This statement is an excellent example of "leakage."

Here is how:

Consider that Ryan Braun did use exogenous testosterone. This means putting a large needle in his gluteus Maximus muscles, something athletes report as very painful. Consider just how painful, and now put yourself in his shoes.

In Statement Analysis, we ask you to presume innocence, and then look at the statement. In "leakage" it is the polar opposite. Presuppose guilt and now listen to his words. While you read his words, think of the painful needle and you'll see why more than a few people laughed over his deceptive response.

What follows is the analysis I posted at the Statement Analysis Blog.

Ryan Braun may win the MVP this year in the majors. He was originally suspended for using performance enhancing drugs, but won his appeal on a technicality.

Question for Analysis: Did Ryan Braun use testosterone?

While awaiting the hearing, he said, "*This is complete B.S. I am completely innocent.*" He told radio announcers that he would "*tell my side of the story*" at the hearing. He had this opportunity and may others to say "*I didn't take testosterone*" or something similar, indicating a reliable denial, but he did not.

Statement Analysis rule: If the subject cannot bring himself to say he did not do it, we are not permitted to say it for him, even if he hits an awful lot of home runs.

MLB hearing revealed that his attorney argued that the chain of custody was compromised because the sample sat in the fridge over the weekend. MLB testers testified that it was late on Friday and they did not think Fedex delivered on Saturday, but swore that the sample remained untouched in the fridge. There was no evidence of tampering.

MLB overruled the suspension. This is what Mr. Braun had to say about it:

"*If I had done this intentionally or unintentionally, I'd be the first one to step up and say I did it,*" Braun said. "*I truly believe in my heart and I would bet my life, that this substance never entered my body at any point.*"

Headlines interpreted his denial as "vehement" and "strong" and "emphatically denies", yet Statement Analysis views it differently:

"*If I had done this intentionally or unintentionally, I'd be the first one to step up and say I did it,*"

1. "If I had..." allows for the possibility. Innocent people generally do not allow for any other scenario to be examined. They did not do it, and there is nothing else to be debated. That he allows for the possibility is noted.

2. "this" When there is the word "this" instead of "that", it is indication of closeness. We expect to hear, "I didn't take testosterone" but the use of the word "this", indicating closeness, goes against innocence. This is the 2nd red flag for us that is noted.

   3. "I did it" forms the very words of an admission. This appears to be an embedded admission where a guilty person is able to frame the words of guilt. An embedded admission is not something an innocent person does unless the person is entering into the language of another, quoting an interviewer or another accuser. Here, in context, it appears to come from the free editing process.
   4.

"*I truly believe in my heart and I would bet my life, that this substance never entered my body at any point.*"

Deception indicated.

Instead of saying, "I didn't take testosterone, the subject uses additional language to indicate the need to persuade:

1. "truly" weakens the assertion, as it calls for emphasis
2. "believe" weakens the assertion more so; as it acknowledges that others may "believe" differently
3. "in my heart" weakens it even further, as it is only where he believes, in his heart, and not in his head. Others, in their "hearts" will "believe" differently. It is also an indication that he "beleives" differently in his head, or intellect. It is a phrase used when someone wishes to persuade, but even in persuasion we don't see additional qualifiers added.

4. "would" is conditional tense and a further weakening of an assertion.

In the beginning of a denial, we have four qualifiers used.

"I am happily married" is a straight forward sentence.
"I am very happily married" uses one qualifier. This is due to either attempt to persuade, or that the subject was previously unhappy, and did not expect to be this happy.

"I am very very happily married" will lead a therapist to inquire about his unhappiness.

"I am very very very very happily married" will lead a divorce attorney to write up a bill.

To qualify 4 times is extreme attempt to persuade. Ryan Braun qualified his sentence four times to this point, but wasn't done. He is a poor liar:

that this substance never entered my body at any point."

1. "This" substance, chooses the word "this" bringing him close ("that" shows distancing language) to the testosterone.

2. "Never" when substituted for the past tense verb, "did not" or "didn't" is unreliable.

3. "Extra words":

Extra words are those in which a sentence works should they be removed. They give us additional information.

"at any point" is unnecessary extra words making them "doubly important" for the analyst. It is interesting to note that not only are these extra words weakening a weak denial, but the word "point" is used. Testosterone use is, in high dosages, administered via needle.

If you had injected testosterone painfully into your rear end, might you use the word "point" in your language?

Analysis Conclusion:

Ryan Braun's test indicated testosterone levels three times higher than the normal limit for athletes.

He does not issue a reliable denial consisting of the simple three elements of First Person Singular "I", past tense verb, "did not" and event specific, "I did not use testosterone", in his statements. He was unable to bring himself to say these words; therefore, we cannot say them for him. He does not deny using testosterone, instead, he gives a deceptive response that, even though it is a short sentence, has an abundance of red flags.

Deception Indicated.

Ryan Braun used testosterone.

MLB will be forced to consider this should he continue his MVP-like season and come up for voting.

When the appeal was made in his favor on the technicality he said, "The truth prevailed" but did not tell us which truth. He also avoided saying, "I did not use testosterone"; something an innocent person will say, easily and without qualification.

The "leakage" that caused laughing was not just his terrible need to persuade, but the word "point" in his language.

Point well taken.

Braun sought to blame others. Did the employee who did not know that Fedex had Saturday pick up disciplined by MLB? Later, did he receive redress from Braun?

In the case of Lance Armstrong, he did severe damage to others' lives, and even their businesses. As a multi-millionaire, he could "outlast" anyone in a law suit, and force others to settle, wrongfully, because they could not maintain the lawyer fees.

Imagine having your small, family run business bankrupt by Lance Armstrong, only to see him put on a performance of a lifetime on the Oprah show?

I can only imagine how his former masseuse felt, or how Greg LeMond and his family felt, or the others of whom Armstrong attacked just for being honest.

Sometimes there is a price for honesty and for those who have children to feed, and a mortgage to pay, the liar can put them in life-changing positions where no easy answers exist.

Lastly, do not compromise yourself. You are all that you have, when it comes down to it, and your dignity is not worth what a liar might put your through.

Go slowly; do not "rush from the presence of the king", that is, do not be quick to say "that's it, you won't listen to me, I am outta here!", as you may accomplish more good in your presence, than in your absence. It may be that you will win more wars, by strategic retreats than by protest.

Of course, there may come a time when you are no longer able to abide the liar, but this is a decision that must be made carefully, and while seeking the multitude of counselors that wisdom demands.

When the situation is not one of criminal activity, careful thought is needed. Some battles are worth losing to prosecute the war.

Your own personal revenge should be negated.

It is the liar that has placed you, others and perhaps even an entire business in jeopardy and wisdom is desperately needed.

I spoke with a woman who had run a successful business since 1979. Her dedication to those less fortunate in life had been her passion. She was one of a rare breed who's steady hand kept the company afloat throughout the years, staying with the same company since she first accepted the position more than 35 years ago. She outlasted both liars and thieves (it was my contention that they are, both, one and the same), and watched trends come and go.

She said that there were many times in which she thought of personal revenge upon those who had deliberately sought to harm her through the employment of deception.

She is glad she did not.

It was one thing to be victimized by a liar, but it was quite another to be re victimized by the liar, over and over, through personal bitterness.

It wasn't simply taking "lemons and making lemonade" but stepping back and waiting, knowing that, one way or another, the injustice will be held to a higher bar and court, one day, instead, focusing upon what she, herself could do, for the enrichment of her clients' lives.

She said that there were many times when she thought to take action, but as she counted the cost and carefully took the time to weigh things out, she was repeatedly glad she trusted in a higher authority and "moved on" with her own work.

It is never easy dealing with a liar, but there is comfort in knowing that, once discerned, you are now able to be in a more careful position, not letting your guard down, and be well aware that the liar's own nature may attempt to pull you into criminal activity. In your case, with your knowledge, you have both eyes wide open, which is a lot better than being blindsided.

Chapter Nineteen: The Deceptive Among Us

It's never good.

"The Lord hates lying lips…" said Solomon quite a few years ago. Why? Why would the Lord hate?

If good is intended towards us, than it is that we see that those of lying lips intend harm towards us.

Neville Chamberlain is often quoted as one of the most famous men unable to discern the liar who stood before him.

This inability to discern the lie of Adolf Hitler, buying the Nazi regime time for mobilizing its armies, became a grandstanding embarrassment when Chamberlain took the paper signed by Hitler, waved it before the camera, and said, "Peace for our time!" even as Hitler told his subordinates: "It's not worth the paper its printed upon."

Poland would now be divided between the Germans and the Soviets, and once Germany invaded Poland, under the false flag of deception, what did England and France do? They declared war against Germany.

Since World War II was declared to be in defense of Poland, one might ask, "So, how did that turn out?"

Poland was all but destroyed, and those that were left alive were under the iron rule of the Soviets for the next half century.

The Deception was not just man to man, Hitler to Chamberlain, but of the German people who "listened" to a "radio broadcast" of "Polish invaders", portraying Germany as the victim in a deceptive radio broadcast followed by deceptive news reports. Prisoners in Polish uniforms were forced to "attack" a German radio station and Hitler had "no choice" but to defend "German nationals under attack."

All this while England and France were disarmed by Hitler's deceptive agreement.

Measure the cost of deception? Hardly. Historians today debate the number of dead from the cataclysmic blood letting that took place merely 20 years after the "War to end all wars" was fought.

Japan claimed to have been deceived by the United States shortly after World War I, in which Japan was an ally of the United States, but felt squeezed out during the Treaty of Versaile's dividing up of the spoils.

Deception upon deception.

Franklin D Roosevelt had imposed an oil embargo, knowing an attack would take place, preparing America, and arming German's enemies, even while proclaiming neutrality. This deception is often looked at in a positive manner because America obtained victory over Nazi Germany and Japan in the war, but quickly led to an entire eastern continent, including Poland, under the very cruel despotism America fought against with Hitler and the Japanese Imperial Army.

Deception in large scale; deception in small scale; both have its impact.

A deceptive pedophile charms the lonely, single mother, simply so he can get close to her children. His language must give him away, and in meeting those who have fallen prey to this destroyer of lives, I have found a principle of Statement Analysis well worth applying:

Note the words one chooses even when jesting or joking.

Remember, words come from somewhere. It may be that the humorous words are taken from a movie. "We're gonna need a bigger boat" or "time to go to the mattresses…", or, as having been quoted for what will soon be a century, "Frankly, me dear, I don't give a damn."

The intent, humor, may be simply words chosen from a movie.

Or, maybe not.

Women who became involved with child predators later reported that there were linguistic signals (and behavioral) which they only picked up on later.

Most of these signals were in the form of jokes.

Joking, or jesting, teasing, or attempts at humor, like every other aspect of communication, comes from the brain which "knows what it knows."

Let us take as our example the brain of the pedophile. He desires to have sexual relations, in his words, with children (that which we call sexual abuse). This is what his brain knows. When he speaks, he must be on guard to not let these thoughts become articulated and slip out.

They usually do.

This is the good news.

The bad news is that nobody seems to be listening. Well, not "nobody", as those reading this book may become trained in Statement Analysis and learn how to ask "analytical" questions, that is, questions that flow from analysis.

We teach to ask questions based, not upon your words, but upon the words of the subject, as if it could be done exclusively. This is how strict we attempt to be.

Mothers have said, "I knew something was up. I hated the way he teased my daughter, saying how "sexy" she was, but he did it in a way that was so absurd that everyone laughed!"

It was absurd to the mother. It is absurd to you and me, but it is not absurd to the pedophile; it is his leakage.

Mr. Sapir describes a training in Washington, D.C, in which he commented on just how many murders take place there. A policewoman jokingly said, "Oh, I should drop off my husband here!" and caused the class to laugh.

Mr. Sapir said, "You have been thinking about killing your husband."

She said, "No, that is ridiculous. It is just a joke."

He said, "Ok, then. Let's move on…"

During the break she approached him, rather sheepishly and said, "well, we are going through a bad divorce and sometimes I just think it would be easier if he died."

She wasn't planning on killing him, but because it was a thought in her brain, it came out, via joking.

Sometimes deceptive people will deliberately joke about something sensitive, almost as if they are trying to address the "800 lb gorilla in the living room", thinking that if they joke about it, it will appear absurd to all.

Listen to what people tell you, and follow carefully their words.

I had reported a serious crime and was visited by two detectives, both on the force for decades. Neither appeared trained.

I gave some fairly sensitive information to them and said, "if this information is shared with the suspect, the business owner, innocent employees are going to get hurt."

"Ha, ha, we'd never do that!", one joked.

2 hours after they left, the suspect appeared to take a form of revenge, as if the suspect gained the information I just shared.

I emailed the detective, with the direct question, "After leaving here, did you stop at the suspect's place of business and share the information with her?"

This gave him plenty of time to think of an answer. My suspicion was that he did.

He did not respond.

Therefore, I called, twice, leaving the same message on his voice mail.

He finally called me back.

I asked, "Did you go to the suspect's business after leaving here?" Did you go there and talk to her?"

I should have not asked a compound question, but was a bit angry.

He answered, "Did I go to the suspect's business and talk to her after leaving your house? I have spoken to the suspect."

I said, "Did you tell her what I told you?"

He said, "I would never tell her what you told me, no more than I would tell you what she said."

He gave several signals of deception in his answers:

1. He answered a question with a question.
2. He avoided given a direct answer. Note also the passivity of "have spoken…"
3. He avoided using the past tense verb "did not", instead used "would not."

He was deceptive.

If he did not want to answer, he could have said, "I am not at liberty to answer your questions", regardless, he lost trust with me, and I will not have confidence in his ability to do his job. Even after 25 years on the job, police often score poorly because they often think everyone is deceptive, and, in this detective's case, he was deceptive with me. There will be no trust moving forward.

Deceptive people will always put their own interests above yours, but more so, will put their own interests above the truth and above what is right.

I have interviewed thieves and gotten confessions after listening to them "joke" about what it would be like to steal this or that from their company. They are nervous in the interview, and may not show it in the usual way:

They show it linguistically.

I like humor and I am told that it is part of my Irish heritage: to embrace and use humor. If you've ever been to an Irish wake you are likely familiar with Irish humor. Next to the "Irish goodbye" (which can linger for hours), the Irish wake is rife with morbid humor, with nothing sacred. I find it sometimes quite helpful, especially when it is a relief from incessant tears.

Yet I listen always.

Thieves will telegraph their plans. They may do so jokingly, or may talk outright, in which others think they are joking, but they are not.

I remember when the Baby Ayla case first broke. Another missing child, and another uncooperative parent, yet, another brain that "leaked" information.

Baby Ayla was reported missing while under the care of her father, a single, unemployed man who had a child with one woman and another, Ayla, with another. Only Ayla was with him.

The father, Justin DiPietro, met with police who set up media in the usual way: so the parent can appeal to the kidnapper.

This is the "expected" much like what any parent would do if they could not find their child. Statement Analysis deals with the "unexpected."

For example, let's say you were grocery shopping in Walmart with your toddler, when she suddenly wandered off. The first thing you would do is look for her, and call out to her. This is the expected. This is what parents do.

Justin DiPietro refused to "call out after Ayla" releasing a statement saying that he was "emotionally incapable" of doing so.

Huh?

That's like the parent who's toddler wanders off at Walmart, but the parent, instead of looking and calling after the child, decides that he, the father, "comes first."

He finishes his shopping.

He helps pack the groceries.

He brings them to the car.

He drives home.

He unloads the packages from the car.

Perhaps he has dinner first, and then, maybe then, he is comfortable enough to call out to his missing daughter.

This is the "unexpected."

Deceptive people become tigers when they are seen as deceptive and will trip over their own prideful words when they go to defend their own selves.

When Ayla's mother told media "Justin is not cooperating!", he fumed. He released a statement to be read to media, by police. It began,

"Contrary to rumors floating around out there…" and went on and on how he did speak to police.

I read the statement to Avinoam Sapir. He said, "What does the father do for a living?"

I said, "He is unemployed."

He said, "Well, what is he trained to do?"

I said, "He's trained in nothing. "

Frustrated, Mr. Sapir said, "Did he have any plans for training or employment?"

I could not tell what the genius analyst was getting to but then I remembered that his mother said he was trying to pay for a class to be a truck driver.

"Truck Driver?", Mr. Sapir asked, "Uh, oh, that's not a good sign. That baby is in water."

He explained that truck drivers have "their wheels firmly on the ground" and that since we had other statements by DiPietro, including one in which he referenced his missing child in the past tense (a strong signal that he knows or believes she is dead), any metaphor or expression should be something more "concrete" but by choosing "floating out there", it was very likely that little baby Ayla was dumped in water.

Later we learned that police revealed that Ayla was likely dead, due to the blood found in the house, and that they had found some items that may have belonged to her…

In the Kennebec River.

If he had disposed of his child in water, these are the thoughts that would be in his brain, even while he is attempting to speak about something else. This is the "leakage" that the brain does, revealing itself through words, even when trying to be deceptive.

It is like a job applicant offering, "I don't have a drinking problem" when no one asked, "Do you have a drinking problem?" This is called a "negation", or that which is offered (positive) in the negative, and in analysis, it is to be deemed "very important information."

Incidentally, Ayla's mother reported that in the weeks before Ayla "went missing", the father had sent text messages to the mother expressing "concern" that someone might "take" or "kidnap" Ayla.

We then learned that not only was her blood found, but the unemployed single father of two had purchased life insurance: not for his two kids, and not even for Ayla, but against Ayla, betting that she would die before he did and that he would stand to gain significant money.

The case, officially, remains unsolved, though police have accused DiPietro, his sister, and his girlfriend, of deception.

The deceptive among us range from Hillary Clinton and the "Benghazi" scandal, to the President Obama's claim that a spontaneous protest emerged from a documentary, when it was, in fact, a well rehearsed military and terrorist strike against United States citizens, all the way down to the fast talking door-to-door salesman who does his best to get a signature on the bottom line.

Being prepared can mitigate the nightmares that can follow.

I volunteer to assist women who are victims of Domestic Violence, and worked with the indefatigable heroine Susan Murphy Milano, who has since succumbed to cancer. I counsel victims of Domestic Violence to be unafraid to ask questions on that first date. I insist that the "ex wife" or "ex girlfriend" be interviewed, particularly if the man refuses to take responsibility for his own actions.

As questions. Listen for answers.

A broken marriage is a failed relationship and there is plenty of blame to share: will he take responsibility? This, itself, can go a long way to protecting a woman from domestic violence.

Ask him if he has assaulted her.

Listen for the answer.

In "yes or no" questions, count the number of words that come after the first "no", and begin to get a feeling of whether or not he is truthful, or he is attempting to persuade.

If he is attempting to persuade you, he has a need to persuade you. This is not good.

Note also, as said repeatedly, that when one lies when there is no apparent cause to lie, it is an indication of a personality disorder in which the subject is likely a habitual liar from childhood, and one who can mean nothing but trouble for you.

Listen to his jokes.

Are his jokes violent in nature? Does he joke about what harm he would like to bring his ex wife? Do you recognize the genesis of his jokes? Are they TV or pop references? Or, do you get the sense that they are coming, instead, from his own life's experience.

Addicts joke about drugs, knocking off drug stores, and will sometimes even "jokingly" "seem" to be asking to borrow someone else's pain medication.

Are these jokes repeated?

Remember, anything repeated is sensitive. Why is it sensitive? This needs to be found out.

Liars bring damage and destruction and leave a wake of pain that can ripple for generations. The lying lips that are hated, should be avoided.

By now, you've come to the conclusion that little good comes from liars, and you are correct. But what about law enforcement? Aren't they experts in lie detection?

Chapter 20: Crisis in Confidence

In speaking with companies, I have found a universal complaint: nothing gets done when a report is made to law enforcement.

In speaking with victims' families, the same theme can also be found: the lack of justice can be maddening.

If a suspect in the disappearance of a child makes incriminating statements, and fails his polygraph, how is it that years go by, and he remains still not arrested?

When a large theft takes place and a company makes a police report, why does the company continually feel that the lost money or merchandise will not be recovered, and that the insurance company should not be contacted because it will only increase the rates we pay.

The frustration can be acute.

Let's step backwards a bit, and take a larger view of law enforcement.

First of all, the polygraph is not generally admissible in a court of law unless both parties stipulate to it. Therefore, when someone fails a polygraph, it does not "prove" anything.

Regarding the polygraph, if the prescreening interview is conducted according to the language of the subject himself, that is, no interpretation, is should be highly accurate. If the subject "tickled" the little girl, rather than "molested" (in his personal, subjective internal language), he should not be asked, "Did you molest…?", but "Did you tickle?" in the polygraph.

When a polygraph uses only the language of the subject, it is highly reliable.

Now, the cops may feel, "We know who did it" and can focus their investigation accordingly.

This does not prove he did it.

There is also the element of political change in law enforcement over the past few decades, beginning in the early 1980's, in earnest, where police test scores were "rescored" according to "racial sensitivities" and later "other sensitivities."

This meant that the possibility existed that not the necessarily best and brightest would be chosen for the police force in America once politicians became involved.

Then, there is the call of the dollar. Many good police officers have left law enforcement because security or insurance companies pay up to 25% more salary, and cops must feed their families.

Has there been a general 'downgrade' in law enforcement opinion in the past half century? Certainly, Hollywood has had its say.

In the 1930's, 40's, and early 50's, law enforcement was often overplayed as if the federal law enforcement (FBI) had all-knowing, all –righteous qualities, and scandals were few and far between. It these famous scenarios, the "G-men" always won out, and the "bad cop" did not exist, or if he did, did not survive the closing credits. The let down was inevitable.

Then as we moved into the Hollywood of the 60's, 70's, and beyond, we found stories of dirty cops, killer cops, Dirty Harry mixing coffee with sugar while shooting down three bad guys, yet still paying his check.

Whereas the early Hollywood movies may have drawn in those with high and lofty expectations, the latter part of the 20th century portrayed a very different cop, one, perhaps, who could be a hero if only he would "turn on his fellow cops" and "break the blue wall of silence" once and for all.

Today, it may be a mixed bag of sorts, with some departments having lower educational standards than others, for entry, and many with lots of arms and vehicle training, but little interview training.

Next, when we speak of law enforcement, we must speak no longer of police officers, but of lawyers; lawyers who are now called "assistant district attorney" or "assistant attorney general" and, fresh out of law school, love to build a career with a winning record in court.

Thus, they want cases from police in which they feel they can win.

But what happens to the young assistant district attorney who strings together a bunch of wins in court?

The call of money echoes once again, and he may find himself or herself in private practice, making many times more money than in public service.

Lastly, with a movement in our country where parental discipline and authority is under question, and upholding a child's self esteem taking precedent over a moral compass, we have not only filled our jails and prisons, but we have left law enforcement, desperate for money, having to triage what cases to take, and what not to, and when one is chosen, how much time (and money) can they dedicate to the case?

I don't believe any little boy grew up saying to himself, "I can't wait until I am older and am a police officer and can hide behind a bush and ticket a speeder for a hundred bucks!"

Departments are underfunded. Good cops are underpaid. Even in establishing a training seminar, there is the constant haggle over the money, and once established, do the attendees have the intellectual capability of handling mentally vigorous training?

Where does that leave the dedicated police officer?

Where does that leave the dedicated assistant district attorney?

Lastly, where does that leave the public's confidence in the system being able to bring perpetrators to justice?

A friend once told me that he would just as soon not call the police on theft reports. "It's just not worth it. It satisfies the insurance company but beyond that, it is just a lot of hours lost."

Companies are doing what they do best: evolve due to need.

Necessity is the mother of invention.

Companies are using Statement Analysis training in two distinct ways:

1. They are using it to hire better workers
2. They are doing their own internal investigations

When Human Resource professionals are trained in Analytical Interviewing (interviewing from the analysis of the statement), they are "way ahead of the curve" in terms of crime prevention. They can weed out those who are more likely to fraudulently file suit, steal, be disloyal, and in short, put their own selfish needs above the material needs of the company.

I have watched companies see year by year drops in criminal activity, and in unemployment claims (honest workers stay longer!) since implementing Statement Analysis Services in their business.

But what about when something does happen?

The answer is clear: Do a joint investigation.

If not a joint investigation, a parallel investigation.

If police, or the insurance company wish to do their investigation with you, it is a joint investigation. If they prefer to do it on their own, you authorize your own worker to do a parallel investigation.

Later, you can compare notes.

Here is an example of such.

A small company served adults with special needs. In this particular case, there were 7 workers coming in and out when an expensive iPad went missing.

The young man who owned the iPad could not speak. His grandmother had purchased it for him, and it was by this iPad that he found a new world of instant communication and the joy of music. His iPad was with him day and night, and was, as is said, "his life."

Indeed, it was his life's connection to the outside world and its wonderful aps allowed for not only faster communication, and the delight of music, but of challenges for his mind through the use of games.

He loved it.

One day, it went missing.

The company was upset, as this was a "loaded iPad", that is, one in which held the most memory and had many games and special features installed.

The police were called and did an investigation. They told the company owners, "we are unable to solve it; there were just too many employees who had access to it. We're sorry, but it is gone."

The company decided to pay for a new one for the client, though it would appear difficult in not only finding out all the games and music he had installed on it, but now they had to be suspicious of one of these 7 employees.

They called me, as a Statement Analyst, for help.

In typical Statement Analysis confidence, I said, "Sure, I'll help. In fact, you have each employee write out what they did from the time they arrived, until the time they left work, and I will tell you who did it, when they did it, and maybe even how they did it."

There was no uncertainty in my voice.

The voice on the other line, however, laughed.

I said, "I am not joking. Get those statements right away."

The company asked that I conduct the interviews. They knew from working with me that interviews can be several hours long, as I am patient and let the subject speak for as long as he wishes to, while I listen carefully for clues.

"You'll have 7 interviews, and with each interview several hours long, you might have to…"

I interrupted. (Interruptions are forbidden in Analytical Interviewing) with "I apologize for interrupting; don't worry about it. I will likely only need to interview one person, perhaps two if there was an accomplice, but not all 7."

Again, the chuckle; again, my response: "I am not joking with you."

The next day, I received all 7 statements and did my analysis, of which I am going to show you here exactly how it was done, as we now use it in training law enforcement and corporate investigators.

I said, "I found your iPad. Miss Jones stole it."

They were surprised. Out of all the workers possible, Miss Jones was at least 30 years older than the rest, and the young employees were far more into electronics.

"Are you sure, Peter?", they asked. "I will bet my reputation on it."

"It can't be her. It has to be one of the young ones. They are so into i-everything!"

"Nope, it was Miss Jones. Set up the interview."

Later, I got a call from Sgt Smith (also not his real name). Sgt. Smith was not pleased to talk to me. He said, "I just got a call from the company with the stolen iPad and they said you are going to be interviewing Miss Jones. I have 25 years experience on the force and let me tell you something, buddy, Miss Jones not only didn't do it, but she doesn't even know what an iPad looks like. She even let me search her vehicle. You're barking up the wrong tree."

I knew that by calling me "buddy", he was being disrespectful, likely because he felt threatened.

"Sgt., did you see her written statement?" I asked.

"I did."

"Sgt., there are distinct indicators of deception within her statement and I am going to conduct the interview based upon my analysis of her statement. I invite you to sit in, however, I caution you that in this form of interviewing, I say very little, and I let her control the interview."

This made his laugh at me.

"I never let a suspect control an interview!"

He declined to participate in the interview.

In fact, so did Miss Jones. She quit her job instead, but, as is my habit, I called her on the phone. I generally do this to reluctant interviewees to see if I can get them talking.

I was polite to her as I am polite to everyone.

I am polite to all suspects because of several reasons, but chiefly because I attempt to treat others as I would like to be treated. I invite the suspect to have a lawyer present. I do not violate anyone's rights.

I also speak politely so that I do not hinder the flow of information.

Miss Jones knows about the iPad, if she did take it, and not me. Therefore, since I do not have the knowledge, my talking will only get in the way. I need to get the information from her.

Thirdly, is my "you never know" factor.

You never know the consequence of speaking harshly to someone.

Once, with a social worker, I was interviewing a man who had been accused of sexually molesting a 3 year old girl, the daughter of his girlfriend. He said to me, "She was walking. You know. She was walking in that way. You know that way they walk?"

The social worker I was with quickly left the room. She felt as if she could fly across the table and slap his face for the disgusting innuendo he was giving us.

Instead, I said, "Continue." And "I'm listening."

Later, I told her, "If I had shown disgust on my face to him, the flow of information may have stopped. In this case, we were able to safely remove the mother and child from his home, but what if we did not have enough evidence? What if we just angered him with the moral repugnancy on our faces? What if it angered him and he went home and took it out on the three year old little girl?"

Point taken.

Miss Jones answered the phone and said, "I *really* don't want to talk to anyone about this. I've already talked to police and they have their answers. I feel so accused by the company that I quit."

I was taking notes and wrote down the word "really" which told me, "she'll talk under the right conditions."

I said, "I am sorry that you feel accused. You don't have to speak to me. I understand. It must hurt to be falsely accused."

She appreciated the kind sentiment and began to talk.

As she spoke, I took notes.

I had her statement before me, and now I share it with you, just as it was written, so you can see what questions I asked, and what areas that I targeted my questions towards. My handwriting was in my own sloppy abbreviations, which I encourage trainees to develop their own. Mine include:

IDHAI: I don't have any idea

IDK I don't know, and so on. I make a circle at dropped pronouns so that I write:

"O didn't take nothing", meaning that she was not able to say "I didn't take nothing" but dropped the pronoun, "I", as indicated by my circle, as it is a missing pronoun.

Here is her statement, along with a few principles of Statement Analysis:

How it is entered here, is exactly how it was written. Remember, in Statement Analysis, every word, every letter, and even every jot or mistake, is to be analyzed for information.

To Whom It May Concern:

Arrived at ***** House app 7AM Entered building stated my name and sat at the table. Kinda waited for someone to at least speak to me. When they didn't I asked where the green books were. I read the green books. Did dishes sat back down with a client while he ate. Went out to my truck to smoke. Took my bag with me because it was not locked up and my wallet with cash was in my bag so I felt better leaving with it or putting it in my locked truck.

The clients had lunch sat

and watched how they did it

after lunch I did dishes

Went for a cigarete. Sat

at the table with client

and staff. Fix a clients

Pipe so he could go smoke. on

the porch. Went out with him

a min. Came back in sat

at table and read my book.

At 1:30 nothing was happening

so I left to go home.

Libby gave me hell for leaving

didn't know I couldn't said I

was sorry and wouldn't happen

again.

Miss Jones

Here is the same statement, but now I am adding such emphasis elements to help you with the analysis. This is not complete analysis, but is a sample of what you can get in training. As an analyst, you do not want to know anything more than the allegation. You do not want to know any detail that might influence your analysis.

Allegation: stolen iPad

Arrived at ***** House

app 7AM

1. Notice first that "Arrived at ***** House (it is redacted) begins without a pronoun. The overwhelming number of statements that begin with a missing pronoun are statistically likely to contain deception.

Also keep in mind: deception is primarily through withholding information, and rarely through direct lies. Many deceptive statements contain no lies at all. Since she knows what she is accused of, I am looking to see her write, "I did not take the iPad" or "I did not steal the iPad."

2. Beginning without a pronoun: "Arrived at…" does not tell us who arrived there. We can interpret it being as her, but in Statement Analysis, we do not interpret; we listen.
3. Beginning without a pronoun indicates that she is, for some reason, not willing to place herself there. This is distancing language. I want to know why she does not want to place herself at the scene of the crime.

Entered building stated

4. Who entered the building? She does not tell us, and since she does not want to say "I arrived" and "I entered", we cannot say it for her. There is a psychological reason why she does not want to be there, and I am going to trust her statement to guide me into the answers I seek.
5. Notice that she has mentioned entry twice. I jokingly wrote, "Who is she, the Queen?", which, in my humor, actually was hitting on the point, though I did not realize it at the time.
6. Her entry, or appearance is very important to her. I know this for two reasons: a. where a person begins a statement is always important   b. repetition shows importance.

7. Time: Did you notice that she gives an approximate time with "app 7am"? "app" reminded me of an "aps" or "application" and it caused me to wonder if she really did know about iPads and aps, and things of that nature.

my name and <u>sat</u> at the table.

8. Stating her name, alone with the two descriptions of arrival, has further pressed my "Queen arrival" status in my mind. Note that "sat" is body posture. Body posture in a statement is often a signal of an increase in tension for the subject.
9. Here, Her Majesty enters the building and states her name and appears to be waiting for the coronation ceremony of sorts to begin. I had a thought of Downton Abby that made me smile again, but the next sentence wiped the grin off my face. (don't forget, this is over the telephone)

Kinda waited for someone to

at least speak to me. When they

<u>*didn't*</u>

10. This woman craves respect. She is upset and I am very glad that I have maintained a respectful tone with her. It might be why she is speaking with me. At this point, I raise my level of more formal language.
11. "at least" shows frustration
12. "whey they didn't" is to report what did not happen, making this very important to the subject.
13. I did ask if she had been working there long. I did not want to say "Are you a new worker?" for fear of making her angry.

She confirmed to me that she was a new hire and did not know anyone No one would even give her the time of day.

As I said earlier, where one begins her statement is often the reason for writing. Still, the "Queen" status and where she chose to start her statement did not settle into me as of yet. It would, however, make all the sense in the world.

Principle: Where one begins a statement is often the reason for writing.

I asked where the green books were. I read the greenbooks.

14. "I asked where…" and "I read the greenbooks" are both truthful, reliable sentences. She signals to me that she does know how to use pronouns when she wants to! In fact, in the interview, she confirmed that she read the greenbooks, completely, hence, the strong pronoun. I did not need to know what greenbooks were, as we are studying language, not the event itself.

<u>Did</u> dishes sat back down with a client while he ate.

14. "Did dishes" drops the pronoun. Later in the interview, she admitted that she only dis a few dishes and even those, were not very clean. This is why she dropped the pronoun "I", while using the pronoun, "I" in the reading of the "green books." Dropping the pronoun over dishes is distancing language and in the interview, she showed me why: She distanced herself from the dishes due to poor work.

There is always a reason for distancing language. Next, however, came the solving of the case.

The Reason Why

When a subject is writing out a statement explaining what he did, there should be no need to tell us why something was done.
This is critical and one of the highest levels of sensitivity in Statement Analysis.

When a subject has the need to explain why she did something, it is where we must target our interview questions. It indicates that she expects to be asked, "Why did you…?"

We color this in "blue" and it is in the area of "blue" that we solve cases. Mr. Sapir says that when we have 2 or more "blues" close together, we have a "cluster of blues" that solves the case. Here we have it:

Went out to my truck

to smoke. Took my bag with me

because it was not locked up

and my wallet with cash was

in my bag so I felt better

leaving with it or putting

it in my locked truck.

This is the critical passage that told me everything I needed to know, except motive. Here is how. Let's look at it again:

<u>Went out to my truck</u>

to smoke. Took my bag with me

because it was not locked up

and my wallet with cash was

in my bag so I felt better

leaving with it or putting

it in my <u>locked truck</u>

Thus, the case is solved!

Wait, not so fast, Petey! Explain!

Ok.

1. "Went out to my truck" drops the pronoun. We already know that she knows how to say the word "I" when she wants to put herself in the picture. She really did read the "green books" (client records), cover to cover. She was proud of that because it was not deceptive and her brain gave her the "ok" to use the pronoun "I" in less than a microsecond. But, uh, oh, here is the problem: She wants to distance herself from the truck. She does not want to be at the truck and I want to learn why not.
2. "to smoke" The "truck" is so important to her that she felt the need, without even being asked, to explain to me why she went to the truck. This means she anticipated that I, or the police, were going to say "Why did you go to your truck?"

Remember, the brain knows what it knows, even when trying to cover things up!

"To" tells us the reason "why" and is given the coded color blue for the highest sensitivity in analysis.

Next, not only did she feel the need to explain, without being asked, why she went to her truck, but why she took her bag with her. I did not ask "did you take your bag with you?" I didn't even know she had a bag! She is "leaking" out highly sensitive information and it is about her truck and her bag. She anticipates someone like me saying, "Ma'am, when you went out on your break, why did you take your bag?" as if this was something anyone might even have known!

The bag wasn't locked up. This isn't something I would have thought of asking but she offered it in the negative, making it very important.

3. "so I felt better" is now imputing emotions, and explaining to me why she was feeling better. This tells me that in order for her to feel "better", something had to be bothering her before that.
4. What might have been bothering her about her bad and her truck? I don't know, but her brain knows. I don't have the information, therefore, I keep my big mouth shut and let her control the interview, even on the phone!
5. "So I felt better leaving it or putting it…" is a deceptive trick (we call it the "either / or" trick in which one does not have to commit and can change her mind later. Casey Anthony was big on this trick.
6. Locked truck.

Bingo!

Change of Language.

Remember our principle of change of language?

A change of language should represent a change in reality. This change should be found in context, and if not, may be a signal that the subject cannot remember her own words beause she is making them up.

In this case, there has been a change in reality.

Let's review our two samples:

a. "The officer drew his <u>gun,</u> fired his <u>weapon,</u> and put his <u>gun</u> away." The "gun" became a "weapon" while it was in use, but once completed, it returned to being a "gun" again, and no longer a "weapon." This is a signal of a truthful sentence.
b. "Peter is a <u>good man</u> to work with." Later, "Peter is <u>a good person</u> to work with." What changed me from "man" to gender neutral "person"? It was the presence of Heather in the work place.
c. "I drove my <u>car</u> down 95. It died. I left the <u>vehicle</u> on the ramp. " When this guy picks it up after it is repaired, I bet you it will no longer be a vehicle, but a car.

The question now being:

Q. What is it that caused the "Truck" to turn into a "locked truck"?
A. Answer: the presence of the iPad.

At the end of the interview, the subject felt respected by me and agreed to meet me for a formal interview. I again asked if she wanted an attorney present and she said "no" and actually "thanked" me for being so polite to her. I knew that she had felt slighted by the other workers, but I did not know what the motive for the crime was, even though it was there, staring me in the face, via Principles of Statement Analysis!

She called me back to by-pass the second interview and said, "Let's just talk on the phone. I haven't slept in nights. I want to return the iPad."

She confessed.

Mr. Sapir had taught me that when a subject confesses, it presents a unique learning opportunity for the investigator, and to ask them two questions:

1. Why did you confess to me?
2. Why did you confess now?

She said that she confessed to me because I had treated her so respectfully and that "I could tell that you knew I did it, but you were still respectful about it." She did not realize that I was ready to pounce on her language at several points, but did not because I was letting her control the flow of information.

Why now?

She said she had trouble sleeping.

I dared to ask her the motive. I know that principle teaches that where a subject begins her statement is sometimes the reason for writing, but that did not make sense to me, so I simply asked, "Why did you take the iPad?"

I expected something along the lines of poverty, or having a son or daughter who could not afford it, or something along the lines of expense.

Nope.

It was right in the statement and right where the principle said it would be!

She said, "I took the iPad because I was the new worker there. They were all young girls in their 20;s, and no one would talk to me. They were having girl talk and excluded me as if I did not exist. I was so hurt that I took it knowing that they would never blame me, the old woman, but one of those snotty girls would be blamed."

I was shocked. I struggled to believe that she could be so callous and risk prison for one of the young females, over a social slight!

She then added, "I've never been in trouble before. I've never stolen anything in my life before this and I just couldn't sleep."

Uh, oh (again).

The word "never" is not reliable until I ask, "have you ever…?"

I find not only the sentence, in the negative, to be unreliable, but the notion of having never stolen anything before, to suddenly graduate to a $700 item just to get someone else arrested, seemed too harsh for a amateur.

"Really?", I asked, with the first signal of less tha respectful tone within me.

She was displeased that I dared question her, especially after she had been so "honest" with me. It wasn't that she was so honest, but more that I kept right on asking questions such as:

"Tell me about your truck"

"How many miles on your truck?"

"What color is your truck?"

"How long have you owned your truck" until she finally started to crack and knew I was on to her.

She wrote our her confession and said she was "sorry" for what she had done. (Did you notice the word "sorry" in her statement? This is something we flag for leakage).

I know I shouldn't have, but I could not resist. I asked her about the Sgt.

"Oh, him! He was so easy to fool! I told him that I didn't even know what an iPad is. I have one at home! I put it in my bag and my bad in the truck. He searched the truck but not the bag. He even handed it to me to make room to search the truck. He was not very bright."

An interesting end to the story:

I alerted the company that the iPad was being returned to them and that the thief had written a confession and a letter to the patient's guardian.

The guardian received the letter and iPad and called police to press charges.

The Sgt. Refused. He said, "You got it back, case closed."

The guardian fumed. You have a thief!"

He said, "We don't really know if she did it."

The guardian said, "You have a signed confession!" and demanded to speak to his superior. To her dismay, his superior did not want to press charges either, so it took the guardian calling the District Attorney's office, demanding justice to be done, to get something done.

A month later, the thief called me back and said that the Sgt brought the summons to her home and served her, saying, "this is bullshit!"

Another month later, I received a call from a co worker. "Hey, your iPad lady is in court today."

"Really? That doesn't make sense. It's too soon to answer for the iPad!" I said.

She said, "Oh, no, she is here for a prior theft!"

6 months later the iPad thief called me to chew me out. "You ruined my life. My husband said "this was the last straw" when that Sgt brought the summons and he has left me. Now I am sick and I don't even have medical insurance. It is all your fault."

Indeed.

Analytical Interviewing is non confrontational, non stressful and is based upon the use of legally sound, open ended questions, such as:

1. What Happened?
2. What Happened, Next?

Where the answers, themselves, are not interpreted, but heard.

We then ask questions based upon the language of the answers, and seek to never introduce new words.

We then ask questions based upon the analysis of the statement, such as "Tell me about your truck?" learning the difference between a "truck" and a "locked truck", and the difference between a "hoody" and a "sweater."

It takes intense study, and a good deal of practice, but participants can revolutionize their solve rate, while companies can reduce shrinkage, poor employees, unemployment claims, and in short, wherever the damage of counterfeit language is seen, it can be mitigated through the use of careful and methodical training.

It is not Hollywood's "Lie to Me" where one bends over in an funny and awkward state and says, "there it is!" only to walk away with a huge smile and a case of money.

Oftentimes, learning the truth about deception, itself, can not only be painful, but can put you in an ethical dilemma you wish you hadn't known about.

Chapter Twenty One: Even The Guilty Call 911

I still get many questions about the case of Haleigh Cummings, the beautiful 5 year old girl who went "missing" from a small town in Florida, reported to police on February 10, 2009.

Haleigh Cummings was left in the care of her live in teenaged baby-sitter, Misty Croslin. The Croslin-Cummings gang of characters would soon be etched into the minds of the American public via the Nancy Grace Show in which the case was not only highlighted, but sadly, provided 'entertainment value' of the lowest sort.

The Croslin-Cummings clans were generational poverty, uneducated and incarcerated people who's slow speech, heavy accent, and bizarre culture showed the seedy underbelly of rural American culture, one in which, I was to learn, was not well known to the nation.

In a day of great medical and scientific advancement, we had Misty Croslin's own grandmother, Flora Hollars, speaking of a child being molested, saying, "*if she was molested, she musta' liked it.*" Her accent was so heavy that sub titles would have been useful. "*Maybe she got into one of them pills and she swallored it...*"

The father, Ronald Cummings, took to calling Nancy Grace, "Miss Nancy" and bragged that she had given him her private cell phone number. Writer and journalist Simon Barrett covered the case extensively through Internet Radio, and was able to interview many of the peripheral characters that were someway connected to the case. His blog updates provided insight and further fueled interest in the case. Simon and his wife, Jan, were somehow deeply emotionally committed to finding Haleigh, and even after they interviewed me on radio, in which I showed the linguistic indicators of Haleigh's death, Jan refused to give up hope. This case touched not a few people in our country, and overseas.

A few hours after making the 911 call, Misty Croslin was interviewed and said, "I loved that little girl like she was my own."

I noted how quickly Misty was able to reference Hailey as if she was dead, using the past tense, "loved" rather than, "I love…" I also noted that Misty used the distancing language of "that little girl" while avoiding Haleigh's name. Even though Misty was not the mother, her instinctive use of past tense and distancing language gave verbal indication that Haleigh was dead. Misty's 911 call provided a great deal more information.

On February 10, 2009, Misty Croslin, then 17, called 911.

Analysis of 911 calls is no different than any other statement, as it is set up as:

The Expected versus The Unexpected.

The Expected.

Put yourself in the position of the caller, presuming innocence. If you were babysitting a 5 year old girl and awoke to find her missing, what would you say to the 911 operator? What would be the first thing you want police to know?

The order in which one speaks shows priority.

Can you imagine your own child gone missing? This is a horror for parents across the nation and the 911 calls indicate the priority within their own hearts:

"My child is missing!"

Simply, this is The Expected.

Statement Analysis is "confronted" by that which we did not expect to hear.

The Unexpected

Picture your child missing. Would you begin your call with a greeting? This is not expected, and, in fact, appears to be a psychological attempt to 'make friends' with police. With a child missing, pleasantries are dispensed with as urgency and hormonal rush take over.

Here is what Misty Croslin said:

911: "911, what's your emergency?"

Misty Croslin: *"Hi…umm…I just woke up…and our backdoor was wide open and I think…and I can't find our daughter"*

Note the call begins with a greeting. This is not expected and shows up in 911 calls of domestic homicide in which the caller was guilty or had guilty knowledge of the crime.

Next, note the order in which she speaks. Order is important to note. Whether it is the chronological order in which you name your children, your siblings, or even the names of friends, order has reason. It an "excited utterance", order speaks directly of the importance.

Here, Misty tells the 911 operator 3 things that she wants police to know:

1. That she was asleep. This is the single most important element for the caller: that the police know she was asleep and has now just woke up. This is "The Unexpected" for an innocent caller. The first thing she wants the police to know is that she was asleep, therefore, could not possibly be involved. It is the first signal of guilty knowledge of the crime of the disappearance of Haleigh Cummings.

2. That "*our backdoor was wide open*".

Notice that the 2nd most important thing for the police to know is about the backdoor being wide open. Misty says "our" backdoor; not "the" backdoor. Pronoun gives us ownership. "the backdoor" would be a common phrase used by any caller since the caller is from the residence. For Misty, the most important fact for the police to know is that she was sleeping; secondly, that the backdoor was open; not just the backdoor, but "our" backdoor, plural. This is an indication that she was not alone or that she has a need to share guilt of what happened to little Haleigh.

3. Thirdly, and lastly, she reports a missing child.

It is commonsense to suppose that if your child was missing, it would be the very first thing out of your mouth. It is a reflex by not only a parent, but a step parent, a relative, a caretaker, a babysitter. In Misty Croslin's mind, it is low on the list of priority.

We deem this 911 call to be deceptive; even from the onset.

Why did Misty say "our daughter"?

When a parent says "our" daughter, or "our" son, this is an indicator that a step parent, (or step caretaker, etc) is likely involved. When biological parents speak, it is not the norm for them to say "our daughter" as they, even when speaking together, still use the natural, "my" daughter.

The exception may be when parents have already discussed divorce and will lead, eventually, to step parenting because one of the parents may have been involved with another love interest.

President Clinton, after the Monica Lewinsky scandal, said he need to repair things with his mother, his wife, and "our daughter"; a strong indication that he and Hillary had discussed divorce. (Another strong indication at that time was the black eye that President Clinton sported after he told the country that his definition of sexual relations was not the same as most others; Hillary included).

Why did Misty rely upon the plural in both "our back door" and "our daughter"?

Had Misty already considered herself a step parent, it makes sense. She said, "them kids loved me like they was my own..." (past tense language noted).

But why "our" door? The norm would not have been "my back door" unless the person lived alone. Even then, the common: "the door".

Note: When someone says I must make the bed, they are likely married. When someone says they must make "my bed" they are likely single. When a married person says, "I must make my bed" they are likely headed for divorce and are already taking ownership. For married couples, "the" is the norm. "The" dog is a family dog, but "my" dog is taken care of by one person more than the others.

Since Misty is in her residence, it is a red flag that she does not use the norm.

This leads to the question: why?

could it be that Misty has been coached? This would explain the plural use here and with "our" daughter. Or, if instinctive, it tells us that Misty was very likely not alone.

Misty also began a sentence with "*I think...*" but did not complete it. Fragmented sentences show stress as they are fragmented thoughts. What did she think? Was an explanation of what she thinks happened about to follow?

"I think" is a reduced commitment. If your child is missing, you would not "think" she is missing: she is missing . You know this. Whatever it was that Misty was going to say, she 'self-censored' indicating that she was withholding or suppressing information from police.

911: "you can't find what?"

Misty Croslin:"our daughter"

Misty revisits the plural language of step parenting, or a prepared or coached call. She does not use the little girl's name, which suggests distancing language.

911:" OK, what's your address?

Misty Croslin: "(inaudible)"

911: "OK, what's the numerical?"

Misty Croslin: "The numerical…what's that?"

911: "the number…green lane?"

Misty Croslin: "Yes"

911: "OK when did you last see her?"

Misty Croslin: "Um, <u>we like</u> just, you know…it was about 10 o'clock- she was sleeping- I was cleaning…

Here is another indicator of deception.

Remember that pronouns are instinctive. "We" indicates that she was not alone. Was she referring to herself and the child? Or, was she referring to someone else?

Remember also to keep in mind the question she was asked.

The 911 operator asked about the last time Misty saw Haleigh.

This is a sensitive question.

Misty was asked when was the last time "*you*" saw her. Misty is unable to take ownership and begins with "um" stalling to think (a parent or babysitter on high alert has adrenaline pumping overtime and has strong recall) and then weakens her statement with "we like just", "you know" ("you know" is often a phrase, but it is also employed to convince rather than report. This is supposed to be an informative call; not an editorialized story nor a building of an alibi. Misty began the call building her alibi; not reporting a missing child)

Misty said she was sleeping, but did not answer the question precisely, but immediately changed the subject back away from the missing child to herself:

"*I was cleaning*"

NOTE: cleaning, laundry, bathing, showering, washing of hands: when enter into a statement further exploration for sexual abuse must begin, as these phrases are commonly used in cases where sexual abuse has taken place. In a child's language (or an adult recalling childhood abuse) we often have the mentioning of blankets, coverings, opening of doors, and closing of doors.

Like the school teacher who notices that a child is incessantly washing where once she did not, and becomes concerned, so it is linguistically that such references should cause child protective caseworkers and police to explore for possible sexual abuse.

What would Misty's cleaning have to do with Haleigh's disappearance?

The brain knows what it knows.

This is not only building of an alibi for Misty, even if it does not appear sensible, but possible leakage into sexual abuse of Haleigh, something that, later on, became more and more likely to have happened, as more information came forth.

Who is this call really about?

Look at the number of sentences that Misty spoke reporting a missing child.

How many sentences were about the missing child?
How many sentences were about Misty?

911: "OK- how old is your daughter?"

Misty Croslin: "She's five"

911: "Ok…what was she last seen wearing? Ma'am…?"

Misty was silent at this point, prompting the 911 operator to ask, "Ma'am?"

Misty Croslin: "She was in her pajamas- she was sleeping…"

Misty mentions now, for the 2nd time, that Haleigh was sleeping. The question was answered, but additional information is given. When information appears unimportant, in Statement Analysis, we consider it doubly important. It is vital that the 911 operator understand, from Misty's viewpoint, that Haleigh was sleeping. It was initially a priority that the police knew that Misty, herself, was sleeping, but now we have repeated information: Haleigh asleep.

This could have been an indication of a drugged overdose of the child.

We later learned that both families were heavily involved in drugs, and in the drug trade (currently Misty, Ronald and others are incarcerated for drugs, as other relatives have been in and out of jail for drugs).

I believe from Misty's emphasis that Haleigh was, at this time, not so much as sleeping, but looked that way as she was likely unconcious. For Misty, Haleigh being asleep is too important. I do not believe that Haleigh died in her sleep but, as others were involved, and sexual abuse was not only generational, but verbally indicated in the interviews with Misty, I believe that Misty had allowed Haleigh to be drugged first, and then sexually abused by another, possibly her own brother.

911: "OK...alright...You said your back door was wide open?"

Misty Croslin: "yes- it was bricked- there was a brick on the floor...when I was asleep it was not like that."

Here, in Misty's language, enters a brick.

Even as I look back on this case, I feel the heaviness of heart, recalling the interviews with Simon and Jan.

The brain knows what it knows. Why is a "brick" so important to Misty that she repeats it?

Although I am veering from the strict analysis as this point, subsequent interviews with Misty, her brother and Ronald, all indicate to me that Hailey's death came as a result of overdosing her with drugs, to make her compliant to sexual abuse. She was carried out of the home (see Misty's description of her hair, as it may appear that her long hair hung out from being wrapped in a sheet), and her body was "bricked" or weighted down, when thrown into the water, to be devoured by the Florida wildlife, particularly, the gators.

Let's return to the analysis of the 911 call:

 "it was bricked"; not "it was open" nor even "it was held open by a brick". For Misty, being "bricked" means the brick had control over the door.

This is passive language.

Remember that passive language seeks to remove responsibility.

"The gun went off" avoids responsibility of who pulled the trigger. "The door was bricked" avoids saying who put the brick there. It is awkward language.

But as quickly as Misty mentions the door and the brick, she immediately states again that she, Misty, was alseep, and that at that time, there was nothing "bricked". I believe that this language may suggest the manner in which Haleigh died or was disposed of. It is in Misty's language for good reason.

911: Ok...the back door...listen to me...your back door was wide open...what are you talking about a brick?"

Misty Croslin: "(inaudible)"

911: "what is a brick?"

Misty Croslin: "it's almost like– on the stairs- we have a walkway..."

911:" uh huh....and there was a brick laying there?"

Misty Croslin: "yes...it's still there"

Misty identifies the cinder block for the 911 operator. She now identifies where a block may be found, at the crime scene.

(background) tell them they've better come on...

911: "we've got em coming- tell him we've got them coming"

Misty Croslin: "they're coming"

911: "Ok what's the color of your house ma'am?

Misty Croslin: "blue"

911: "blue, OK(pause)
OK- what does she look like? How tall is she? Give me some description of her."

Misty Croslin: "How tall she she? Like long hair like curly...with curls..

Misty answers a question with a question, meaning that this is a sensitive question to her and she needs time to think. Even with Turner's Syndrome and doctor appointments, Misty likely does not know Haleigh's height and weight. The parent that brings a child repeatedly to a doctor knows this instantly. Usually one parent knows and the other doesn't, as both generally cannot make regular doctor appointments, but Haleigh was a special needs child and the height and weight is likely taken at every appointment. Misty will struggle if asked for specifics. Misty does not answer how tall she is, nor eye color, or hair color. All she can say is that her hair is curly.

This is the excited utterance and reference for Misty: seeing Haleigh's curly hair.

Was Haleigh wounded in the head? Was the head used to attach a brick? Was she hit with a brick and "shut up" by someone? Was she face down in the bed with curly hair showing? Curly hair is the answer Misty gives to how tall is Haleigh. This is what was in her mind.

911: "long curls...what color?"

Misty Croslin: "(inaudible)"

911:" ok- what color hair? Brown hair?"

Misty Croslin: "Yes...oh my gosh...."

The 911 operator struggles to get answers. Misty appears to be in a panic over these questions, but was not in a panic when she first reported Haleigh missing. These are specific questions but they are not difficult questions. The 911 operator is now asking compound questions; likely out of frustration. Compound questions are to be avoided. They allow the subject to answer any question that is easist to answer. It is often done by television hosts who enjoy hearing their own voice more than the answers by the subject. Here, it is a sign of frustration as questions are not being answered in a timely manner.

Misty would go on to fail polygraphs, lie on television, marry Ronald Cummings and eventually end up in prison with a lengthy prison sentence for her involvement in the drug trade.

Haleigh's remains were never found, nor do I think they will be. Certain statements made by the family indicated veracity about disposing of Haleigh in water.

Police were not able to get a confession out of Misty, and Ronald seemed to hold a strange aura of control over her, and her brothers. Ronald played the polite good ole' boy with "Miss Nancy" on television, but gave indications of his own violent temper, not only with Haleigh, but with reporter Geraldo Rivera.

Officially, the case remains unsolved.

The 911 call of a missing child is about as "straight forward" as a call could be: my child is missing! My child is missing!

The expected is that this would be the priority, and that the parent would be truthful, while being understandably upset.

The expected also is urgency. "Tell me what to do! I will do anything!"

The expected is that the innocent caller will attempt to recall any detail that might help.

The unexpected is things like, "That's all I know", thus, ending the flow of information.

But what about a chuckle?

Would you expect a father of a missing 7 year old girl to actually laugh on the 911 call?

Before you answer with, "well, maybe it is nervous laughter", the context of which the laughter arose, along with other details of the case would be helpful.

I am referring to the case of missing 7 year old, Isabel Celis, who's father, Sergio, reported her missing.

In this case, we begin with the 911 call, although behavioral analysis should also be noted: Remember the example of the toddler wandering off while grocery shopping at Walmart? The parent calls for the child, rather than waiting, or continuing shopping, checking out, and going home first.

In the same sense, we look for parents to immediately call out for the missing child. The parents will do anything asked of them, appeal to the kidnapper, cry out to the child, and do whatever is asked of them.

When 7 year old Isabel Celis was first reported missing, not only did investigators have to come to grips with the strange 911 call, but also with the fact that they struggled to get the parents to agree to "call out to Isabel" and speak to the "abductors" who Sergio alleged had Isabel. Behavioral Analysis of the parents showed an unwillingness to help police find Isabel.

Here is the 911 call, along with the analysis. You may, like me, find it difficult to believe that the father of a missing little girl could laugh on such a call, but as you read his words, you may, also like me, begin to understand the case in context.

Here is the *entire* 911 call made by Sergio Celis regarding his missing 7 year old daughter, Isabel.
Statement Analysis is in bold type. Emphasis by underlining, italics and color added.
Please note that the color blue is given for the highest level of sensitivity.

Dispatcher:911 what's your emergency?

Sergio Celis: *I want to report a missing <u>person</u>, my little girl who's six years old, I believe she* *was abducted from our house.*

Please note that additional or extra words give us additional information. The added word "want" actually reduces commitment.

Please note that he is reporting a missing "person"; it is not expected that a father would refer to his child as a "person"

Note the order:
1. He wants to report a missing person
2. "My little girl"
3. He "believes" she was "abducted" from "our" house. That she may have been abducted is third.

When someone calls their home "our" house, it shows a desire to share ownership. This is often seen in divorces, or can enter the language of those who rent a room in the home, or live with others. That he feels a need to share the home while reporting a child missing should not be missed. We find that the pronouns "we" and "our" come from parents who wish to share guilt (Dillingham) especially since parenting a child is a highly personal ("I" and "my") relationship.

Note the assertion of abduction is only "believed" which is weak. If he believes that she has been abducted, he should have a reason for his belief. An abduction is conclusionary and does not hold the same meaning as "kidnapped" where ransom and contact may be expected. That a father of a missing child could jump to this conclusion should alert investigators to withheld information.

Dispatcher: What's the address?
Sergio: 57 or 5602 E. 12th Street.
Dispatcher: Okay. Stay on the line for Tucson Police.
Sergio: I will.
Dispatcher: Tucson Police Department, Gabhart
Sergio: Hello, I need to report a uh, missing child. I believe she was abducted from my house.

Please note that his call to the police who will be investigating the "abduction" begins with the greeting, "Hello."

People in a hurry to report an emergency may not think to be polite, unless there is a reason to 'befriend' the operator.

There may be a psychological reason for this: some guilty parents will seek to make friends or be at peace with those who might later suspect them. This is why guilty parents will often "thank" police for their work in searching for the missing child, rather than show impatience and frustration. They are, literally, "thankful" for the police failure to locate the "missing" child. This shows itself early in an investigation, and then turns to rage (or disappears) as time passes and the public is aware that the police now suspect the same parents who once thanked them.

This should be seen as a red flag for guilty caller, and an attempt to portray him as "friendly" with the police. Urgency on the part of the innocent parent is expected; not a casual greeting.

Please note the change of language. When language changes, it should reflect a change in reality. If not, it may be an indication of deception as the subject does not speak from memory and is not keeping track of his words:
"missing person" and "my little girl" and "our house" is now:
"missing child" from "my" house.

There does not appear to be any justification for the change in the context, therefore, it may be that it is not coming from experiential memory.

Note how he refers to Isaabel:

To him, Isabel is not "Isabel" but a "person" and a "little girl" and a "child."

Person: gender neutral

"little girl" specific gender

"child" is often used when at risk. While "missing" she is a "person" (non specific) and "child"

Dispatcher: Okay. How old?
Sergio: Six years old.
Dispatcher: Okay is it your daughter or?
Sergio: Yes
Dispatcher: Why do you think she abducted?

That the subject said he thought his daughter was "abducted" was not expected by the 911 operator. An "abduction" is a conclusion, therefore, the subject must have good reason to say what he did, especially given a father's instincts.

Sergio: I have no idea. We woke up this morning and went to go get her up, start her baseball game and she's gone. I woke up my, my sons, I, we looked everywhere in the house and my oldest son noticed her window was wide open and the screen was laying the backyard. We've looked all around the house, my son…

Deception indicated

1. Please note that "I have no idea" is not expected. He asserted what he thought but now claims to have "no idea" what caused him to say so? This is not credible. That she is "missing" would show an "idea" why. A child is missing and a parent says that they have "no idea"? We saw the same deception from Justin DiPietro, father of Ayla Reynolds, who's blood was found in his basement.

2. Please note that he reports that "we" woke up; not "I" woke up. This is an indication of deception. Note that he does not say who the "we" are here. Pronouns are instinctive and guilty people seek to share responsibility with the word "we", no different than a guilty teenager runs away from commitment in hopes of sharing guilt with the word "we"(Dillingham)

3. Note the highest level of sensitivity is found in two specific parts of language:
A. "Left" (departed) when used as an unnecessary connecting verb
B. Reason Why: "to, therefore, so, since, because..." and so on. This means that the subject, when reporting what happened, has a need to explain why he did something. These two parts of language are given the highest level of sensitivity in Analysis, and are color coded with blue to highlight specific areas of extreme sensitivity. When more than one is found, we know we are at a highly sensitive
He tells the reason why he went to get Isabel, of whom he avoids using her name (distancing language)

4. Pronouns are well practiced by humans since the earliest days of speech and are completely reliable. When someone cannot keep track of pronouns, deception is present. Note: "I, we looked everywhere"indicates deception.

Dispatcher: Okay, hang on.

Sergio:...are running, yeah, my sons are running around the house looking for her.

This should not have been needed to be said and is an attempt to portray the family as united and searching. There is no need for him to say that the house has been searched unless...
Unless he has a need to persuade police that they searched the house. Who would not search the house? This was expected before calling 911.

Dispatcher: the screen was on the ground outside?
Sergio: Yes

His daughter was not in her bed, and the screen was on the ground outside, yet he had "no idea" why he thought she was abducted? This does not make sense, unless it is a false report: as a false report, that is, not coming from experiential memory, it makes sense.

Dispatcher: What's her address?
Sergio: 5602 E. 12th Street.
Dispatcher: What's your name sir?
Sergio: My name is Sergio, S-E-R-G-I-O, middle initial D, last name is C-E-L-I-S,
Dispatcher: I-S as in Sam?
Sergio: Yes.
Dispatcher: Okay, what's her name?
Sergio: Isabel, I-S-B-E-L, uh, I-S-A-B-E-L, M as in man is the middle initial

Here is when her name enters his language, but only in response to a direct question.

Dispatcher: Okay, same last name?
Sergio: Yes.
Dispatcher: Okay what's her actual birth date?
Sergio: Is (removed by TPD), of uh, (removed by TPD). I'm sorry. (removed by TPD) and she's going to seven this year, so uh, (removed by TPD)
Dispatcher: Okay. Is mom there also?

This is a yes or no question. Anything beyond "yes" or "no" is sensitive.

Sergio: Uh, she had just left for work, I just called her and I told her to get her butt home. (chuckles)

Here he established his wife's alibi. Whatever happened to Isabel, instead of answering "yes or no" there was a need to explain that it happened while his wife was not home. If he had "no idea" what happened to her, how is it that she had "just" left for work? Please note the word "told."

The word "told" is used in authoritative sentences. "My boss said to be at work at 9" is one way of saying it, while, "My boss told me..." is stronger. Here, he portrays the sentence as if he had to exercise authority to "tell" her or "instruct" her to come home.
Is this reasonable?
No.
A mother of a missing 6 year old would not have to be "told" to come home from work: she would leave immediately. Here, the subject wants us to believe that he had to impose authority over her, as indicated by the word "told" in his language.
Next, this is buttressed by his wording "get your butt home."
By his language: He is portraying her reluctance to come home. Is this how he wanted it?
Is this how Becky wanted it?

Please note that he is heard chuckling on the call made to report his missing child.
In statement analysis we say that we do not analyze the person, but the words, and that

people who analyze voice inflection are often wrong as often as they are right. But it is here that it is so ridiculous that it sounds cartoon like and is impossible to ignore:
He laughed while reporting his daughter missing, while he is being deceptive. His nervousness is likely due to the deception and need to portray himself as authoritative and helpful.

Dispatcher: Okay, mother.
Sergio: But she was...
Dispatcher: What kind of vehicle is she going to be en route back in?
Sergio: Uh, in our Lexus RX300, and it's red.
Dispatcher: Okay.
Sergio: And she's coming from TMC, so she should just be coming straight down Craycroft.
Dispatcher: Okay. How tall is she?
Sergio: She is five two.

This indicates where his mind is: he is concentrating on "pleasing" the operator and not about his missing daughter. His language reveals that she is not a priority. He thought of his wife in the "get your butt home" comment and his mind is still on his wife, not daughter, who, if truly "missing" or "abducted" would be all he cared about. This is a parental instinct to care only for the missing child. He is more concerned with image and alibi than he is with his missing daughter.

Dispatcher: No the, I'm sorry, you're daughter
Sergio: Oh *my daughter*. Um...forty inches. Thirty, yeah 36 to 40 inches.

If your child was missing, would a 911 operator need to redirect your attention back to your daughter? This is the reason in an interview, we do not "redirect" anything: we listen.

Dispatcher: Okay. Is she black, white, or Hispanic?
Sergio: She's a fair skinned Hispanic with uh, clear eyes and light brown hair.
Dispatcher: And what do you mean by clear eyes? Like...
Sergio: Uh, well they're a little bit green...
Dispatcher: Are they hazel or?
Sergio: ...green, green, hazel, sure.
Dispatcher: Hazel, okay. And you said she's about 40 inches tall.
Sergio: Yeah.
Dispatcher: Do you remember what she was wearing last night when you saw her?

**The expectation is "yes" followed by what she was wearing. It is a yes or no question, but it has the expectation of commentary for the purpose of helping locate her. His answer reveals that he saw her two times.
Please note this.**

In Sergio Celis' answer, he dilineates different times he saw what she was wearing. He should simply report what pajamas the six year old had on. This is where extra words give away the information needed:

Sergio: *Uh, <u>before she went to bed</u> I believe she was wearing little navy blue shorts and, and a pink uh, a pink like <u>little</u> uh, tank top type of a shirt.*

He reports what she wore, not to bed, but "before she went to bed" indicating that this may not be what she was wearing when she went to bed, or when she went missing.
Also note that besides not reporting what pajamas she had on, he describes her shirt and shorts as "little":
She is six years old.
Not only does she have on "little shorts" and a "tank top" but a "little tank top" type of shirt.
The dispatcher reflects back the language, without the additional and "unimportant" information of the size of the clothing:

Dispatcher: Pink tank top? Okay. Navy blue shorts. Has she ever tried to sneak out of a window or anything?
Sergio: Oh no.
Dispatcher: Have you guys...
Sergio: Hu-uh
Dispatcher: ...been having any weird phone calls, anything like that, somebody hanging around?
Sergio: No. <u>We</u> got home late from uh, <u>my</u> son's baseball game.
Dispatcher: Uh-hm
Sergio: <u>You know</u>, about 10:30 last night. (clears throat) Everyone took their <u>showers</u> and they all went to bed. I <u>even</u> was in the living room watching uh, the Diamondbacks game <u>at midnight</u>.
Dispatcher: Uh-hm.
Sergio: And I feel asleep and I <u>never heard</u> anything <u>weird</u>. So I was like just on the...
Dispatcher: Okay.
Sergio:...other side of the wall from her.
Dispatcher: How, how many siblings does she have?
Sergio: Two.
Dispatcher: Okay, and those are brothers you said?
Sergio: Yes.
Dispatcher: How old are they?
Sergio: 14 and 10.
Dispatcher: And you said they're out looking or they were <u>looking all over</u> the house?
Sergio: *Oh no, they, they just, they just went right now, my oldest son, the 14 year old, he went running around just to make sure um, but I, she's nowhere...*
Dispatcher: Okay.
Sergio:...to be seen...
Dispatcher: Outside or inside?

Sergio: He's outside our property wall.
Dispatcher: Okay. And where is the ten year old?
Sergio: He's in the garage. He's just out in the garage just waiting for...
Dispatcher: Okay.
Sergio: ...my wife.
Dispatcher: Okay and what's mom's name?
Sergio: Becky.
Dispatcher: Okay. And what's your birth date sir?
Sergio: (removed by TPD)
Dispatcher: Okay. And what's mom's?
Sergio: Uh, (removed by TPD)
Dispatcher: Okay. Any you're both natural parents of the child?
Sergio: Yes.
Dispatcher: Okay. So no, no step-parents, any, any problems with any grandparents?
Sergio: No.
Dispatcher: Okay. So you're not having any family issues, anything like that?
Sergio: No.
Dispatcher: Okay. And you haven't noticed anybody hanging out in front of your house?
Sergio: No.
Dispatcher: Okay. You're son that's 14, what's his name?
Sergio: (inaudible yelling in background) Uh, *I'm sorry,* my wife just walked in and, and she's speaking to somebody. I don't know if she's speaking to the police also. She might have been calling on her way. You asked me about my son, what did you ask me?

In a 911 calls and in Statement Analysis in general, the words "I'm sorry" entering for any reason, are flagged for interest. It is often found within the words of the guilty. We saw this in the 911 call of Casey Anthony.

Is this leakage of the brain knowing what it knows?

Dispatcher: Yeah the, the 14 year old that's out looking for her?
Sergio: Yes. What about him?
Dispatcher: Um, well hang on a second. Okay, actually I think one of your sons is trying to call. Um, I'm sorry, what was your 14 year old's name?
Sergio: (Taken out by Tucson News Now)
Sergio: My wife just got home and she's kind of <u>hysterical</u> and <u>freaking</u> out, so.
Dispatcher: I, okay. Tell her we are on the way, we've got a...
Sergio: Okay.
Dispatcher: ...bunch of officers on the way, I want you guys to stay there in the house.
Sergio: We will.
Dispatcher: Okay.
Sergio: *Bu-bye*

Analysis conclusion: Although the case remains official unsolved, the father was said to be removed from the home, in an agreement with child protective services, and many thought the case would break, but eventually, he returned to the home and no arrest was made.

The following is my opinion of the 911 call, based upon analysis of the words Sergio Celis used:

This is a deceptive call regarding an "abduction" that did not take place, made by a subject with willful and guilty knowledge. Specifically, the caller is deceptive about what happened to Isabel Celis, of whom he distances himself, and is deceptive about his own actions. It is a tragic case that police appeared very close to proving that Isabel did not leave that home alive, and that the parents were not cooperating early on for good reason.

There were also linguistic indicators of possible sexual abuse, which echoed, somewhat, the Jonbenet Ramsey case; another case in which the 911 call appears scripted, and the case remains officially unsolved.

911 calls are as you would expect them to be: Emergency calls in which the caller's priority is the emergency, itself.

The unexpected is when the caller attempts to, even gently, guide the police away from the truth, by any means possible, including alibi building.

Justice for Isabel, just like justice for Haleigh, remains unrealized.

For now.

Chapter Twenty-two: The Conclusion of the Matter

Deception hurts.

It undermines confidence in language, just as it does in human nature itself. For one, it is deception that destroys a life, while in another, as in the case of Adolf Hitler, deception resulted in the destruction of millions of lives.

Deception destroys businesses.

Small businesses can be rocked right out of business by a single deception that is undetected.

Larger businesses can be "nickel and dimed" to death, slow death, in which the costs of shrinkage and insurance are passed down to both the customers as well as to the employees, via wages.

Where is the breaking point?

How often can quarterly unemployment payments be sustained before an employer must cut wages, or raise prices? Or, worse, go out of business?

How many times must one "fall" in a company, grab a few unearned dollars through a frivolous suit, until other deceptive employees see it, and join in?

I've seen companies in which suits were "all the fashion", that is, something that "everyone does."

In one company, a working pair husband and wife, both submitted outrageous time sheets for overtime that appeared to be deceptive.

I interviewed them both.

Separately.

I asked the wife to tell me what happened, on the overnight shift, that warranted so much overtime, as the patient sleeps through the night.

She said, "She throws things. She can be a danger to herself and others. She needs supervision."

I said, "Yes, she does. Now tell me what she did Thursday night."

She said, "Thursday night? Well, as I said, she throws things, and she is a danger to herself and others."

The woman remained in present tense language, making her statement unreliable. I asked her about her bills.

"My bills are fine."

Now, I don't know about you, but my bills are either paid, or not paid, but they are never "fine." Bill collectors had been calling the office looking for her.

I then interviewed the husband and was surprised how quickly an admission emerged.

"It was my idea, not hers. Just blame me."

I thought he was confessing, but I was wrong.

"Everyone does it. Why shouldn't we?"

Hence, the difference between a confession and an admission. A confession not only admits what was done, but includes remorse and acknowledgement of what was done was morally or legally wrong.

He did not confess. He made an admission, and was bitter to have gotten caught, not penitent for having attempted to have stolen from his employer.

While awaiting determination, I sought ways to allow them to keep their jobs, but his wife was so incensed at being caught in a lie, that she convinced him to quit their jobs, together.

Thus is the anger of a liar when caught.

There are times in my life where I could have said, "ignorance is bliss", and not have known the truth, or at least, ignored it.

There are times in all of our lives where we learn that Santa Claus is not real, and it can be unpleasant, but not much beyond that. But what of learning the truth about someone you or I looked up to, admired, respected, and believed in?

These are those times where you and I might wonder if we would have been better off not knowing the truth.

Heather and I love old movies, especially from the 1930's and 1940's. She is fond of saying, "When you find out about that movie star, do me a big favor and do not tell me anything!" We laugh over such.

Yet in reading about some of the movie stars who's movies we admire, there is the inevitable bursting of childhood balloons, and the learning of how some of the "stars" of yesteryear were so terribly depraved, or had mistreated others, or have done other notoriously rotten things to their fellow man. Yet on screen, they appear heroic, always moral, and always winning.

So, while laughing at Bob Hope and Bing Crosby, I let my love of biographies stand aside, and don't tell her about how Bing treated his kids, or how Bob, a multi millionaire, would throw a dollar on the ground just to watch his maid have to bend over to pick it up. Yeah, I leave that stuff out. She likes her illusions in tact: no one before 1945 ever sinned. I'm with her on that. No Judy Garland stories, or Marilyn Monroe drug accounts, or the countless other lives exploited by the Hollywood moguls in their quest to make money, while portraying America in its best light. We still love "It's A Wonderful Life" and "The Philadelphia Story", just the same. It's like a kid watching "The Brady Bunch" and hearing that "Mom is dating Greg." It just doesn't work.

Many years ago, when my son, Peter was at the age of wanting a sports star's jersey, I said, "not a chance. As soon as I pay an arm and a leg for a jersey with a player's name on it, the player will be arrested for something horrible. Nope. I will get you a jersey with your own name on it. This will remind both you and me of carrying that name appropriately and being careful how we conduct ourselves.

My brother-in-law, a huge sports fan, had his son near the same age, and was in the same dilemma.

He chose his favorite professional football player's name on the back of his son's jersey (which was more expensive than using his own name).

It did not take long for his son's favorite player to be arrested…drugs, rape…well, you get the picture.

The reality is that we live in a fallen world.

In this fallen world, it is men of clay, like Terry Elvis, who's ability to believe, itself, is a gift. For Terry, the injustice of the trial of Christ, the Innocent put to death for the guilty, gives him the reason for his hope of reunification with his darling Heather. Or that of Kelly Osburn, who saw her daughter's reputation smeared by a botched and shoddy investigation, wanting to close the book on the case as 'suicide' when it was anything but, who continued to fight on, even when loved ones told her, "Enough, let it go!" but she knew she could not.

There are heroes all around us, so much so that there is no need to look to Hollywood only to see Sean Penn, "Rescuing little black children from Hurricane Katrina" except his boat was sinking from too many cameras aimed at him, leaving room for not a single child. There are real heroes, every day, facing life with courage and conviction.

Among other heroes include Susan Murphy Milano, who's fight for justice, particularly for women who were victims of intimate partner violence, was unwavering, in spite of her own frail humanity.

The heroes on the movie screen are pretend. They earn a fabulous living pretending to be someone else.

The real heroes, warts and all, are those who work endlessly to help others, like Monica Caison, of the Center for Missing Persons, who's willingness to help others far exceeds all natural ability and time allotted in life.

Or like Avinoam Sapir, who immigrated from Israel, and brought with him the genius of not only facilitating a system of thought, but the courage to share it, around the world, while remaining accessible to answer any question of any student. He is unique in his own humility and bearing.

It is men and women like these mentioned here that are "treasures in clay", that is, subject to the same human fragility as others, yet within them, find the strength to push for justice.

It is the victims of sexual abuse, like my wife, Heather, who are followed by a voice, every day of their existence, that whispers to them that they should end their own lives, yet press on, recognizing the lies imprinted upon them during the years that they were too young to do anything about.

Yes, these are the heroes of truth. They are the ones to whom we may look, even when hurt by deception, and press on.

We must become a discerning people, as a nation, and demand honesty, for from our own selves, and then from others.

We must be willing to be discerning in business, even as politicians portray any type of critical thinking as "judgmental" or "unfair", and hire the best and brightest. We are Americans. We want the best and to have the best, we must not only be the best, but hire the best, regardless of inconsequential factors.

We must be willing to ask questions, and when we do, we must be willing to listen. To listen is to learn.

Learning presupposes humility, for without, we do not see our need. It is when we see our need, we are inspired to grow and learn.

Discriminatory thinking has been given a bad name, simply because it has become associated with foolish discrimination and a rush to compete to appear "compassionate", which has come to mean showing compassion to the perpetrator, but not the victim.

We must listen.

We are fearfully and wonderfully created, and we have been created to be industrious and to communicate one with another.

Faith stands the tests of vigorous questioning and allows for sense in our fallen world.

We need to ask questions.

We need to listen to the answers.

Printed in Great Britain
by Amazon